Wisdom from the Monastery

In the present book, the concept of "monastery" stands for the women's communities as well. For pragmatic reasons, we use this name also for religious orders that, strictly speaking, do not lead a monastic life in the sense of a *stabilitas loci* (staying forever in one place), as for example the Franciscans (lesser brothers), Augustinians (canons), and members of other communities.

Wisdom from the Monastery

A Program of Spiritual Healing

Peter Seewald (Editor)
Bernhard Müller
Lucia Glahn
Simone Kosog

North Atlantic Books
Berkeley, California

Published by
North Atlantic Books
P.O. Box 12327
Berkeley, California 94712

Cover photo by zefa/F. Damm
Cover design by Claudia Smelser
Interior typography by Konecky & Konecky, llc.
Printed in the United States of America

First English edition: Konecky & Konecky, 2004.

Wisdom from the Monastery is sponsored by the Society for the Study of Native Arts and Sciences, a nonprofit educational corporation whose goals are to develop an educational and cross-cultural perspective linking various scientific, social, and artistic fields; to nurture a holistic view of arts, sciences, humanities, and healing; and to publish and distribute literature on the relationship of mind, body, and nature.

MEDICAL DISCLAIMER: Any information given in this book is not intended to be taken as a replacement for medical advice. Any person with a condition requiring medical attention should consult a qualified physician or practitioner

North Atlantic Books' publications are available through most bookstores. For further information, call 800-733-3000 or visit our website at www.northatlanticbooks.com.

Library of Congress Cataloging-in-Publication Data

Müller, Bernhard.
  Wisdom from the monastery : a program of spiritual healing / Peter Seewald (editor) ; Bernhard Müller, Lucia Glahn, Simone Kosog.
     p. cm.
   ISBN 978-1-55643-923-0
   1. Spiritual healing—Catholic Church. 2. Monastic and religious life.
I. Glahn, Lucia. II. Kosog, Simone. III. Seewald, Peter. IV. Title.
   BT732.5.M59 2010
   248.4'7—dc22
                                                        2010037140

1 2 3 4 5 6 7 8 LAKE BOOK 14 13 12 11 10

With special thanks to Father Rhabanus
Petri OSB and his brothers of the priory of
Jakobsberg on the Rhine, to the Franciscan
nuns of Oberzell and of the Holy Baths of
Krumbad, and to Sister Annunziata and her
fellow sisters at the Cistercian convent of
Oberschönenfeld for their friendly support.

Table of Contents

PART II:
Healing in the Monastery

PART III:
Silence in the Monastery

Fasting
in the Monastery

Bernhard Müller

Preliminary

"Fasting makes the way easier"

"Teaching something old is harder than teaching something new."

Hebrew proverb

*H*ow can angels fly?," my four-year-old asked me one day. He looked at me inquisitively, but before I was able to give him an answer he blurted out: "I know, it is because they are so light."

How I too would like to be lighter. Light as an angel. Or at least as light as my son. Most of us are slow and heavy from too much eating and drinking, weighed down by too many worries and unfulfilled ambitions that often lie heavily on our shoulders. I wanted to make a change. I wanted to rid myself of this burden — and fortunately I had a good friend who helped me along.

"Go and spend some time in a monastery," he said, "fast with the monks! The path to lightness is through fasting. Fasting gives you renewed strength and confidence. Everything looks different. What was blurred and insoluble becomes transparent and clear. You feel optimistic again. Often it feels as if you only have to wish something for it to come to pass. You are filled with a feeling of happiness. You feel so light, so free. And this lightness is not just a product of your imagination. After your fast, you are truly lighter, both physically and mentally."

For a long time the religious practice of fasting in Europe seemed not only unfashionable but practically forgotten. But today people are again coming to realize that fasting is more than merely a question of dieting. Many only decide to fast when they are already ill, have lost their figure, and have paid a heavy price for their extra weight. It is never too late to learn to fast. But you should remember one thing: you should attend the right school, the school of the monks who have been practicing fasting for almost two thousand years. Praised by doctors as the "cure of all cures," fasting is the royal way to physical and spiritual health, to a new sense of well-being and happiness. Try it for yourself — you will discover your inner self and come closer to the truth. I promise you that it will do you good. And you will realize why monks have been praising the benefits of fasting for centuries, and still do so today.

Bernhard Müller

Welcome to the monastery

The steps up to the priory of Jakobsberg

We accept everyone!

"The sea does not refuse entry to even the smallest river, hence its depth."

Chinese saying

*I*t was a bright summer's day, the birds were twittering, and in the distance I could see the sparkling of the River Rhine. With a slow and heavy tread I began my climb up the mountain. But it was almost as if every step that brought me closer to the monastery took some of my worries away. My path led me past vine-covered hillsides and through colorful forests of deciduous and coniferous trees, then up some wooden steps until I finally reached my destination, the pilgrimage church of the fourteen Auxiliary Saints with its promise of new beginnings. Here, on this sacred mountain, I would fast for a week with the Benedictine monks, renouncing too much food, noise, and visual stimuli, and attempt to find myself again.

Jakobsberg near Rüdesheim has been a refuge for pilgrims since 1720. Originally it was inhabited by hermits, but now the priory has been renovated by the Missionary Benedictines of St. Ottilien, the youngest offshoot of the ancient tree of monastic life. Here every year thousands of people find what they need to quench their mental and spiritual thirst. As I made the short ascent, I had the impression that I was entering a deeply spiritual environment.

"Give me answers to the questions of my life!"

My first outing took me to the church. This is built in such a way that the eye of the visitor is inevitably drawn to the chancel, where in the apse Christ as ruler of the world and in the form of the risen God gazes upon the visitor. In his left hand he holds the book with the seven seals that only he can open. Looking at this sight one is tempted to cry out, or even groan loudly, as generations of pilgrims have probably done before: "Open the book for me, answer the questions of my life!"

In the front part of the chapel there is an almost endless row of figures painted on the walls. They are people from all nations, and somehow I too felt that I was part of this continuing line of doubters and questioners. I too was looking for answers to my questions. Later I learned that the fresco painted by the Benedictine brother Lucius Glazner depicts a scene from the mysterious Book of Revelation: "I looked, and there was a great multitude that no one could count, from every nation, from all tribes and peoples and languages," wrote St. John the Evangelist, "they cried out in a loud voice, saying: 'Salvation belongs to our God who is seated on the throne.'"

I closed the door of the church slowly and carefully, and as I walked through the door I remembered Leo Tolstoy. On a windy, stormy night the Russian poet had knocked on the door of a monastery asking for help. Hesitantly, he asked whether he could spend the night there, even though he had been excommunicated. The door-keeper's answer was simple, exemplifying the Christian spirit: "We accept everyone!"

When eventually I stood before Father Rhabanus, a monk about forty years old who would teach me what I needed to know about fasting, I saw a slim, clean-shaven man with alert eyes. His name comes from the Old High German word for "raven." He was a rather ascetic looking figure, cheerful and down to earth. To think that I, a man of the world, had been afraid that I might not understand him, the cloistered monk, because our worlds were so different! It very soon became clear that my fears were completely unfounded.

Father Rhabanus

The lanky monk welcomed me warmly. His words and manner of speaking put me right at ease. "Have a rest first," he suggested. No sooner had I put my case down in my room than I realized that I had entered a universe that could help me with the pressures and anxieties of daily life.

So that our heart may have ears

The story of Jakobsberg near Rüdesheim on the Rhine goes back to pre-Roman times. The discovery of tools, household objects, and other artifacts indicate the existence of a settlement on this site going back to 4000 BC. In Roman times, Ockenheim, situated at the foot of Jakobsberg, was the intersection of several military roads. Much later, in 1720, the then parish priest Blasius Caesar founded a place of pilgrimage on the Ockenheim mountain in honor of the celebrated fourteen Auxiliary Saints, or Holy Helpers — a series of patron saints for all kinds of problems — and this soon developed further. The site of the sanctuary has always attracted settlers, and in 1921 Trappist monks from the Dutch abbey of Echt came and settled at Jakobsberg. From 1951 to 1960 the monastery housed the novitiate of the East German Order of Jesuits. Since the late 1960s the monastery has been run by monks of the arch abbey of the Missionary Benedictine monks of St. Ottilien.

Through the open window of my new cell I could hear birds singing, although sometimes it sounded more like quarreling. Over a hundred kinds of birds come here to winter or simply to fly through this part of the world, and this flourishing bird population is complemented by 230 species of rare ferns and flowering plants that thrive at Jakobsberg because of its unique soil conditions. Father Rhabanus encouraged me by saying: "You'll see, fasting is good for you! It liberates you from the constraints of everyday life. This will help you to find yourself. There is much, much more to fasting than not eating."

Listening is not a skill that one learns once and then has forever. It requires lifelong practice. Fasting helps here too.

Shortly after my arrival at the monastery the monk told me a little about the founder of his order, St. Benedict, who in the sixth century wrote down the Rule for his community at Monte Cassino in southern Italy. This Rule of St. Benedict became the foundation for all the monastic orders in Europe. The Rule begins with a single word: "Listen!" And this is for a reason. "Listening," Father Rhabanus explained, "must actually be practiced." Only a person who is really free can master this fundamental aspect of spirituality.

Thus the prayer: May our hearts have ears. An unusual image but a very important one.

Curious to learn more, I allowed myself to follow along this path. On the day I arrived, Jakobsberg was like a land filled with flowers. The fields of ripe corn stood in profound silence, and the grapes were nearly ripe. I had stepped away from everyday life and its pressures — including the need to eat. I hung up my jacket on the coat rack in my little room in the priory's guesthouse. As I did so I felt as if I were taking off not just a heavy garment but a suit of armor that until then had protected me. I reflected that fasting might leave me defenseless and naked, and I immediately thought of Adam and Eve. Perhaps this was childish, but somehow I was also confident that here on the mountain, in spite of the great variety of fauna, there were no serpents.

Monks in the refectory

In the foothills
of Eternity

The Meteora monastery in Greece

A short history of fasting —
and what you can discover in the process

W hat do we really mean when we talk about fasting? Is it only a kind of fitness program? A reduction in calories that unfortunately has to be repeated over and over again because it never works for long? Or is it much more than a mere declaration of war against excess weight? Is it possible that it is connected with something that we have lost sight of? Why is it that fasting exists in every civilization in the world? Why is fasting so important in all religions?

"Through abstinence, what is tired and weak and sick becomes strong."

Hymn sung by monks during Lent

Then too: what about our own Western, Christian tradition of fasting? Where does the concept come from and what can one achieve with it? Is the practice of fasting really so important that it not only influences the condition of an individual but also that of an entire society? "In Europe," the journalist Paul Badde wrote in a report from Jerusalem, "it appears that fasting fell into oblivion a long time ago, first in the church, then in society as a whole." But as this critical observer warned, "no one should think that this loss of moral substance in humans would not have fatal consequences for society at some time or another."

Myths of Fasting

Fasting is a battle against the temptations of evil and at the same time a source of comfort, cheerfulness, and joy. It is a wonderful means of achieving concentration and sharpening the senses, a way of discovering the self and one's own soul. It is an exercise of reflection, repentance, listening, and sharing. It is the rediscovery of feelings and the sense of what is really important. And finally, beyond the self, it is the path to the light, to God, to the basis of our creation without which we can live only half a life.

Fasting has countless facets. It is letting go and relaxation. It is cleansing and turning round.

Fasting is the quintessential paradox: gain through reduction, increase through decrease, less is more... Throughout the ages this renunciation, usually carried out in a ritual manner, has been one of the essential mysteries of human heritage — an ideal way that through the act of renunciation leads not to weakness but to renewed clarity and strength.

Fasting as a cultural achievement

In contrast to what happens in northern latitudes, fasting in the Holy Land, the cradle of the Christian tradition of fasting, takes place at a time when nature is more bountiful than at any other time of the year. The hills are a delicate green, and the air is scented with the fragrance of thyme. The bazaar in Jerusalem is overflowing with fresh herbs and the produce of the harvest from the mountains of Judea: sage, chamomile, wild oregano, parsley, shallots, fresh fruit, and vegetables. It is a time of abundance. Here, the regular lengthy fast before Easter was never a virtue arising out of necessity but always a renunciation prompted by reason, and consequently a cultural achievement.

According to St. Basil the Great, the true father of monasticism in the East, "fasting is as old as mankind," and to be precise, "because it was ordered in Paradise." The Bible is full of stories about times of fasting and the fasts of prophets and saints. Moses fasted for forty days and forty nights on Mount Sinai before he was allowed to receive the tablets of the Law. The prophet

St. Catherine's monastery on Mount Sinai

Jonah was only able to avert God's judgment that threatened the city of Nineveh by inducing its inhabitants to observe an all-embracing fast. As for the prophet Elijah, he went to the desert where he fasted for forty days in order to prepare himself for his important new mission.

It was in this desert, where the earth is usually rust-colored with slate-grey reflections, that Jesus came to fast for forty days in order to gather the strength he needed before embarking on his public ministry.

The man from Nazareth wanted to free humankind of its chains and brought a new Law to the world which repealed almost all of the interminable details of religious regulations. It is well known that the "Son of Man" was very fond of food. The Pharisees called him "a glutton and a drunkard," and when the wine ran out during the wedding at Cana he miraculously produced further supplies from water.

Jesus was one figure in the long fasting tradition of his people. Three things were important to devout Jews: fasting, praying, and giving alms.

They fasted as a matter of principle twice a week, on Monday and Thursday. In the third Book of Moses, at the very beginning of the Bible, fasting is elevated to an everlasting law to achieve atonement and purification. God's order to fast is repeated in many places in the Old Testament. Thus the Israelites fasted to mourn their own sins, emphasizing their repentance and their prayers of supplication, as well to express their commitment to their religion. Also, when a loved one was in the throes of death, the people around him would fast, as David did when his son lay on his deathbed. The power ascribed to fasting is reflected in the Talmud, in which it is said: "He who prays without being answered must begin to fast."

Of course, fasting is by no means an exclusively Judeo-Christian phenomenon. It occurs in all civilizations and religions. We know that in the great religions Christ, Buddha, and Muhammad fasted for a long time before their public appearances. It is said that Buddha fasted extensively in his early years in order to progress along the path to enlightenment. He increased his fasting to the point of only eating one seed a day.

Gandhi's fasting liberates a subcontinent

In Hinduism, fasting is part of religious ritual. It is considered one of the conditions for spiritual progress: there is no praying without fasting. One of the figures most famous for his fasting was Mahatma Gandhi, who through his fasting almost single-handedly brought about the departure of the British occupying forces from his country. Gandhi knew very well that fasting must remain unselfish if it is to have a positive effect: "I can fast for my father to free him from sin," he explained once, "but I cannot fast to receive an inheritance from him."

Gandhi had the same attitude to fasting as is found among monks. The effects of his fasting were so powerful that in the 1930s there was a saying in London: "When rebellion rages in New Delhi people smile in Whitehall, but when Gandhi begins to fast the whole of Downing Street trembles."

For devout Muslims, fasting is one of the five pillars of their religion, together with the pilgrimage to Mecca, the daily times of prayer, the profession of faith to Allah, and the giving of alms. During Ramadan, the annual month of fasting, devout Muslims give up food, drink, sexual activity, and of course smoking, between sunrise and sunset. At the same time, they must be friendly and generous towards other people. Breaking the fast each evening provides an opportunity to eat and pray together, and the end of Ramadan is celebrated with a great celebration. In addition, Muslims also fast on certain "holy nights," on days of remembrance, to do penance, or for personal reasons.

Monks as teachers of fasting

Nowadays fasting is offered in many expensive diet clinics where people go to lose weight successfully or for the treatment of certain illnesses. But it is the monks who can

Mahatma Gandhi

rightly claim to be the original masters of this art. They have been the true guardians of the secrets of fasting for almost 2,000 years. "There is no higher calling than that of being a monk," the Russian poet Nikolai Gogol said after learning the art of fasting from monks. Poets such as Hugo von Hofmannsthal and Gerhart Hauptmann were so influenced by the monastic life that they expressed the wish to be buried in monk's habits. The Swiss Protestant writer Walter Nigg, referring to the unbroken tradition of the art of monastic fasting, observed: "The monastic orders are an inexhaustible well for the Catholic Church into which all the water trickles down and without which Christianity would dry up… It has always been monasticism that has saved the sinking Church."

Indeed, the monastic orders were for centuries a source of priceless spiritual treasure for the Church. Western civilization as we know it would be inconceivable without them. The ordained men and women preserved and guarded spiritual secrets from generation to generation, secrets that otherwise would have been forgotten, even by the Church. And even if many

Desert cacti can survive long periods of drought

monasteries and convents have become deserted in the last decades, they still contain seeds that could suddenly start to germinate again at any time.

How monks preserved an extraordinary treasure

The first Christian monk, who only a few decades after the birth of Christianity left everything behind and withdrew into the desert in the footsteps of Jesus, was not driven by loathing or disgust. In the same way as Abraham had left his country, and Elias and John the Baptist had lived in abstinence and chastity, so the hermit Anthony left civilization and withdrew to the barren desert, which was unbearably hot during the day and bitterly cold at night, in order to dedicate himself entirely to God.

The first monks wanted to open their hearts to God. Fasting will help you control your passions.

The first hermits, or "desert fathers," were looking for three things in the desert: prayer, fasting, and solitude. Their dwellings were uncomfortable and cramped, their clothes were simple, they slept little, and ate simply and sparingly between periods of daylong fasting. It is reported that these men battled "every day like athletes, and as a result succeeded in controlling their bodily need for food, achieving absolute poverty, true humility, and sanctification of the body."

When the soul is no longer troubled by tumultuous distractions, humans become aware of the greatness of their own being and the dangers threatening it. The monks fled the world not because they were disillusioned with life. On the contrary, the desert was thought to be inhabited by demons whom they wanted to defeat through fasting and prayer. It was not unusual for people to consider their inner being as a real battlefield in which the greatest enemy was their own self will. Matthias Grünewald depicted the Temptation of St. Anthony by evil spirits on the Isenheim Altarpiece. It shows St. Anthony lying stretched out on the ground, threatened by terrifying larvae and spirits who torment him and pull his beard, while from above God watches the struggle of the holy athlete. When St. Anthony asked

The desert of Judea, the site of the first settlement of hermit monks

the Lord why he did not come and help, God replied: "Anthony, I was here but I was waiting to watch your battle. Because you have won the battle without giving in, I shall always help you from now on, and I shall make you famous everywhere." It was believed at that time that he who resisted the demons knew all the secrets of the soul.

When fasting, monks strive towards the salvation promised by Christ in order to be more and more filled with the richness of life.

The greatest experience of a seeker after God is nothing less than an encounter with God himself. Through fasting one renounces all of the desires and needs that might obstruct one's vision. That this is a lifelong task is reflected St. Anthony's words to his pupils: "The fruits of the earth do not ripen in a few hours but need time and rain and care. In the same way the harvest of a life will only be fruitful through asceticism, austere, lifelong practice, perseverance, self-control, and patience."

The foundations of life

Fasting is one of the fundamental elements of life itself, not confined to human beings but characteristic of other species as well. Migratory birds cover long distances without eating, and salmon swim for hundreds of miles up rivers to spawn without taking any nourishment. The male penguins in the Antarctic refrain from eating while they are incubating their eggs. In the insect world, the pupa stage could also be considered a time of fasting. Then, at the end of the period of renunciation, the pupa transforms itself into a wonderful butterfly, the young penguins emerge from the egg, and the migratory birds and salmon reach the destination of the longest journey of their life.

Naturally the fasting of monks has a meaning that goes far beyond the fasting encountered in nature. From the very beginning Christian monks fasted in homage to God: "They were worshiping the Lord and fasting," according to the Acts of the Apostles (13:2), because believers wanted to become better people.

But neither the monks nor the Church left precise directions for Christian fasting. It was up to each person to devise an individual approach to fasting. This was because, for the monks, it was not a matter of having an empty stomach but of a deeply felt sacrifice. That is why the renunciation of someone who gives up smoking for a week may be greater than that of someone who lives on water and tea for the same period.

Tips and tricks in monastic life

It was the theologian Buchard of Worms who in the eleventh century defined the rules of fasting in strict terms and coined the technical concept of "abstinence," including abstention from meat dishes. While ordinary believers observed the days for fasting laid down by the Church and loyally followed the rules it dictated, there are enough credible reports to show that there were many monks who knew how to comply with the rules of fasting while at the same time sidestepping their spirit.

Perhaps it was only human that even monks would look for loopholes in order to make the harsh periods of fasting a little more bearable. As a result

The Fasting of the early Christians

The early Christian communities adopted the fasting tradition from the Jews and reinterpreted it to satisfy their needs. They fasted two days a week, on Wednesdays and Fridays, to commemorate the death of Jesus, and they considered it a sign of a devout life that would please God. Soon they introduced a period of fasting before Easter. In the second century, this fasting period lasted between one and six days and later a whole week. In the first half of the fourth century the church scholar Athanasius specified a period of fasting lasting forty days, known as Lent. In the same way, the church later introduced a corresponding fast just before Christmas, Advent. Very early on, fasting also came to be seen as a preparation for special rituals such as baptism or the appointment of a bishop. Fasting before receiving the Eucharist goes back to the third century.

Praying pretzels

Did you know that pretzels were a food invented for periods of fasting? They were considered an ideal tonic during periods of abstinence, being both meat-free as well as nourishing and tasty. The word "pretzel" is derived from the Latin *bracchium*, "arm," because the shape of the pretzel symbolizes the crossed arms of a monk: the posture of monks when they pray.

the monastic culinary tradition became extremely inventive. Everything that swam or came into contact with water was not considered meat and could therefore be consumed during periods of fasting: swans, peacocks, common herons, otters, and beavers were there on the menu of "meatless" meals.

Monks also used certain tricks: they cooked and boned pork, game and poultry. Resourceful cooks kneaded the chopped up meat together with fat and spices and shaped it into a malleable mass which could then be kneaded into the shape of carp, trout or crustaceans — a miraculous transformation to delight and surprise everyone. Then there is the story of the bishop who loved hunting. Having shot a beautiful roebuck, he quickly threw it into a nearby pond. "Look, it's swimming!" the excited dignitary cried, and he renamed the roebuck "carp."

About St. Francis and his oil

Necessity is the mother of invention, so monks devised a special drink for periods of fasting, following the principle that "drinking does not break the fast." In Bavaria there are beers still known today by the names Franziskaner, Paulaner, or Augustiner, thus clearly revealing their connections to monastic orders.

In this way, many monasteries escaped the harshness of long periods of fasting by using their brewing skills. Apart from hops, beer contained the same ingredients as their basic bread, namely water, barley, and yeast. If brewed strong enough it could also satisfy hunger. In addition, the monks of the

Beer and pretzels, the fasting food of the monks

Paulaner order, which was dedicated to pastoral care with strict fasting rules, were "obliged" to celebrate the feast day of their founder, St. Francis of Paula, on April 2, right in the middle of the fasting period of Lent. So what could they do? In the end, the loyal monks decided to brew an extraordinary feast day beer, even stronger than the strong beer "Einböckischer Art" as it was brewed until then in the Munich court brewery. Thus the "Doppelbock" extra-strong beer was born. In honor of their founder this strong beer was renamed and given wonderful names such as "Oil of St. Francis" or "Holy Father Beer" (*Salvator*). As Johann Wolfgang von Goethe said: "The first time you shudder but after you have been drinking it for a week you can't stop."

During periods of fasting the monks were forbidden to eat meat, eggs, and some dairy products, but desserts were not expressly mentioned. Many lay brothers in monasteries kept bees because they needed wax for their altar candles. Since wax was only a byproduct of the bees' main activity there was almost nothing in medieval monasteries that was not sweetened with honey. The most delicious delicacies were made from almonds and honey. It is reported that the founder of the mendicant orders, St. Francis of Assisi, asked for some of Sister Jakobine's almond pastry as he lay dying. When Spanish nuns in South America produced what we know today as

Beer mugs from the Schussenried monastery

chocolate from an awful-tasting Indian beverage, Pope Pius V declared emphatically that anyone who consumed chocolate was not breaking a fasting rule. This had unintended consequences; for instance, many monasteries in Europe held out-and-out chocolate orgies even during periods of fasting.

Ideals and realities

Originally monks who ate meat during a period of fasting could be punished with death, but a few hundred years later there was nothing to prevent St. Thomas Aquinas from becoming extremely corpulent: he was so fat that a semicircle had to be cut out of the tabletop where he sat. This shows that asceticism is not always popular. For instance, a thousand years ago in Saint-Germain-des-Prés, an abbey just outside Paris, an ordinary monk would consume almost 7,000 calories a day. In comparison, a teacher today is said to consume about 2,400 calories.

The fasting regulations of the Church

The new 1983 ecclesiastical law of the Catholic Church includes only a few rules on the subject that should be observed by everyone throughout the world. The details are left to the national churches. While there are in general no specific regulations in the Protestant Church regarding fasting, in 1986 the German Bishops' Conference stipulated in its regulations concerning penitence: on fasting days people are allowed one nourishing meal and, if necessary, two small refreshments. But all Catholics between the ages of twenty-one and sixty are obliged to fast. Those who are unable to fast because of physical weakness, poverty, or strain are released from the obligation to do so.

In addition, the Church had defined two obligatory fasting days: Ash Wednesday and Good Friday. Abstinence from meat dishes should also be observed on days of repentance, meaning all Fridays of the year that do not fall on feast days. By extension, the rule of abstinence also involves a general reduction of food consumption, abstinence from alcohol, coffee, tea, tobacco, etc., and performing works of charity and devotion (for instance, going to mass on weekdays). All Catholics can decide for themselves whether they prefer to give up meat on Fridays or consider a reduction of food more important. All Catholics who are of sound mind and have reached the age of fourteen must obey the rule of abstinence.

But as the former Dominican monk Hans Conrad Zander asked in his *Little Catholic Calorie Counter*, why did these men of God who strove so hard towards the lofty ideal of renunciation eat and drink so excessively? The simple answer is that the ideal and reality do not generally go together. The ideal at that time was represented by people such as the monk St. Romuald, who only ate a handful of peas a day, or St. Celestine, who had not one but six periods of fasting in the year, or the hermit St. Anthony who

Nuns praying at the canonical hours

never ate or drank anything before sunset. The reality was that, whether they were monks or not, everyone in the Middle Ages was terrified of starvation. If weather conditions were unfavorable or if war broke out, whole countries were threatened with famine.

The gluttony of aristocrats and that of monks should be looked at in different ways. While knights reveled in eating large amounts of food, the history of eating in medieval monasteries is not a story to be proud of. Decadence is never without consequences. Monasteries in which no one prays or fasts are "dead monasteries," and their inhabitants all too easily become tragic caricatures: comical figures wrapped up in themselves, who, as St. Benedict said, "lied to God with their tonsures." The French author François Mauriac coined the phrase "snobbery of the great orders," whose "mental condition is not very different from that of a member of the Jockey Club." Indeed, where gluttony took over, it was not just the monastery that went downhill. Because monasticism played such a central and vital part in the Catholic Church, the whole church suffered when the orders forgot or betrayed their ideal.

"In fact, it was a healthy, natural instinct of self-preservation that caused people in the Middle Ages to gobble down as much as possible if the food was available."

Hans Conrad Zander

About the best in people

In the Christian tradition, fasting is never mentioned on its own. The triad of the monks and their church ran as follows: praying, fasting, and sharing. This is why, on Ash Wednesday, at the beginning of each Lent, monks were reminded in religious services of the words of Jesus in the Sermon on the Mount, exhorting people not only to observe these three rules but to practice them, especially when out of the public eye. "When you give alms, do not let your left hand know what your right hand is doing… whenever you pray, go into your room and shut the door, and pray to your Father who is in secret… when you fast, put oil on your head and wash your face, so that your fasting may be seen not by others." (Matthew 6:2–18)

For monks, fasting did not mean going through life without merriment and with as little joy and as much suffering as possible. The ideal of monastic fasting and the asceticism of the monks, when elevated to the highest level, essentially reflects a spiritual dimension that reaches beyond boundaries that one may "die with Christ." As the apostle Paul wrote: "[they] deal with the world as though they had no dealings with it." (1 Corinthians 7:31). The monks appreciated the good things of this world but they were prepared to let go of them. Fasting was considered an exercise in not having to have, a declaration of an absence of need by which a limit was imposed on one's desires. Sometimes our escape into noncommitment, distractions, bustling activity, or resigned sadness can reflect our anxiety in the face of what is mysterious in our inner self; it is an escape from who we really are.

For the monks, fasting means rediscovering the self in order to be able to give their lives a new direction.

The priorities when monks are fasting are not beauty and health. Particularly welcome are people who want to clarify their inner life and examine their goals, who have the courage to give up something, to distance themselves from long-established habits, and who are prepared to change their ways. In fact, people who fast are a little like "Adam before the Fall of Man," as the great preacher St. John Chrysostom said in the fourth century. In paradise only the essential counts. This means that overindulgence or the excessive pursuit of success and power will prevent a person from achieving great and lasting happiness, and that without abstention one cannot remain completely human. "Seek what you are seeking," the church father St. Augustine advised, "but not where you are seeking it." Even when we can satisfy our senses to excess, our soul will continue to yearn. What we are really looking for is a glimpse of heaven.

Seen in this light, fasting in monasteries is like stepping into the foothills of Eternity.

"Seek what you are seeking but not where you are seeking it." (St. Augustine)

How to prepare
for a fast

A monk walking in Jakobsberg

What to expect

"Fasting is the food of the soul."

St. John Chrysostom, the greatest preacher of the ancient Church

*O*f the many reasons for fasting, the most important was as familiar to the ancient monks as the Lord's Prayer: its healing effect on body and soul. People who want to fast must first have a clear idea about their motives for fasting. Losing weight should not top the list. The main goal of fasting in the monastic Christian tradition is the purification of the whole metabolism and inner, spiritual growth. Admittedly, fasting will not get rid of the end products of diseases (such as gallstones), but many diseases which could develop can be prevented.

People who fast can see things more clearly and can, when necessary, change their ways more easily and chart a new course, freeing themselves from dependencies. The small, difficult steps of fasting allow us to gradually consider new possibilities for life in the future. How far these new experiences can carry the person who is fasting varies according to the individual. But the spiritual experience will give everyone something to think about.

The vital importance of fasting in people's lives

was expressed by St. Ambrose as follows: "You turn to medicine and ignore fasting, as if you could find a better remedy!"

The best doctors in the Middle Ages, such as Avicenna and Paracelsus, firmly believed in fasting cures to heal their patients. The concept of the "inner physician" who becomes active during the fasting process dates back to that period. Current medicine confirms that fasting is the best way of preventing certain illnesses. In many cases it works like "an operation without a knife." No surgeon's scalpel can remove what is harmful to the body as carefully, skillfully, and painlessly, while preserving what is useful, as the fasting body itself.

The person who fasts feels more cheerful, refreshed, and efficient after fasting.

That fasting does not result in a reduction of the body's efficiency is clearly reflected by what happens in nature. Weeks and months of fasting are part of the normal life cycle of many animals in the wild. Animals that live in high mountainous regions, such as the ibex and chamois, put on winter fat during autumn, which gets them through the snowy "fasting period." In the words of Dr. Hellmut Lützner, an expert on fasting: "The fact that this fasting period falls right in the middle of the rutting season clearly shows that fasting in no way reduces the body's vital energy, but on the contrary, increases it!"

What fasting does for you. It...

- strengthens your character
- makes you feel more liberated
- brings spiritual clarity
- promotes a new view of life
- contributes to weight loss
- has a rejuvenating effect and helps prevent diseases
- gives energy and strength
- relieves the strain on the digestive system (liver, gall bladder, stomach, bowels, pancreas), locomotor system, heart, circulation, and kidneys
- has a diuretic effect, desalinates and detoxifies the body
- is helpful in many diseases

Fasting will help in the treatment of the following diseases

Rheumatism, arthritis, arteriosclerosis, gout, high blood pressure, low blood pressure, disorders of the heart and blood circulation, varicose veins, asthma, skin disorders, diseases of the stomach-bowel tract, constipation, diabetes mellitus, receding gums, glaucoma, migraine, nephritis, acute chronic inflammations, and infections.

Fasting is thus an outstanding "universal remedy" that is without damaging side effects. At a time when so many people are suffering from high levels of cholesterol, fasting can greatly improve individual well-being and the health of whole nations.

If and when to fast

Approaches to fasting vary enormously. For instance, special fasting clinics offer health-promoting fasting cures to people as in-patients. In Catholic communities, special groups are formed in the pre-Easter period in order to fast together. There are many monasteries that offer fasting courses in an atmosphere of tranquility and relaxation.

Five centuries before Christ, the ancient Greek philosopher Pythagoras extolled the virtues of fasting: "It is an excellent way of preserving and restoring good health."

In principle, one should first decide whether one wants to fast alone, with a partner, or in a group. Naturally it is much easier to tackle this demanding task in a group of like-minded people. Joint fasting with your spouse can also have a beneficial and strengthening effect on your relationship as you overcome initial difficulties together and support each other. But anyone who feels unwell or uncertain about the matter should speak to their doctor before undertaking a fasting cure.

On no account should one fast

- during pregnancy and lactation
- in the event of debilitating diseases such as tuberculosis, Graves' disease and cancer in an advanced stage, gastro-intestinal and duodenal ulcers
- in the event of psychosis and severe depression
- in the event of treatment with certain medication (for instance, drugs for high blood pressure and diabetes)
- in the event of addictions such as alcohol and drugs
- children and old people who are weak should not fast

Try to find a good companion

I remember with great pleasure when I called Father Rhabanus at the Jakobsberg priory to arrange my personal week of fasting. The Benedictine monk was very happy with my decision but at the same time he reminded me of the importance of the proper preparation. Fasting is a process, he explained, that starts at least one week before the actual fasting itself. A well-organized preparation contributes greatly to the successful outcome of your fast.

This preparation also includes a "good companion" because, as the saying goes, with a good friend "no road seems too long." You will discover in this book that monks are not only good teachers of fasting but also ideal spiritual guides. Their wisdom can help you to fast on your own. Monastic fasting may appear rather harsh and also a little old-fashioned. But the power that you derive from the deeper levels of fasting will convince even the most skeptical. As Rainer Maria Rilke wrote in his Florence Diary: "Be old-fashioned just for one day and you will see how much eternity you have in you."

Make a clean sweep

Like any deviation from our daily rounds and behavior, fasting requires commitment and inner determination. There are many temptations lurking when you fast at home. There is the refrigerator, and relatives and neighbors can make your fasting more difficult with their well-meant invitations: "A bite of breakfast can't do any harm!" You ought to consider very carefully who you want to tell that you are fasting. It is often better to mention it to as few people as possible — this will save many unnecessary discussions.

Today in the Western world it is definitely easier for people to die from overeating than from starvation.

A very important word of advice before you start your week of fasting: make a clean sweep at the outset. Cancel all your private and business commitments. Fasting is not a computer program that you start with the push of a button. You must get in the right mood and constantly reaffirm your decision to fast. Ideally schedule your fast during your holidays so as to be as free as possible from daily commitments. Because you become slower when you fast, your ability to react is also slower; you become more sensitive, and your circulation is not as stable. For this reason you should take special care, particularly with activities in which your own safety or that of other people is concerned.

If you are fasting for the first time you will not be able to assess the difficulties involved accurately. But for most people, isn't it more risky to continue on as they are, eating too much? Important nutrients such as proteins, vitamins, and salt that were not easily available in past centuries are now consumed in quantities that do not make us any healthier. Even when your fasting arouses various unexpected reactions in the people around you, do not let your resolve be undermined. It will be an experience that will open up new physical and spiritual possibilities. You will feel you are living at a higher pitch!

Practice fasting

Get in the right frame of mind by starting your fast gradually:

- Reduce your cigarette, alcohol, and coffee intake.
- Eat only to satisfy your hunger and no more.
- Try to give up meat and sweet things.
- Try to relax, through stretching, walking, meditation, and prayer.
- Reduce the external stimuli around you: watch less television, listen less often to the radio, avoid loud music and exciting sports events.

Gothic cloister of the Poblet Monastery, Spain

When you are fasting at home, free yourself from everyday commitments as much as possible and "switch off" everything that can be switched off. Remember: the early monks used to withdraw to the desert to fast because they believed that it was the perfect setting for it. The body and mind have important tasks to perform during the period of fasting, so they must not be distracted by unnecessary external stimuli.

The day of relaxation

The last day before you start your personal fast is called the "day of relaxation." That day you should begin to relax physically, mentally, and spiritually, reducing the hectic pace of your life to get rid of as much tension as possible.

The day before my journey to the monastery I ate little and very simply. I abstained completely from animal protein and ate only fruit and salads. To finish off, I treated myself to an apple because it binds metabolic residues and prevents metabolic hyperacidity. I wanted to arrive at the monastery feeling relaxed, not bloated.

There are various ways of carrying out a week-long fasting cure. Depending on preference and inclination, the fasting teacher in the monastery may use proven aids as a setting for his exercise, such as the Buchinger method, the juice fast, the Dr. F. X. Mayr fasting method, or the Hildegard fast. Fashion is also responsible for the development of all kinds of fasting cures, such as the rice pudding diet, the protein fast, Schroth's treatment or dry diet, the Guelpa diet, the fruit diet, the whey diet, and so on. None of these is really a fasting method in the traditional sense of the word; rather they involve reduced food intake, consumption of low-calorie foods, or detoxification regimes.

Fasting gives great strength and brings about great success.

Fasting is power

After careful consideration during the preparation period, I decided to opt for a total fast. It is the most logical application of the concept of the fast and corresponds to the traditional, classic approach to fasting. It has nothing to do with starving oneself but involves the voluntary abstinence from

The four ground rules of fasting

Rule 1
Do not eat anything, only drink. If possible, drink only water and tea, and most importantly, drink more than your thirst requires.

Rule 2
Abstain from everything that is not necessary. Forego the pleasures of alcohol, nicotine, candies, and coffee.

Rule 3
Get out of your everyday routine. Distance yourself from professional and family commitments, from stress caused by deadlines, modern means of communication, and the media. Avoid over-stimulation and rediscover yourself.

Rule 4
Do what is good for you. Find out what your body demands and please it: have a good sleep, go out in the fresh air, read a good book, or pursue one of your hobbies…

food, supported by the consumption of "empty" drinks, namely water and nonmedicinal teas.

When you merely reduce your intake of food — sometimes by drinking fruit juice only — you may experience pangs of hunger, but when you fast completely you will notice a loss of appetite that will make the rest of your fast much easier. However, it is extremely important that you should drink enough liquid while fasting. Strict fasting is in many respects much pleasanter and easier than "merely" eating less. This is also the reason why so many fasting cures that actually consist of a reduced food intake and the consumption of low-calorie foods fail more often than true fasting.

When we fast we are in fact following an ancient Christian monastic tradition. We are returning to the "source of our being." To make sure that these words do not remain just an attractive concept we must open up to the "adventure of fasting." Dr. Ruediger Dahlke wrote in his guide to fasting: "You will not learn anything conclusive about an apple by merely reading and hearing about it, you must take a bite of it." Trust in the promise made by St. Athanasius, who brought the first monks across the Alps in the fourth

Fasting starts with a day of relaxation, with fruit and salads

What to do on your day of relaxation

- Eat very little.

- Decide whether you will have a **fruit day** (3 pounds of different fruits, spread over three meals), a **rice day** (3 helpings of 2 ounces of whole-grain rice without salt, cooked only in water; in the morning and evening with cooked apples, at lunchtime with cooked tomatoes), or a **raw fruit and vegetable day** (in the morning, fresh fruit alone or with cereal; at midday and in the evening, a plate of raw vegetables and fruit). Chew the food properly. Also, make the shopping for this day a pleasurable experience.

- Say goodbye to: sweet foods, coffee, cigarettes, and alcohol. After all, this cure is only for a few days.

- Motivate yourself: "I have decided to do this and I know that I can do it! I am setting off on a little journey. It will be relaxing. I will learn something. I will be safe and secure, and afterwards I will be healthier and stronger and feel like a new person!"

- Relax. Don't worry. You have a warm house. You have plenty of time for yourself. Also, you can be sure that mother nature will guide you in the right direction. You have a good, well-filled food cupboard at your disposal — within yourself.

century and who spoke of the "great power" of fasting. It is worth taking the risk.

You must organize your week of fasting very carefully. Bring along some spiritual reading about fasting for that week, because you will probably have some important questions on the subject. You probably know what kind of questions you will ask yourself. The book of books, the Bible, will probably be helpful, as well as other spiritual literature. Read every day at set times.

Another point: exercise every day. You will find suggestions at the end of each chapter. The recommended exercises are suitable not only for that day but for the whole period of your fast.

Before you set off: your shopping list

- warmer clothes than usual
- enough underwear
- sports equipment
- hot water bottle
- enema bag
- body oil
- brush
- hand towel
- a few bottles of mineral water
- several kinds of herbal tea
- a few lemons
- a laxative of your choice
- good books
- a fasting diary

Starting the fast

A monk in the cloister of Zwettl Monastery in Austria

The process of detoxification

"Fasting is an irreplaceable training to ensure victory in the battle of life."

Pope John Paul II

Father Rhabanus had a very calming effect on me when we met for our first "session." His carefully considered words — "Now that you are in a monastery, you can take things one step at a time" — brought some order to my mind. I was bursting with questions, with excitement, wondering how I would fare here over the next few days.

In a very real sense I was coming "from outside," from a society that has very little understanding of a way of life dedicated to God. There was a time when monastic life was considered the true life. Ascetics were admired as masters of the art of living, but today things are very different. Anthony, whom people in early Christian Egypt called the "Star of the desert," must have known this when he prophesied: "There will come a time when people will become mad. And when you see one who is not mad then you will go up to him and say, 'you are crazy!' because he is different from you!" I asked Father Rhabanus whether he did not feel like a prisoner in the monastery. He replied: "Here the key is always on the inside, that is the difference!"

Perhaps the difference between fasting and hunger is a little like that between a monastery and a prison. Fasting has nothing to do with enforced abstinence. It is a natural part of our life in which the body switches over to self-regulation. The voluntary decision "not to eat anything" is quite different from not being allowed to eat or having nothing to eat.

Those who "take a holiday from eating" attach "their wagon to a star," Leonardo da Vinci once declared. They are, in a way, the true sensualists. This might seem crazy to some. But a growing number of people now recognize that they are living more and more at a remove, and that the rediscovered tradition of fasting will enable them to rid themselves of addictions and other compulsions.

Giving up instead of taking in

I decided to spend the first day of my fast cleansing the bowels. There are various ways of doing this, ranging from a glass of sauerkraut juice to saline solutions and enemas. The latter might seem rather old-fashioned but an enema is the best and "most productive" way of cleansing the intestines.

From this point, the body switches from external nourishment to internal nourishment. It extracts its vital energy from the energy stored in the fat that has accumulated in the body over the months and years. At the same time the body turns to some extent from "taking in" to "elimination." The body's own refuse service comes into action. All the sluice gates open up and the body starts to rid itself of its metabolic residue. The toxic substances in the body are normally bound to the protein and fat in connective tissue. The

The jewel of life

"Fasting is peace for the body, the pride of the limbs, the jewel of life. It is the power of the mind, the strength of the mind…
Fasting is the school of virtues… the remedy on the road to Christ."
Petrus Chrysologus, Bishop of Ravenna, fifth century

breakdown of fat and protein through fasting destroys this bond, so that the toxins can now be eliminated through the bowels, kidneys, and skin. In addition, fasting also breaks down the excess of proteins absorbed by the body that has accumulated in the walls of the smallest blood vessels in all organs. In this way many metabolic disorders, such as heart attack, cardiac infarction, or strokes, can be avoided.

The body now breaks down everything that burdens it and that it does not need, as well as what makes it ill. The process is a little like an oil change in an automobile. Naturally, this cannot be achieved without effort. Father Rhabanus knows how difficult it is to free oneself from what one is used to. "The first days of fasting are often very difficult," he warned me. You may suffer from headache and dizziness, and the pangs of hunger can be quite severe. You can alleviate these symptoms by drinking a lot. You should drink at least a dozen cups a day. Drinking liquid flushes out toxins. It is best to drink slowly, in small sips, as if savoring a good wine. You can never drink too much, only too little. It is now generally recognized by medicine that many of the ailments that plague our society are related to bad diet. As a result we suffer from various life-shortening diseases that can be avoided.

"Most people dig their graves with their teeth."

Dr. Heinz Fahrner, physician specializing in fasting

Not only do we eat unhealthy foods; we also eat too much, on average one-third more than we actually need. Dr Hermann Geesing, former head of the Schwarzwald-Sanatorium Obertal, notes that: "A person who regularly consumes 100 calories a day too many will accumulate 36,500 calories in a single year." This is a serious burden for body and soul! Just visualize twenty pounds of excess weight: this would represent four standard five-pound bags of potatoes. If a housewife had to carry these four bags of potatoes in her shopping basket she would be extremely relieved to put them down when she got home.

Reaching your soul through fasting

I asked Father Rhabanus why people take part in his fasting seminar. "Many people only want to lose weight," he replied sadly, "but, besides cleansing, the aim of fasting is also the purification of the soul: to ease the strain put on the body by the digestion in order to reach the soul." That pounds will drop off you when you fast is only a welcome side effect. Much more important are the experiences that involve the mind and soul. According to the monks and doctors of the past, fasting heals both body and soul in equal measure.

In Germany health fasting is usually linked to the name of Dr. Otto Buchinger. The Bad Pyrmont doctor developed the method after World War I because he firmly believed that it was above all a great "cure for eliminating and cleansing all the body fluids and tissues." Indeed, fasting cleanses the body and rids it of many diseases. Very old cells are broken down and the formation of new cells is stimulated. Doctors specializing in fasting cures say that fasting alleviates rheumatism, arthritis, arteriosclerosis, and skin disorders.

But Buchinger was not only interested in the purely physical effects of fasting. Like the monk Athanasius who was convinced that fasting drove away bad thoughts and clarified the mind, Buchinger was also aware of the spiritual and mental benefits of this "cure."

When in 1962 Pope John XXIII urged all believers to fast for the forthcoming Second Vatican Council, Dr. Buchinger wrote him a letter to thank him. In it he emphasized that fasting was an "essential element of Christian asceticism." At the same time he regretted that "athletes, the cosmetics market, and the wealthy sick" had taken over the world of fasting "which was in reality the sacred domain of the Church." He also added: "As an eighty-five-year-old convert, I hope that God will grant me the joy of seeing the tradition of fasting revived in the Holy Church."

"Mother Mary": Pray and fast!

High-ranking church dignitaries constantly reiterate the fundamental importance of fasting in the Church. "Without fasting the Church is not the Church any more," said Cardinal Joseph Ratzinger, "because it becomes like the world." But something happened in Bosnia-Herzegovina some two decades ago that led to a revival of the fasting tradition.

In the little village of Medjugorje near Mostar, children had since 1981 been reporting that the Virgin Mary was appearing to them — "Mother Mary," as in the Beatles' song. Those children have now grown into adults but the appearances continue. Millions of believers as well as those who are simply curious have made a pilgrimage to this little village to hear the "message of peace," a call to pray and to fast in order to rediscover the inner self.

The Virgin's message is not new. She is simply reminding us of the twin powers of prayer and fasting, and the link between them. According to the teachings of the Bible and the Church, they are essential for spiritual growth. In the words of one of these messages: "Fasting and prayer are the means by which we open ourselves to God, who can cleanse us of all the sins in our past." He who "fasts and prays with all his heart" will bring joy back into his life and solve many personal problems. The combination of prayer and fasting has the power to prevent wars and bring peace back into the world.

The Franciscans in Medjugorje who look after the pilgrimage site have, "on divine instructions," revived an ancient Christian tradition,

In the priory at Jakobsberg

that of fasting on bread and water twice a week, on Wednesday and Friday. An unexpectedly large number of people have joined them, thus reinstituting a form of devotion that had almost fallen into oblivion. "I have been a priest for thirty years," said one of the Medjugorje monks, "and I am certain that in all the years I have been a priest I have celebrated mass and preached to the faithful on every Sunday during Lent. But it was only in Medjugorje that I became aware that I had completely forgotten about fasting. I never preached about fasting. Nor did I try to encourage the people to fast, nor to explain why one should fast. But now that I have discovered fasting, I wonder how it happened that I did not really know about this biblical tradition and its message or preached it to the people."

When the stove stops working

My first day in Jakobsberg was not without consequences. I did get through the day all right, but then I was tired and hungry, and when I went to the dining room in the monastery where the other guests were enjoying the delights of its cuisine to get my tea, I felt cold. Somehow my inner stove had stopped working. I could still hear Father Rhabanus's words ringing in my ears: "It must be cleaned thoroughly because it is completely clogged up with soot."

I was becoming aware of perspiration on my skin and a bad smell in my mouth; my tongue was furred. At this stage the fasting doctor used to say to his patients: "You cannot muck out a stable without it stinking." The body's refuse is disposed of not only through the bowels and bladder. This is why you should not wear synthetic fibers when you are fasting but underwear that will absorb the sweat. Most importantly, you should shower and bathe more often than usual.

The unpleasant physical symptoms resulting from fasting are waste products of the "internal cleansing," which you must assist from the outside. Now that you have plenty of time to pamper your body, your skin is waiting to be scrubbed with a dry brush and rubbed with oil. You should not wear any foundation or powder that can block the pores. It is important that they remain open to allow the toxins eliminated during the fast to emerge. Because the lungs also expel metabolic residue, you should air out your room regularly and go for long walks outdoors.

"The first few days are the road through the desert. Those who want to reach the oasis must follow this road," says our doctor comfortingly. Father Rhabanus also encourages the participants in his lectures to tackle the first few days "not only from a physical but also from a spiritual point of view, and to rid yourself of unnecessary burdens." Fasting is also "spiritual hygiene." In the same way that we must pay special attention to personal hygiene and pamper our body when fasting, we must make the time to look after our soul.

A new Creation

As Basil the Great described it in the fourth century, the monks consider the practice of fasting as an "ancient gift, which does not age or become obsolete but which rejuvenates itself constantly and continues to flourish." Father Rhabanus expresses it in a more modern way. It is, he says, "the chance to make a completely new start." And it is no coincidence that at the beginning of every period of fasting the monks at Jakobsberg sing the following hymn in vespers: "Now the right time has come, the time that God's favor has bestowed on us."

In the twelfth century, Hildegard von Bingen taught that through fasting, pathological disorders could be eradicated and the healing powers of the soul present in each person released and strengthened. The experience of the monks themselves has always been that the so-called "divine virtues," faith, hope, and love, grow more intense through fasting. And why? It is simple.

My fasting master in the priory opened the Bible and began to read the first words in it: "In

Benedictine nuns in the refectory of Kellenried Abbey

the beginning when God created the heavens and the earth..." Then he compared the seven days of the Creation with the seven days of my fast. Body and soul, "desolate and dark" because of the rubbish and overload of everyday life, weighed down by weariness and illness, will revive through this kind of inner purification, because through fasting and our voluntary abstinence from food we allow God to speak to us the words "And there was light" from the story of the Creation. A good image: we separate light from darkness within ourselves, as on the first day of the Creation. Things that are poisonous, harmful, oppressive, and unnecessary in the body and soul are eliminated, and clarity can grow in its new space.

Exercise of the day: Introduction to writing a fasting diary

Start a personal fasting diary. Every day write down what you have enjoyed, what you have done, what has depressed you. This will make the examination of your inner self easier. You can write all kinds of things "about the soul." You can read it all again later and this will motivate you again. The fasting diary is like a mirror in which you can see yourself. Write down your experiences and encounters of the day, your personal thoughts and feelings. This has a liberating effect.

The right balance

Monk praying in the monastery of Beuron

Learning from doing without

"If you want to fill
your hands with gold
you must first let go of
the stones that you are
holding."

Proverb

*I*t was morning. The second day of my fast was beginning, and when I opened the window, the summer wind blew smells of frying food into my room. I had slept a little longer than usual, and as a result I missed the monks' morning prayers. I felt rather dizzy when I first got up, but I had a good stretch and soon felt better. I did some morning exercises in front of the open window, and that stimulated my circulation. While doing the exercises, I discovered that the monastery kitchen in which the monks were already preparing lunch was right under my room. The faint dizziness soon disappeared, but the seductive cooking smells continued to distract me. Fasting requires self-mastery and effort. Even though you have freely chosen to embark on your fast, it still entails renunciation and abstinence. "Fasting is a thorn in the flesh," Father Rhabanus had said. Now I could see what he meant.

About Anthony and basic questions

In the third century, a dramatic conversion led St. Anthony, the founder of Christian monasticism, to

Tips against dizziness and weakness in the morning

- Stretch well before you get up.
- Activate your circulation using the following method: shower in cold water, directing the jet of water inwards from the hands and feet to the middle. Then return to bed to warm up.
- Take an "air bath" in front of the open window.
- Massage your body with a brush, always brushing towards the heart.
- In the morning do five minutes of gentle stretching.

live the life of a seeker after God and withdraw to the desert. The son of a prosperous, respected family in Egypt, he was about twenty years old when he heard the words of Jesus read in a religious service: "If you wish to be perfect, go, sell your possessions and give the money to the poor, and you will have treasure in heaven; then come, follow me" (Matthew 19:21). This time the words hit him like a bolt of lightning: *You are the man, these words are for you!* was the thought that suddenly flashed into his mind.

Anthony reminds us of the fundamental questions of human existence. Do we not sometimes want to leave everything behind in order to be free? Do we often hang on to things that we do not need? Do we live as if our happiness depended on possessions?

Perhaps we should remember more often that it is not skills that make a person valuable, not wealth but — and this is what the monks teach during the fasting week — the gift of being a human being. Learning this is one of the "gifts of fasting." What makes you valuable and kind is always associated with voluntary renunciation, because with it you must give: your friendship, your love, your forgiveness. We become better people when we give of ourselves: when we smile, reach out to another person, and say a kind word.

The words of Jesus that so struck St. Anthony say exactly the same thing:

there is no true happiness in owning and taking, but only in giving. Isn't this always the case? Indeed, a hot-air balloon only rises when it sheds ballast. A heavy-laden ship has to abandon cargo overboard in stormy seas. We are doing the same when we fast. As we already noticed at the beginning of our fast, fasting makes us freer and lighter as well as more sensitive, more awake, and better listeners. It not only relieves problems and tensions, as Paracelsus had already discovered, but by changing our habits we can discover new approaches to living.

Anthony acted on the spot. He did not even wait for the end of the service but immediately ran back home, sold all his possessions, and began a life of asceticism that he never abandoned.

Why you should start fasting gradually

To follow St. Anthony's example, Father Rhabanus advised us to start fasting gradually and gently. It is important to listen to "the voices that speak in your soul." Fasting is a dialogue with your body, with your own behavior. Much that was hidden will come to light, and things that were buried deep in the unconscious will bubble up to the surface.

But as well as the advice to start fasting very gradually, we should concentrate not only on ourselves but also look at others and learn from them. According to the oldest biography of this great Christian hermit, recorded by St. Athanasius: "Anthony noted the friendliness in one person, the fervor in prayer in another, he noted the silence in someone else, the humanity in another, alertness in one person, knowledge in

"Our life is like a candle: as we burn we become light."
Father Rhabanus

another, he admired one for his steadfastness, someone else for his fasting and for sleeping on the bare earth." Anthony grew and developed because he did not envy the skills and virtues of others but rather sought to emulate them.

The spirit of our time, marked by a passionate desire for life, makes it difficult to see asceticism as anything but dreadful self-torment. It calls to mind emaciated faces and images of life-despising self-chastisement and inhibition. Wilhelm Busch described it well in his poetry: "In front of his cave in the high mountains sits the ascetic, his body and soul now a mere relic of

Praying nuns in the convent of Lilienthal

himself because of his extreme diet." Yet the early desert monks only sought to increase the "vigor of the soul." This increases considerably as soon as you have realized that "the desires of the body have no power over you."

Finding the right attitude

When fasting, we have to be clear about our motives and, if necessary, be willing to reexamine them; it is also very important to find the right attitude. Because we are not fasting simply to lose weight or for selfish reasons only, we need to cultivate humility and detachment.

"And whenever you fast, do not look dismal, like the hypocrites, for they disfigure their faces so as to show others that they are fasting. Truly I tell you, they have received their reward. But when you fast, put oil on your head and wash your face, so that your fasting may be seen not by others but by your Father who is in secret; and your Father who sees in secret will reward you." (Matthew 6:16–18)

For the monks, fasting has always had something to do with a change of heart. In the monastic tradition, fasting, prayer, and giving alms go together. St. Augustine, who had written a rule for monks about a century before Benedict, called prayer and giving alms the "wings of fasting." Without these wings one drags along the ground with difficulty; with them one suddenly becomes light. He wrote: "Fasting puts a strain on you. In itself that is not enough, if you do not strengthen your brother. Your privations only become fruitful if you offer them as a gift to another. How many poor people can eat of the meal that you have just foregone? Therefore, fast and rejoice that someone else can eat his fill thanks to your abstinence."

It is true that fasting does not change the world, say the monks. But fasting changes people. And people change the world.

In this simple truth lies a great secret. The help you give someone always comes back to you. Everything that you share becomes not less but more. As the saying has it, "A problem shared is a problem halved," and "A pleasure shared is a pleasure doubled." When someone fasts and offers his renunciation to another, he fulfils the commandment of compassion that Jesus describes as the yardstick by which we will be measured at the Last Judgment. ("Just as you did not do it to one of the least of these, you did not do it to me.") He also "sanctifies" and heals himself when he helps others. The one who has learned to give to others can also accept help more easily; he can overcome the pride and egotism that often make it so difficult to ask for help.

The monks know that we cannot live on bread alone; living on bread alone, we will die. At a time when unchecked consumerism is so prevalent, monastic concepts such as abstinence and moderation may seem foreign and provocative. All the same, "You cannot live indefinitely off refrigerators, politics, finance, and crosswords. It is just not possible. You cannot live without literature, or colors, or love." So said Antoine de Saint-Exupéry, author of *The Little Prince*, who had an affinity to the monastic attitude towards life.

Diseased cells disappear, healthy cells remain

It has been said that only half of all the cells in the body work at full capacity; a quarter are in a formative stage, and the remaining quarter are sick or degenerating. Fasting tackles this last quarter. "The diseased cells disappear, the healthy ones remain," Otto Buchinger laconically observed.

This rule of thumb can also be applied to the soul. So "Rend your hearts and not your clothing. Return to the Lord, your God!" (Joel 2:13) describes what the monks call "holy fasting." We overcome ourselves when we fast. Without this desire to go beyond ourselves, to reach for something beyond the ordinary, we would remain stuck in the realm of banality, never understanding beauty, wisdom, and the purity of things. We may have enough to live on, but much too little to live for. "The purification of the heart through fasting" is therefore seen as an important aspect of the quest for the meaning of life. It helps us to grasp something of our origin, which is greater than ourselves.

Do not go overboard!

Monasticism in the Egyptian desert was marked by ascetic exercises and deprivations aimed at approaching as close as possible to the divine sphere, as the monks moved to the highest levels of mysticism. At monasticism's high point there were thousands of lay brothers living as hermits in caves or in enclosed complexes in the desert.

But however much St. Anthony praised fasting, he also warned against overdoing it: "There are some who weaken their bodies through fasting; they are far from God because they do not exercise moderation." There is a charming legend about the hermit and a hunter: "Set an arrow in your bow," Anthony said, "and draw it." The hunter did so. Upon which the monk said: "Pull it back further!" And the hunter did so. And Anthony said again: "Pull it back even more!" The hunter then replied: "If I pull the bow too far it will break." The old monk then explained: "It is the same with the work of God and fasting. If we pull the bow too far, the brothers will soon break. This is why we must make allowances from time to time."

St. Benedict's Middle Way

In his Rule, St. Benedict warned against immoderation and excessive zeal that eventually work against the body itself and as a result become counterproductive.

Benedict, a member of an aristocratic family from Nursia, spent time studying in Rome. Finding himself disgusted by the degenerate mores of the city, Benedict fled to the solitude of the Sabine mountains to live the life of a hermit, exactly like the early monks in the desert. He fasted rigorously, completely withdrew from the outside world, and devoted his time to prayer. Soon rumors spread about his extraordinary lifestyle in the mountains, greatly enhancing his reputation. One day he was approached by the brothers of a nearby monastery who asked him to become their abbot.

An evening walk

Hans Memling, St. Benedict, *c. 1485*

But the monks disliked Benedict's strict rule so much that they finally put poison in his wine in order to get rid of the troublesome abbot. Benedict, sensing the danger, escaped death and left the convent to return to live as a hermit in the mountains. Again, his seclusion did not go unnoticed.

Young men soon gathered round him. As a result, he founded twelve small cloisters for them. They did not as yet have the Benedictine Rule that was later to spread throughout the world. Instead they were more like the early colonies of monks in the desert. Benedict was already over fifty years old in 529 when he left the enchanting countryside of Subiaco with his brothers and founded his first large monastery on Monte Cassino, between Rome and Naples. There he wrote the celebrated Rule, which is still followed by 9,000 Benedictine monks.

St. Benedict's Rule provides a real middle way and affirms the bases of human dignity. It has been in existence some 1,500 years, longer than any constitution. Benedict's approach is summed up as *Ora et labora,* meaning "Pray and work." Indeed, serving God and serving people were so closely linked and related in the Rule that throughout the centuries Benedictine monasteries became not only centers of prayer and religion but also focal points of the cultural life of their time.

Where you can find your liver

While I was listening to Father Rhabanus telling me about the history of the order, I became aware that my blood sugar levels and blood pressure had suddenly dropped. I felt wretched and would really have liked to lie down. My fasting master reassured me that this was a completely normal reaction on the second day of fasting. He told me that I should drink more water, more than my thirst required, and put a hot compress on my liver. This was because the liver, the most important detoxification organ besides the kidneys, was now working at maximum capacity.

In my cell I filled my hot water bottle and wrapped it in a wet towel. *But what should I do with it? Where should I put it on my body? Where exactly?* I was wondering. Where is the liver exactly, the body's own washing-machine that was now overheating? Isn't it curious how little we know about our own bodies and the processes that take place in an organism on which we rely

The liver compress

Next to the kidneys, the liver is the most important detoxification organ in the body, which is why it must work so hard when you are fasting. A liver compress is therefore very helpful in supporting it.

- Take three hand towels and a hot water bottle:
  1. Place a dry hand towel on the body where your liver is (at the bottom of the rib cage on the right side).
  2. Now place a moist, hot towel on top.
  3. Then cover with another dry towel.
  4. Finally a hot water bottle goes on that.
  5. Tuck up warmly and remain like this for half an hour.

- You should always lie down when you apply a liver compress. The blood flows better through the liver when you are in a horizontal position than when you are standing.

- You can apply a liver compress every day while you are fasting (it is best between 1:00 P.M. and 3:00 P.M. because that is when the energy supply to the liver is at its lowest).

day and night? Heart, lungs. liver, kidneys — what do they all do? How do they work? What should we pay attention to? We spend so much time on useless things and so little trying to know ourselves!

If you are healthy and are not studying medicine you would never wonder about your liver and what it does. Now, thanks to my fasting experiences, I have become a little wiser. I know where to put a liver compress, namely at the bottom of my rib cage on the right side.

One-third of energy goes to digestion

Father Rhabanus told me that my whole body needed time to heal and strengthen itself, especially during fasting. The energy necessary for the healing of sick cells and the formation of new healthy cells is found in the body's own food storage. When fasting, the body saves the energy it spends on digestion, which is usually thirty percent of its overall expenditure of energy, and concentrates the now unused energy on healing.

Everyone knows from their own experiences that *In fasting there is no* strength, speed, stamina, and ability to think do not depend *pressure to succeed.* directly on eating. You often think better and more quickly on an empty stomach. People involved in sports know the link between fasting and performance. Indeed, no mountain climber would ever consider climbing a mountain on a full stomach.

These explanations by the Benedictine monk allayed my fears that my fast, which I felt was really draining, could seriously weaken me. Also I realized that I didn't have to do anything during my fast. It was not a question of having to lose eight or ten pounds successfully. Fasting should only give us the tranquility to concentrate on life: a tranquility that Father Rhabanus could not stress often enough was one of the most important of the monks' healing treatments.

In the same way that God separated water from water and created heaven and earth on the second day of the Creation, so we must establish boundaries in our life in order not to be overwhelmed. One point had become very clear: the middle way has nothing to do mediocrity.

Exercise of the day: more about drinking

Drinking liquid is particularly important while you are fasting, and you should take more than your thirst requires. Prepare at least four pints of mineral water for each day and also drink some nonmedicinal fruit and herbal teas. In the morning or early afternoon you should also drink some black tea or maté in order to boost the circulation. Your body needs a lot of fluid to support the detoxifying organs and flush out the toxins. Always sip when you drink. Warm each sip in your mouth or let it cool down, depending on what is necessary. Drink slowly and in measured sips.

Cravings

Carthusian monks in the monastery of Marienau

Why things go wrong, and bearing up under adversity

A few small clouds were appearing on the horizon in the morning sky. Rather bad-tempered, I looked out of the window: "The weather will be bad today!" I felt lousy and ill at ease in my own skin. After getting up, I found my tea was too hot, and I tripped over my shoes. Little things irritated me. Fasting was wearing me down. I was frightened by own reactions: why did I blame fasting for my bad mood? Perhaps I was always in a foul mood and just had never noticed it before?

I hung around tired and depressed. My physical weak points and focuses of old diseases seemed to be coming to the fore again. What was happening to my body? Why did I feel so powerless and downright lousy? Was it a process similar to that which takes place in homeopathy, whereby chronic illnesses develop backwards through all their phases in order then to disappear for good with the original illness? Practitioners of natural medicine speak of "original worsening." My concentration, my powers of observation, my physical condition, everything was getting worse. Where were all those euphoric feelings that had been promised to me? Would I never experience them? Was I not the right type? Or was it literally all invented?

The "sweet yoke"

My unease and doubts were increasing, so I decided to go to Father Rhabanus for advice. When you give the engine polluted fuel, my fasting master explained, it does not work very efficiently. The organs were becoming stuck in the process of eliminating toxins. As a result the toxins were circulating through the body; after the body had flushed them all out I would feel better, he said. "Do not give up," he urged me. "Do not break your fast on any account!" It was not a serious problem, just a temporary crisis caused by the toxins.

A temporary crisis! That was easily said. My monk recommended that I not only drink a lot of liquid but also have an enema. That would help to lighten my mood. He suggested that I treat myself to a good rest and keep warm. He also explained to me that when fasting one undergoes not only a physical but also a spiritual detoxification. Bad dreams and mood swings were all signs that unresolved problems were being pushed up to the surface and required clarification. I could now understand that fasting prevented disease in the truest sense of the word: I could see not only how my body was getting rid of toxins but also that how I was undergoing a spiritual "spring cleaning." In the end I willingly gave in before illness forced me to do so.

The monks were also quite aware that when we confront our weaknesses,

Smells and furry tongues

During your fast you will often suffer from bad breath and your tongue will feel furry. This results from metabolic residues being eliminated through the mucus membrane of the mouth. Clean your teeth often and chew fresh herbs (chives, dill, parsley). Brush your tongue with a toothbrush, rinse your mouth frequently with water, or suck a piece of lemon several times a day.

What to do in a fasting crisis

- Drink a lot in order to increase the elimination of toxins.
- Take an enema.
- Get a lot of rest and make sure you stay warm.
- Do not exert yourself.
- If necessary drink a glass of buttermilk.
- In the case of a serious complaint (for instance, biliary colic) call a doctor immediately.

we become nervous and irritable. Father Anselm explained candidly: "When a brother in our convent says during a discussion on fasting that it is better not to fast and be in a good mood than to fast and be a nuisance to others because one is constantly in a bad mood, another brother will invariably reply that this is the wrong conclusion. If we overcome our ill-temper by eating and drinking well we shall never get to know ourselves."

I began to think about this. How often had I eaten and drunk well and still ended up feeling irritable and aggressive? Perhaps my current bad mood had nothing to do with my fasting. Perhaps I had become more sensitive and more aware, so that I noticed my unpleasant behavior more easily, and it troubled me to see how I really was — something that had not struck me before.

In Medjugorje, a pilgrim who had just started to fast on Wednesdays and Fridays told the Franciscan monk Slavko that he was only fasting on two days, but when he was fasting he was an "unbearable man." Slavko replied: "I congratulate you!" At this the pilgrim asked incredulously: "Father, did you understand what I said to you?" The Franciscan replied: "I understood very clearly: I congratulate you!" The pilgrim was astonished: "Why the congratulations?" Slavko replied: "I congratulate you because you are only an unbearable person on two days; whereas the others, although they are not fasting, are unbearable seven days a week, but they do not notice it." Because

A banquet arranged by the devil in an inn, to lead the Dominican monks into temptation. Detail from a medieval miniature painting

fasting is an uphill path, it is also exhausting. In this respect, Jesus spoke of a "sweet yoke." The monk St. Anthony also reported that, like Jesus during his forty days in the desert, he was visited by the devil. Ghostly apparitions unrolled in his mind and dominated his awareness. Memories of events from his earlier life came to the surface again. The thought of delicious food enticed him. At night he was approached by the erotic shapes of young girls, plunging his mind and thoughts into a kind of spiritual typhoon. "The temptations flooded over him like waves of water and threatened to engulf him," wrote Walter Nigg. What had happened? The inner disturbances that wracked his soul made Anthony the prototype of man as seeker.

Growing through temptation

According to the masters, when we fast we become aware that our true human destiny is temptation and not security. Millions of Christians say the Lord's Prayer every day and pray: "Do not lead us into temptation." Yet Anthony the monk answered the question of why there should be temptation: "Remove temptation, and no one would be saved."

You will not arrive at your destination without inner struggle.

Fasting is to a certain extent a test of life. It prevents us from lapsing into the indifference that arises when there is no longer any intellectual struggle.

That we must experience and endure something different in this extreme time is far from easy. For many people there is nothing more painful than to see, hear, and feel their plain, unvarnished selves. Through temptation I was becoming in some measure purified, like "gold in fire."

In the early afternoon I was driven out of my cell by a rush of negative thoughts and temptations. I walked quickly across the convent courtyard to a slightly remote garden where I expected to find Brother Daniel, next to whom I had stood at morning prayer that day. As soon as I greeted him, he noticed my inner turmoil and told me that the constant absorbing of evil images and bad thoughts — for example from television and newspapers — makes us ill. But fasting flushes out all the negativity in our bodies.

Brother Daniel, who was in the garden looking for healing, medicinal herbs, put his spade to one side and invited me to visit the Stations of the

Carthusian monks at the dining table, monastery of Marienau

Cross on the hill with him: the fourteen stations of the passion of Christ, represented on pictures the size of a school notebook, set on small columns. We looked at the sad images and Brother Daniel prayed in front of each one: "We adore you, O Christ, and we bless you, because by your holy Cross you have redeemed the world! ... O powerful God, O Holy God, O Immortal God. Have pity on us!" There are things in life that we cannot describe. The enormous power and inner comfort of these Stations of the Cross are among them.

"Abstinence does not take, abstinence gives. It gives the inexhaustible strength of the simple person."

Martin Heidegger

The monks use fasting as a means of purifying their hearts. With their fasting they engage in the fight against evil, against the enemies of their soul that are experienced as demonic temptations. They encounter the enemy and face what is trying to capture the soul, namely the sins of gluttony, fornication, and greed. The three solemn vows of the order are poverty, chastity, and obedience, vows which the monks make to another person. And nowhere is the spiritual struggle to fulfill this threefold promise fought as fiercely as it is here.

When the stove is out

When fasting you will often suffer from cold hands and cold feet. Because the "inner stove" is turned off, you may feel extremely cold. You can help yourself as follows:

- Wear warm, airy clothes made from natural fibers
- Take a lot of exercise
- Put a hot water bottle on your feet
- Have hot foot baths

I was in the monastery shop with Father Rhabanus as he filled the shelves. He explained: "Fulfilling these vows, which we call 'evangelical counsels,' makes us mature people." The monks' renunciation contains much of what makes life worthwhile. We practice virtues such as loyalty, abstinence, restraint, purity, and humility — things that can only succeed if we have inner freedom. All this is far from easy, Rhabanus explained as he moved a heavy box filled with jars of honey from the apiary of a French monastery; it always remains a "sweet yoke" for the monks to stumble back into the supposed pleasures of the world. We are always challenged and we could always fall.

Finally, as the Benedictine monk and author Father Anselm Grün put it, the aim of the monks' fasting is "to bring out the good in us through a healthy asceticism and to transform our urges, so that the strength that is in us becomes available for the future."

What fasting has to do with love

"There is nothing be it so good and holy," said Basil the Great, "that the devil cannot use it to hide in, like the worm in the bud." St. Basil lived in the fourth century AD and, with Anthony and Pachomius, was one of the founding fathers of the desert monks, gathering together all the hermits scattered over the desert into communities. He had firsthand experience of the all too human aspects of these seekers after God.

As soon as they gathered together, the hermits began to compete among themselves: Who was the best faster? Whose asceticism was most austere? Many tied heavy weights around themselves in order to increase their suffering. Others sought to chastise themselves with belts and flagellate themselves. So now the devil was established in the bud of fasting, and Basil had his hands full trying to drive him away. "What you do to show off bears no fruit but only results in praise from people," he warned his brothers, and he made sure that the superiors drew up binding regulations for fasting in their communities. "To want more than other people, even of admirable qualities, is quarrelsome, a passion that arises from a desire for vain honor," Basil wrote in his Rule, and in doing so put a stop to competitive fasting.

Many of our ideas about monasteries are based on clichés, and one should always remember that monks are also people with faults and sins. Real monks try to live up to their ideal; they are not impressed by their own virtuous acts and they do not allow themselves to become slaves of their own asceticism. Fasting is not an end in itself: you can never really fast without humility, which since time immemorial has been seen as a doorway to God. In the end the objective is love.

It is not a question of suppressing one's inner drives but of becoming a new person.

The monks' love towards Creation and the Creator, not the expectations and reactions of others, is the driving force behind fasting. The order of worldly values is overturned at the monastery gates. "Allow us to achieve the highest good: love," the fasting monk prays. "In themselves fasting and keeping vigils are nothing. Without love there is no value in self-denial, because it is written: God is Love." In Corinthians 1:13, the apostle Paul expresses the idea that without love there is nothing. Such sentiments are now rarely heard in a world fixated on success and celebrity. But even today the monks' simple existence reminds us of the cosmic foundations of the world.

I spoke with Father Rhabanus as we walked along the corridors of the

Carthusian monk ringing a bell

monastery and looked at some pictures. He told me a little story that partly explained the importance of fasting and the reason for it. It concerned an old monk who lived in poverty and solitude. A young man approached him with empty hands outstretched and said: "I have come with nothing in my hands!" The monk frowned and cried out: "Drop your nothing immediately!" Rhabanus explained that even "nothing" can be misused; it can actually become a possession and a temptation for the ego to be become inflated.

"When you are fasting you are doing away with all the false pleasures that can so often intoxicate and blind you, and you are able to recognize your deepest inner truth," my teacher told me. "Now it also becomes apparent whether, having given up all external stimuli, you can resist inner pride." It is often like this: the harder we fight our body through fasting the more our pride grows. "We believe," warns Father Anselm Grün, "that we are now capable of controlling our impulses entirely on our own. We want to tame the 'animal' in us, to break its strength, and be admired for it by others."

In proportion as the body grows fat, so does the soul wither away.
Abba Daniel of Sketis

"Someone who fasts only to achieve recognition does not benefit from the positive effects of fasting," explained Father Rhabanus. Physical fasting must be combined with spiritual fasting, refraining from bad thoughts, pride, and the craving for power and recognition. The twelfth-century monk Bernard of Clairvaux wrote: "To ensure that God is pleased with your fasting, you should not think only of God. You have obligations towards other people as well. God wants you to think highly of those he himself admires." Disappointed in love, Bernard founded over 160 abbeys, and as their superior he came to fully understand human weaknesses.

The most exciting time of your life

A day that had started so tediously ended happily. Fasting opened "the doors of my soul," and old wounds came to the surface. It was as if a mirror were held in front of me. It was not an easy day: fasting takes us to our very limits. But I had also realized that many problems that I considered insurmountable mountains were just little molehills and that renunciation brings unexpected relief and new strength. As Werner Bergengruen wrote in his poem "Heavenly Arithmetic": "Yet God loves empty hands and the shortage becomes a gain." And again: "Each pain makes you richer. Praise the sacred poverty."

Monks consider periods of fasting to be the most interesting times of their lives. When they talk about their fasts, you can tell that they regard them as intense, happy experiences. There are paths that lead uphill and paths that lead downhill, towards the good or the bad. There are temptations everywhere. When fasting, these temptations become more obvious to us. We recognize their attraction but also their price: that they result in a diminishment of ourself, in the loss of the essence of our being, without which we are unable to become what we really are.

At the end of this third day of fasting, the monks advised us to meditate on the Bible's account of the third day of the Creation, when God brought the diversity of vegetation to the Earth, such as grass, plants yielding seeds, and fruit trees of every kind. It had now become easier to see how important it is to prune back the rank growth that covers the beauty and colors of the soul so as to reveal the essential again: "and God saw that it was good."

Exercise of the day: Introduction to "looking in the mirror"

Have a hand mirror available. Look in this mirror every morning and evening for five or ten minutes. Take time to have a good look at your face. Look yourself in the eyes: you are a unique person. Smile at yourself. Ask yourself in front of the mirror: Who am I? How do I live? What will I do differently tomorrow? What do I let myself be influenced by? Take yourself seriously, say yes to yourself. You are a valuable person, worthy of being loved. But also admit your weaknesses and faults. Become reconciled with yourself, because it is only when you have sorted things out in your own mind that you will be able to be frank and direct with other people.

Finding oneself
through fasting

The monastery of Melk reflected in the waters of Danube

Cleansing oneself of "sin"

*"Anyone can perform
magic
Anyone can reach his
goal,
If he can think
If he can wait
If he can fast."*

Hermann Hesse

I headed back to the priory from my morning walk along a sandy path. I could hear the sound of bells coming from the tower of the little priory church resounding in the mild summer air. As I came closer to the wall of the church I could also hear the monks singing at morning prayer. I felt deeply moved by the clear voices of these men in dark habits who had taken names such as David, Jeremiah, and Daniel, and who kept the monastery doors open to people like me.

The monks' singing seemed to have a therapeutic effect on me. It put me in a positive mood and made me feel content and stronger. It is for good reason that the monks' prayers are said at the canonical hours and fitting that the Gregorian chant for the celebration of the Eucharist is entrusted to them — a divine music that felt to me like an anticipation of the heavenly realm. A sense of well-being flowed through my body, like a soothing balm on my soul.

After Lauds Father Rhabanus, dressed in his plain habit and without any affectation, guided us in our efforts to better ourselves. "Let go of anything that imprisons you," he recommended, in order to be able to experience the silence of the monastery. In this silence we could survey the whole of our day or the whole of our lives so as to gradually overcome the confusing variety and inconsistencies of our inner selves. But first we had to rid ourselves of the fear of not being able to keep up with fast pace of modern life. The fact is that we do have the ability to deal with time, instead of letting it eat us up. "We are constantly on the run, afraid that we cannot fit enough in. And thus time comes upon us as a thief."

Rhabanus knew what he was talking about; he had been entrusted with many responsibilities within the monastery. So he was the cellarer (that is, the administrator of the whole business side of the monastery), he dealt with the spiritual guidance and care of people, and he was also the choirmaster and organist, and in charge of the monastery shop. "Even in the monastery it can often be quite stressful," he admitted. But the important thing to him was to become more of a monk in order to make his life more meaningful and draw closer to God. This is also why he fasted regularly. Fasting forces us to slow down and changes our perception of time. At this point he mentioned another paradoxical effect of fasting: we become slower, yet we have more time at our disposal. We are no longer fighting for every minute and even have time to waste. What a luxury! It is a wonderful feeling, a real pleasure to be able to waste time instead of having to manage it.

I can hear better and I can see more clearly since I have been fasting.

Long ago the desert monk Cassian realized that overeating "dulls the clear sight of the heart." That is why he praised fasting so highly. Two hundred years later, in the fifth century, Philoxenes, another monk, said that it was only through fasting that the "veil was lifted from the overfed heart." One begins to recognize that "there is something else beyond what we can see and touch." From his long experience with people fasting, Father Rhabanus had arrived at the following conclusion: "Through fasting we come closer to ourselves. Everybody has a story within them. Through fasting we become more sensitive. We become aware of the heaviness within us that we have tried to deny using food and other distractions. We see our woundedness and our shortcomings. And fasting gives us the opportunity to accept ourselves."

The inner home

"A kind of unraveling and loosening of a tensed-up spiritual structure is discernible, a clarification of the situation and a heightened sensitivity. At first analytical thinking is made more difficult, and intuition deepened and heightened. At the beginning of the fasting period we experience a short-lived but clear swing of the pendulum in our moods towards depression.

There is then a clear swing to the other side, the manic side: we experience easier thought processes, and heightened spiritual productivity.… Inner tranquility, the meta-center… is discovered, in other words, the inner home."

Dr. Otto Buchinger, after observing 2,500 patients fasting.

Why we need a "savior"

Father Rhabanus was happy to share his ideas when I asked how his wisdom differed from the teachings of the New Age movement and how the fasting of monks differed from that of esoteric groups. He insisted that the differences between them are quite clear. While many non-Christian "saints" elevate themselves to a godlike status and preach that redemption can be had through one's own efforts, the Christian monk is convinced that salvation can only be achieved through the grace of God. The monk is different from other people but not because of some gnostic or occult science. He knows that he cannot free himself through fasting and other achievements; he is someone who humbly gives himself to God. According to esoteric teachings, man can bring about his own redemption, but the monks say the opposite: "You must find yourself, you must accept yourself — but you can never achieve your own redemption. You need a 'savior,' a 'redeemer.'"

The sacristy in the monastery of Nova Rise, Bohemia

Father Rhabanus continued in his fine speaking voice: "Fasting helps you recognize your actual condition. People who fast properly will become aware of their own fragmentation and realize their need for redemption and forgiveness." Ultimately this is why those who take part in fasts often need to talk about their worries and problems. It is not unusual for those fasting to go to confession, where they are promised spiritual purification. Confession is like a thorough cleansing. Not all those receiving this sacrament of the Church are holy, but saints are always among those who go to confession frequently; so said the celebrated parish priest of Ars, a man who lived two centuries ago and who often sat in his confessional for up to eighteen hours a day because people traveled from all over France to receive the sacrament of confession and blessing from this divinely gifted confessor.

In the first monastery of the Eastern Church founded by St. Basil was a monk who, in the fifth century, came to see his abbot in complete confusion. "What is the matter, brother?" asked the abbot. He replied: "I have committed a serious sin, and I cannot reveal it to the fathers." But the abbot urged him to do so: "Confess it to me and I shall bear it." What a great word, what a help! Instead of merely listening, instead of psychological advice — the burden was taken from him! There can be no greater feeling of solidarity than this.

About the seven deadly sins

Many people nowadays have a problem with the concept of "sin." It is an idea that has become outdated and is perhaps even an "invention" of the Church. The willingness to feel responsible for one's own actions, mistakes, and omissions and to improve oneself is disappearing.

But when fasting, these basic elements of our human existence come right to the surface and it becomes important to consider the full dimensions of such apparently obsolete concepts as "guilt" and "sin." Father Rhabanus explained: "By 'sinful' we monks understand something like 'isolating oneself from others,' or 'missing the point.' Fasting is a means of finding the right path again."

The Benedictine monk continued: "Go through the traditional seven deadly sins. At a time when we all believe that we are not sinners, you will soon notice how often we become embroiled in these seven capital sins." "I cannot remember them all," I said sheepishly. That Father Rhabanus also had to think for a moment made me feel a little better. Then he listed them: Pride, Greed, Lust, Anger, Gluttony, Envy, and Sloth. "Do you see how clever and apposite this selection is? It is like a mirror in front us, helping us to understand ourselves better so as to get on better with ourselves and with others."

"The line dividing good and evil," wrote Alexander Solzhenitsyn in *The Gulag Archipelago*, "is not between classes and not between parties, but it cuts through the heart of every human being. This line moves and varies as time passes. But even in those with a heart filled with evil there is a corner of good. And in the best heart there is an unacceptable pocket of evil."

Thoughts on emptiness

There is an old custom in Munich on Ash Wednesday, the first day of the Christian Church's annual forty-day Lenten fast. In the morning the Lord Mayor and the whole city council make their way to the fountain in front of the town hall. Is this just some belated carnival fun? Perhaps, but every popular show of devotion and tradition transmits valuable experiences and admonitions and advice on important aspects of life; whether it be the fact that when we die we shall not be able to take money or material goods with us, or that we need to rid ourselves of all burdens, if we want to cleanse ourselves.

It is only when we are empty that we can start to think again.

We often forget about important symbols and rituals whose observance is conducive to better self-knowledge and familiarity with life. The period of fasting has many such symbolic associations. It is a time for emptying things out. Don't we all carry baggage filled to the brim throughout the year, containing more than is good for us? During my fast I emptied my "bags" completely and washed them out, right down to the smallest folds of the stomach and intestines. And I emptied more than that. My brain was stuffed with useless rubbish, needless chatter, cheap television kitsch and petty resentments. My heart overflowed with everyday worries and everyday desires, with large and small grievances, disappointments, and expectations. Now was the time to clear everything out.

Gain through loss, the doctor had said about the healing effect of fasting. When fasting, the body breaks down everything that burdens it, that it does not need, that troubles it, or that makes it ill. Naturally the same thing happens on a spiritual level. Do I really need everything that I have accumulated? asks the person who is fasting. "Just look at what is in the shopping basket," wrote Siegfried Lenz in one of his novels, "at what is necessary and what is superfluous."

A view of Jakobsberg in the Rhine valley

About eating and looking

The French philosopher Simone Weil, an atheist who never deliberately looked for God and yet was completely moved by his omnipresence, discovered two fundamental but opposing attitudes in people. She called them "eating" and "looking." This leads to the following questions: Am I an eater? Do I require immediate gratification? Do I want to eat up, consume, and use everything? Is our society a world of eaters? On average, every individual owns 10,000 items. What a vast amount this is — especially when you realize how much you actually need and how little people in poor countries have.

For their part, monks are onlookers. At least they want to keep reminding themselves of this and to preserve this attitude. Benedict showed them how to achieve it. He recommended that they "anticipate each other in respect": "No one should look after his own good but after that of others." Rule number seven is the most extensive composed by the founder of the order. It is the rule of humility. We too can apply this rule to the stopping place that is our fast. Its ladder of twelve rungs can turn an "eater" into a "onlooker": someone who does not feel the need to own everything, someone who can ignore and do without the things of the world, as we are now doing without roast pork and candies. "Self-aggrandizement only leads downhill," Benedict wrote about the divine ladder, "while humility leads upwards."

Humility means sacrificing the self. All the renunciations of the monks, all the sacrifices that they make, are only labels for this sacrifice of the self; and this is not easy, even for a monk. A few years ago, Mother Theresa of Calcutta said to a politician who wanted to do better and asked for some guidance on how to improve his work: "Take a little more time to kneel."

Looking at it more closely, Rhabanus said, we can control nothing apart from ourselves. Everything else — prosperity, family, friends, health — can be lost through misfortune, chance, or one's own stupidity. Only the self is retained. This awareness is particularly important to monastic practice, which in turn serves to remind us of what is most meaningful in life. Power and influence, standing and wealth—none of these really makes us stronger. They deaden us, deprive us of strength, and leave our hearts cold. We live in a pleasure-seeking consumer society, yet ultimately it can be so boring. Nothing that happens really moves our minds and souls. We live, but we are not really alive.

"Fasting makes people perceptive," said the monk at the end of our little meditation. You suddenly see the true reality that lies behind the glitz and sparkle, what no television show reveals — the much maligned and disparaged ideals of truth, beauty, and goodness. The person who fasts and who has become an "onlooker" can see the reality, recognizing it even though it might appear only in a flash. Indeed, the true "onlooker" does not hold on to anything anyway.

A healthy body and a sound mind

When I returned to my cell I continued to ponder what Father Rhabanus had told us. Language is a kind of seismograph registering the kinds of diseases that afflict us. Aren't the needs of our soul "swept under the carpet"? People who bottle up their anger or anxiety become bitter — they can't "stomach" what goes on around them. Others complain that "their blood boils," "their back is killing them," they have a "lump in their throat," or are simply "sick to death."

Father Rhabanus had said: "It is never too late to take the route of fasting and turn back even when one's feet feel like lead." Comforting words. It is always better to calm down and turn back than to complain about what can't be changed. According to Benedictine teaching, fasting leads the monks, and those who follow the same path, to the threshold of heaven. It is only when we let go of everything and break away from all the things that we were relying on for support — eating and everything else — that we can really experience that which brings us internal peace.

After my mid-fast crisis, the experience of fasting was beginning to make me happy. I realized that salvation was ever-present and that I had to do nothing more than offer myself to it. The monks say: "If you let God deal with you, you will be able to say: I want to live in peace with my body because I like it. I am fasting because it is good for me." The body is not the tomb of the soul as the Gnostics taught, quite the contrary — a healthy body strengthens the soul, it brings confidence, and it makes life more secure.

Separating good and evil

While I considered all this, a beautiful sunset was taking shape on the horizon, and I decided that in the evening I would follow the advice of my fasting master. "Exercise and fresh air are indispensable when fasting!" Father Rhabanus had told us. Those who do not play sports regularly should go for walks, swim, cycle, or work in the garden in a leisurely manner, while those

Nuns from the convent of Kellenried

who are more athletic should continue with their favorite sports, without forcing themselves beyond their usual limits. Everything that does not require an excessive output of energy can be mastered without any problem. Those who do fitness training build up their muscles while weight decreases. Those who exercise their muscles will break down fat when fasting. But those who mostly lie in bed when fasting become like greedy eaters who do not move, losing strength and efficiency.

Let us make our fourth day of fasting like the fourth day of the Creation: let us shine a light within in order to separate day and night in our inner selves! Let us find out what is good and what is evil, because our thoughts dictate our actions. What we are thinking today will affect what we are doing tomorrow.

Exercise of the day:
Guidance for keeping fit

Do you really exercise enough? Besides bad nutrition, lack of exercise is one of the main causes of many diseases in modern society. Exercise increases the activity of the heart and improves the circulation, and consequently breathing as well. Through adequate exercise, oxygen is distributed to all the cells, and metabolic residues are eliminated more efficiently. Go for walks, jog, dance, ride your bike, or do yoga.

Whatever exercise you decide upon, it is important that you continue it when you are fasting. You should certainly walk a lot, especially in the fresh air. But it is important to do some warm-up exercises before you take part in sports. When fasting you will not have the energy for sprinting and other excessively energetic exercises. On the other hand, you will have much more endurance.

Transformation through fasting

The table in the refectory of the monastery of Marienau

Arriving at the oasis
and feeling a new freedom

"The periods of fasting are part of my being. I can no more do without them than I can without my eyes. Fasting is for the inner self what the eyes are for the outside world."

Mahatma Gandhi

*H*as this ever happened to you? You wake up, rub your eyes, and you know: I have actually managed to do it. A problem that had plagued you for a long time has solved itself as if miraculously. This morning I had a very similar experience. Everything was so much clearer and more certain than it had been before. When I went on my walk, I noticed things. My imagination was livelier and my senses sharper. I smelled herbs by the wayside. I saw the early birds flying among the butterflies and heard the sound of church bells in the distance — sounds that I had never noticed before.

Back in my room, I looked into the mirror completely nonplussed: I had not seen such a happy face for a very long time.

Had I been asked to paint a picture of what I imagined fasting represented, it would have been a somber painting, with dark colors, stern figures displaying expressions of self-denial, and an oppressive atmosphere. And the music I would have composed would have been more like what is played at funerals than at

Everything dissolves

"At first you only feel the lack of it; then the desire for food disappears… When fasting, a similar process takes place on a spiritual level. The body slowly loosens up. The mind becomes freer. Everything dissolves and becomes lighter. Burdens, inhibitions, and problems are felt less intensely. The boundaries of reality begin to shift. The limits of the possible are pushed further forward and the mind becomes more sensitive. Your conscience becomes more perceptive, refined, and stronger. The sense of spiritual decisiveness grows."

Romano Guardini,
German religious philosopher

weddings. What solemn sounds for a joyous, liberated life! What dark images for such a clear mind!

Today I have the feeling that I have come closer to a mystery. I believe that God likes souls that are like fluffy clouds. Perhaps an angel will descend from heaven and land on it, and, crossing his legs, he will ask me: "Now, my friend, how are you doing?" This morning I am well! I find myself talking to this apparition on my fluffy soul cloud, which seems as tiny as Peter Pan's Tinker Bell and at the same time so large that I might never see it in its entirety. I am overcome with feeling, filled from head to toe. I am like a helium balloon that has been released, no longer involved or dependent on everyday activities and trivial concerns. I feel I could talk to God as easily as I breathe.

Simply put, my senses have become more finely tuned. Words that I have heard a thousand times without thinking about them have suddenly acquired a new and deeper meaning.

In the oasis at last

I do not listen to the radio, I do not read any newspapers, I do not watch television, yet even so — or consequently — I have reached the oasis.

Hymnbook in the library of the convent of Beuron

Fasting has created a space within me. Now I can fill it and recharge myself. I listen to the monks in their morning prayer sing "Lord, you have exalted my strength like that of the wild ox; you have poured over me fresh oil," from Psalm 92, and feel as though these words now apply to me after five days of fasting.

I feel slimmer and healthier, and my sensation of well-being, my strength, and my vigor have increased. Fasting has made something blossom within me. All negative thoughts have been blown away. It is no coincidence that the Church chooses to sing this mysterious song during the fasting period of

Lent: "Now is the time of grace, now are the days of salvation. You help us to overcome evil. You give us back purity of heart. You give your children the strength to achieve immortal salvation in this mortal world." And elsewhere it is said: "Renunciation diminishes selfishness in us and opens our arms to the poor. Your compassion has driven us to share our bread with them. Through fasting of the body, one overcomes sin and elevates the mind. Give us strength and victory through our Lord Jesus Christ." Could greater praise be given to fasting than in this religious service? It is indeed strange that it is so hard for us to rediscover our own spiritual traditions.

Freedom from chains

"Entrusting our lives to a higher power," Father Rhabanus explained, "does not make us needy, rather it opens our eyes and makes us truly free. Accepting that we do not need to do everything ourselves, and indeed that we are unable to do so, is really healthier than arrogantly attempting the opposite. Trust God with your disappointments, even your complaints. You will find it liberating. It will comfort you and give you a place to rest."

"Sometimes fighting with God is also part of this faith, throwing a problem at him when you are completely shattered and depressed," I said in

Harmful substances for the soul

"Curiosity and the restless wandering of the mind will feed the soul with harmful substances. When you abstain from these substances through a particularly blessed fast you will be able to keep the physical fast almost effortlessly and enjoy its benefits. This is because it is not the mortal flesh but a pure heart that is the House of God and the temple of the Holy Spirit."

John Cassian, monk living in the fifth century

reply. Father Rhabanus agreed with me. "Yes, like Job did. That too is a kind of prayer."

The Franciscan monk, Father Slavko, said, "We need to fast in order to pray better. It is easier to pray when you are fasting and you fast better when you are praying." There is a saying: "A full stomach does not like to study." Monks, whose rhythm of life is punctuated by prayers, have reinterpreted this as: "A full stomach does not like to pray." The physical emptiness created by fasting leads not only to a genuine hunger for the divine, it also helps us to perceive the spiritual world better.

Gain is always preceded by loss or renunciation. Or conversely, every pain is followed by a reward. During those days of fasting, I became aware again that the obligations and tasks that were such a burden in my everyday life were in fact not unreasonable or useless. Anyone who wants to achieve something must put some effort into it. *Abstinence reduces* Perhaps this is obvious, but how often do we forget it. Fast- *selfishness and opens* ing has the unique effect of putting all these things into *the heart.* perspective. It keeps at a distance the worldly concerns that seem to constantly intrude upon us. People who fast naturally become humbler because they realize that much of what they thought important in the past is not important at all.

Frequently the reason for our dissatisfaction is that we can no longer see what is important, Father Rhabanus told us. Because we have become blind to what is important, we believe that our happiness and satisfaction depend on the possession of more and more things.

Fasting is simply a way of making ourselves flexible again, becoming less proud, rigid, and arrogant. The Benedictine monk Father Anselm Grün explained it in this way: "Fasting is a means of getting closer to one's own truth, a means of getting on better with ourselves that will allow us to free the good core within us from the shackles that have imprisoned it."

Indeed, so much of what has previously appeared hopeless and sad becomes transformed when you fast. Roger Schutz, the founder the monastic community of Taizé, summed up his experience of fasting by saying: "Everything becomes desirable again." In antiquity it was not unusual to interpret the word *ascetic* as simply "an athlete's way of life." It is the

Nuns in conversation, convent of Kellenried

"athletic" competition of those who fast that gives them new mental strength. It also helps them develop new courage, just as exercise builds up muscles. Pessimism disappears and a new confidence emerges: I can manage, I am strong enough! People who previously tended to hesitate when facing a difficult situation, or young people who after failing an examination might have suffered from depression or dabbled in drugs, find the mental energy to respond and develop a new strength.

Gradually I began to see one of the most important practices of the monks in a different light: the readings and prayers said at the canonical hours. At first I found this daily chanting a little strange. I was always turning the pages to find the selected psalms in the thick black book that was pressed in my hand. The words and content of the psalms, or Songs of David, from the Old Testament, which had been inspired by the landscape and life in Palestine 3,000 years ago, seemed antiquated and even questionable.

But as my fast progressed and I attended more readings, I began to recognize in them those existential questions that people throughout the ages have always asked themselves. We are too attached to the things of the world, it is said in these ancient texts. We cling to what is ephemeral and become paralyzed. People must constantly remind themselves of the fact that life on Earth is only a breath of wind. Here too fasting is helpful: we need to become pilgrims again in the traditional sense. This does not mean we must now give all our possessions away, but we must remember more often that what we have is only on loan.

Live and let live

Fasting motivates us to go on, it strengthens our hope and directs our thoughts forwards. Through fasting we renew our expectations for the future, and we become more receptive to change. "If we see fasting as letting go we shall also realize that all our life is about letting go," Father Rhabanus explained. "Because at some point, whether we want to or not, we shall have to give our life back."

It is true that in the media we are constantly confronted by violent deaths caused by wars and accidents and we experience close at hand how the people in our lives leave the world — yet we behave as if this will never happen to us. In a society dominated by pleasure and instant gratification, one's own death has become more taboo than ever in history. This ignores the fact that someone might want to prepare for death, a practice that was known in the past as *ars morendi*, the art of dying. This act of preparation was highly regarded by society in earlier times.

The thought may seem strange at first, but fasting also involves a preoccupation with death. When we die we must "throw away" everything that we have achieved and have lived for, and, like the person who fasts, we learn to

Fasting is not an attack against the body, nor is it a desperate attempt to raise the mind above the body.

"drop" everything. Seen in this light, fasting is practicing for the last, ultimate letting go. At any rate, we learn that the loss of things that were important to us does not diminish us. Every "no" (to eating or to having to own something) becomes a great "yes" to life itself. St. Benedict, the founder of the order, never tired of admonishing the monks that "they needed to always bear in mind that death can come at any time." We come to see death no longer as a failure or a final defeat in our struggle for life. As Father Rhabanus quite simply put it, "We monks know that we just fall into God's hands."

A sense we have lost

Fasting had made me more alert and more appreciative of the riches around me. I began to comprehend the sense of life anew, more intensely. This sense is an increasingly rare commodity nowadays, because the sense of the Holy, of things that are completely different, of the profoundly secret, has gradually become lost.

Fasting enables us to develop a new life plan.

Increasingly, religious mysticism is often encountered only in superstitious practices. We rely on vague, irrational forces, on our own spiritual energy. Fasting takes us beyond this. It is like a passage through life. Letting go of the "usual" gives us hope of a future. We expect the good and therefore we are optimistic and develop new strength. Fasting enables us to develop a new life plan and give ourselves a future. "Take me up, O Lord, according to your word," the monks sing, "and I shall live. Do not let me fail in my hope."

It is hard to deny that the world today suffers from a strange exhaustion of hope, the strongest of all forces, and perhaps the only true life force. On the fifth day of Creation God spoke: "Let the waters bring forth swarms of living creatures, and let birds fly above the earth." God blessed them and spoke: "Be fruitful and multiply." There is so much future, such blessing in this life. So much good is given to humankind, we only need to use it with reverence.

Exercise of the day:
Learn to become silent

1. Tranquility

Make sure that your surroundings are peaceful, the opposite of the noise and hectic rush associated with your workplace and everyday life. Our grandparents would have sat in their rocking chairs to achieve this.

2. Silence

While tranquility is associated with the reduction of movement, silence is associated with the absence of sound. Before you started fasting you were surrounded by all kinds of noise, but now everything has become more silent because you have switched off the radio and television.

3. Not speaking

Silence is also achieved by not speaking. Lie back, close your eyes, and relax your whole body. Breathing deeply and regularly will further help you to relax. Even ten minutes of this exercise will prove extremely beneficial.

4. Purification

It may happen that you can now hear loud voices within you that until now had been suppressed by external noise. Let them out and write it all down in your fasting diary. This purifies the spirit. After a few days you will become aware of an inner peace, what the monks call contemplation.

Different kinds of fasting

Church vault in the cloister of Poblet in Spain

Fasting with eyes, ears, mouth, and hands

*A*sked about the secret of enlightenment, a master replied: "When I lie down, I lie down; when I sit, I sit; when I stand, I stand; and when I go out, then I go out."

"That can't be," his pupil replied, "I do the same thing." "Yes and no," the master responded. "When you lie down, you are already sitting; when you sit, you are already standing; and when you stand, you are already in thought."

This teacher's advice is widely applicable. Fasting is one of those things that one does completely or not at all. The Spanish mystic and nun St. Teresa of Ávila, the first woman elevated by the Catholic Church to the status of Doctor of the Church, explained it as follows: "When I fast, I fast; and when I eat partridge, I eat partridge!"

One could compare the human heart to a large house in which there are several inhabitants, some of them not very popular, such as Mr. Anger, Mrs. Loneliness, and Mrs. Anxiety, and others much more popular, such as Mrs. Patience, Mrs. Pleasure, and

Mr. Trust. But the doors to the rooms inhabited by these nice ladies and gentlemen are often locked. I found this to be true when I was fasting. The first days of my fast were dedicated to a long-needed self-cleaning. In this way I rid myself of many obstructions that were preventing me from entering these rooms. This required a lot of effort. But as a result, I rediscovered the key to rooms that had been locked.

As the genial Pope John XXIII once said: "Just for today, I am trying to experience the day without attempting to solve the problems of my life all at once. Today I want to do something that I do not feel like doing. Today I want to protect myself from two evils: haste and indecisiveness. Today I want to believe that God is there for me — even when the circumstances seem to indicate the opposite." I could accept this because I felt at ease. I was happy to notice that my body had become more independent — at least from food — and that my mind was more lively. The heart no longer had to pump blood to the stomach to sustain the digestive system.

"I can't get no satisfaction"

Father Rhabanus reminded me this morning of the saying: "To be close to God is my happiness." Everybody wants to find happiness. But what was my own happiness? Where should I look for it? I remembered the blaring advertisements constantly selling things they say will make me happy: delicious gourmet food, expensive clothes and cars, the best plays, fabulous holidays...

Naturally consumption is pleasant. But does it actually create happiness and satisfaction? Sometimes it does, to be honest. But how long does it really last? "I can't get no satisfaction" — over the years, the words of this Rolling Stones song have become the hymn of a spoilt society, because it is so difficult to find happiness. It was therefore all the more surprising that now of all times, the absence of excess, the voluntary, conscious fasting, created in me a feeling of peace and great satisfaction. It was like switching over from having to being. Nothing that in the past had stimulated and captivated me could shatter my wonderful tranquility. I was enjoying the peace that I had often fled from. It was an awe-inspiring sensation to regain a bit of freedom through renunciation.

The story of the wine and dagger

A text of the fifth century tells the story of an old desert monk who was accosted by a robber. The desert monk had lived as a strict ascetic and fasted all his life. The robber stood before him. He did not say a word. He was holding a beaker of wine in one hand and a dagger in the other. The monk drank the wine. Upon this the robber fell to the ground and became a monk. The moral of the story is this: the old monk had the choice of letting the robber who wanted to commit murder be guilty, or be guilty himself. The desert monk decided to take the "guilt" upon himself and drank the wine — unthinkable for a desert ascetic. In this action the robber recognized the monk's greatness and inner freedom. Indeed the monk did not want to make another a victim of his own abstinence. As a result the robber was converted.

In another story, two brothers visit an old man who was not in the habit of eating every day. When he saw the brothers he welcomed them with pleasure and said: "Fasting is its own reward, but when you want to live by love, you obey two commandments because you give up your own self-will while fulfilling the commandment of feeding others."

"May it now be a little less?"

When the butcher says "It's a little over, is that all right?" we usually nod in agreement because we like "to treat ourselves." But during the forty days of Lent preceding Easter, the Church turns this the other way round, saying: "May it now be a little less?" Eloquent preachers, often monks from monasteries, repeatedly warn people against the must-have philosophy in their "sermons on fasting," asking them to pause and consider the true weight of things — and that applies to more than just the butcher's scale. In his Rule, Benedict devoted a whole chapter to the Lenten fast. This demanded a great deal from the monks. During Lent they were required to:

- "guard against faults,"
- refrain from "idle chatter,"
- dedicate themselves especially to prayer, and
- respect their life "in all honorableness."

Wine cellar in the abbey of St. Hildegard

Fasting according to the Benedictine Rule

Chapter 49 of the Rule written by St. Benedict of Nursia in 529 is a summary of how Western monks should keep the Lenten fast:

- The monks should always live as if it was Lent;

- but since few have the strength to do so, we recommend that at least during the days of Lent we should live our life in all honorableness,

- and that during these holy days we should atone together for previous shortcomings.

- This is properly done when we turn away from all faults and concentrate on prayer, reading, repentance of the heart, and abstinence.

- In these days of fasting we should go beyond the usual duty of our work through prayer and abstinence from food and drink.

- Thus everyone can, with the joy of the Holy Spirit, voluntarily offer something to God over and above the duties allocated to them,

- by depriving the body of food, drink, and sleep, and abstaining from chattering and foolishness,

- and by looking forward to Easter with spiritual yearning and happiness.

- The sacrifice that the individual wants to make should be submitted to the abbot and done with his blessing and approval;

- because what is done without the permission of the spiritual father will be considered presumptuous and ambitious, and will not be rewarded.

- So everything should be done with the abbot's approval.

Today, increased health awareness has made us more careful in selecting food that may be affected by environmental pollution. But spiritual nourishment too may be healthy or polluted. Father Rhabanus, who is no prude and is quite at ease in the company of the women staying as guests of the monastery, encourages something that we might call "spiritual hygiene."

The flooding of our society with pornography and violence seriously endangers the mind and spirit. Like the environmental pollutants that enter our bodies through food, images of violence and sex enter our minds through our eyes and ears. The commentator Gabriele Kuby has noted that people go to the barricades to protect the purity regulations of beer but no one thinks it necessary to look after the health and purity of our spiritual nourishment. My teacher in the monastery therefore advised us to fast from these things as well. We were to take responsibility for what we read, listened to, and watched. We could fast with our eyes, watching less television, going less often to the cinema, and reading less. We could fast with our ears: less traffic noise, radio, music, and entertainments. This abstinence would be very beneficial.

It was clear that a week of fasting would allow us time to meditate on the customary urge to own things. But why, you might ask, did Benedict place so much emphasis in his Rule on the fact that his monks should not be driven by the urge to possess? "No one owns anything, anything at all," he stated. "Everything is shared, as it is written in the Scriptures, so that no one can describe anything as his possession or claim ownership to it." In chapter 33 of his Rule, the founder of the order even called personal property a "vice" that "must be removed from the monastery by the roots."

Francis of Assisi, the founder of the Franciscan order, born in about 1182, loved poverty. His radical approach to a life of poverty explains why spiritual giants such as Benedict encouraged renunciation and abstinence so unreservedly. It is said that the bishop of Assisi took Francis to task: "Your

The refectory in the cloister of Beuron

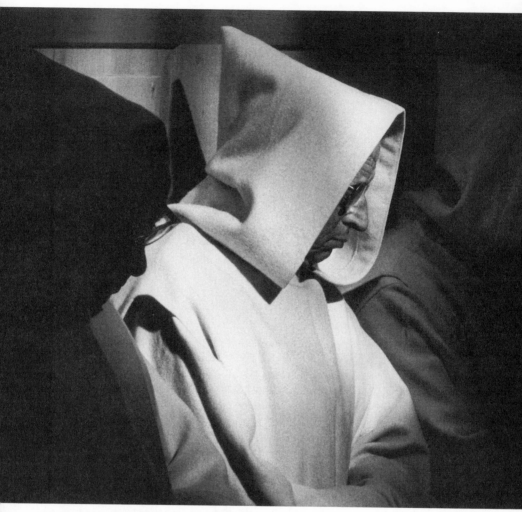

Carthusian monks deep in silence

life seems very hard to me: to have no earthly possessions is very difficult."
Francis replied: "If we wanted to own anything we would need weapons to
defend ourselves. This would lead to arguments and fights that would stand
in the way of love of God and our fellow human beings. That is why we do
not want any earthly possessions." But what Francis despised most of all

was money: "Having abandoned everything, we must protect ourselves against anything that could make us lose the kingdom of heaven. If we were to find money lying on the street, we would pay no more attention to it than to the dust under our feet."

Going for the gusto

People who want to extol fasting hardly know where to begin and where to end. One benefit immediately springs to mind: fasting is a good way of fighting greed. "We dig our own graves with our greed," the calm and collected Father Rhabanus said during one of our discussions. Accumulating money, accumulating books you have read, accumulating honors, accumulating travels, accumulating sorrows: how much I have suffered, how much I have endured. He who accumulates most is considered the best, the most famous, the most educated, the most popular. Is it not so? And instead of being astonished about this we are amazed that someone might question the wisdom and meaning of our behavior. Does not our attitude to possessions and profit often influence our relationship with other people?

"We often keep friends and acquaintances only so long as they prove useful to us," the Swiss sociologist Reinhard Fatke said. "Sometimes we only love children if they are cute and satisfy our emotional needs — and then we discard them psychologically, which leads to emotional neglect, behavioral disorders, depression, and suicide. Partners and married couples sometimes look upon each other as possessions that may be put to one side or thrown away after use."

Ascetic life shows that true human greatness lies beyond selfish efforts and urges. When fasting we have the opportunity not to cling to anything any longer. According to the monks, this means touching "the heart of God."

Looking toward the more elevated realm of the Christian mystics who aim to achieve complete emptiness and nothingness — the *nada* advocated by St. Teresa of Ávila — those fasting do not lose themselves in the meaningless and bottomless pit of the nihilists. On the contrary, their emptiness becomes absolute fullness. As the Spanish founder of the order described the highest level of her enlightenment: *Dios solo basta*, "God alone is enough." But that is another story.

Fasting makes you grateful

It should not be overrated, but fasting naturally also leads to gratitude. People who fast soon discover that they are living off capital that they have not created themselves. They recognize that life is a gift. It is a gift that we accept but cannot cling to. "What is freer than a heart that desires nothing on Earth?" the Augustinian monk Thomas à Kempis asked in his devotional work *The Imitation of Christ*, a guide to spiritual life that he wrote for the men and women in monasteries and convents. Those who fast and no longer concentrate on themselves hear an inner voice that makes them happy. They no longer worry about all the unimportant things they used worry about. As a result they can discover the true meaning of life that so many pundits spend the whole of their days looking for in vain.

Also, the better you fast, the more carefree, childlike, and secure you will feel. Monks in early Christian Egypt wore a kind of hood when they were fasting which at the time only children wore. In doing so they wanted to express that what mattered to them was that childlike quality that Jesus praised as the naturalness of humanity; a childlike quality that now we even take away from children as we fill and cover the playroom with goods mass-produced by the entertainment and consumer industries.

Return to oneself

As we walked through cloisters filled with the fragrance of roses, Father Rhabanus stressed once again that in his Rule, St. Benedict urged the monks during fasting to abstain not only from food but also from other things.

He himself always believed that when the belt of his habit began to feel tight, it was also a sign for spiritual abstinence. "Where do I get my feeling of self-esteem? Do I get it from professional satisfaction? Must I achieve a lot in order to be allowed to live? Should I also fast a little in my work so as to have more time for my fellow men, for myself, and for God?" These were the kind of questions Father Rhabanus would ask himself when meditating during his period of abstinence.

It is an old custom in monasteries on Ash Wednesday for each of the monks

The eye is also fasting

"The eye fasts when it refrains from looking and watching inquisitively; the ear fasts when it stops listening to idle talk and gossip; the tongue fasts when it refrains from slandering, grumbling, and unnecessary talk, and holds silence in high esteem; the hand fasts when it leaves useless things alone; but best of all is when the soul itself abstains from all imperfections."

Bernard of Clairvaux,
the most important monk
of the twelfth century

to give the abbot a *schedula*, a piece of paper listing their resolutions for their fast. These lists are not confined to abstinence from food and drink. In fact, they show the diversity of the monks' fasts. Often they include additional prayers, particularly spiritual reading matter, or the renunciation of things that they feel they have become dependent on. The abbot examines these resolutions in the light of the personal needs and requirements of each monk, adapts them if necessary, then gives them back to help them improve their self-control. If the resolutions are excessively hard, he may soften them a little, but if the resolutions are too easy, the abbot will give the monk a little push in the right direction.

Naturally, abbots also fast. For instance, Odilo Lechner, superior of the cloister of St. Boniface in Munich, abstains from alcohol and sweet foods. But even more importantly: "I watch less television and read the newspaper less often. So far as these are concerned, I feel at risk and tend to excess. And I must admit that I am happy when it is Lent: I live more sensibly and I have more time for important things. This does not mean that I do not rejoice when it is Easter, and I can watch my favorite programs again."

Our sixth day of fasting had come to an end. On the sixth day God filled the Earth with a wonderful diversity of creatures, beautiful and varied like the many-colored splendor of the rainbow in the sky. Then He created the jewel

Cheese produced at the convent of Chamberaud in France

in the crown, humankind, in His own image, as man and woman. He gave them everything, and at the same time He burdened them with the freedom to use the Earth but not to misuse it: to accept the Earth as a gift, not becoming greedy and destroying it in the process, but using it sparingly like someone who is fasting.

Exercise of the day: Guide to contemplation

Choose a picture that you find appealing and that has a positive effect on you. Look at this picture for ten to fifteen minutes while sitting completely relaxed on a chair. Have soft meditative or classical music in the background. You should not try to explain the picture but simply look at it.

You can repeat this exercise from time to time. Soon you will feel the healing effect of this contemplation. You can also carry out this exercise with a short poem or prayer. Read the text aloud to yourself for ten or fifteen minutes. This will create a feeling of calm within you and you will notice its healing power.

The goal of fasting

A sister serving food in the convent of Alromünster

Ending a fast and what it tells us about eating

On the morning of the last day of their week of fasting many people who took part in a class given by Father Rhabanus had a vision. All the poison in their bodies seemed to have been flushed away. They experienced the deep satisfaction of not only having dreamed of good resolutions but of also having fulfilled them: Yes, I can change my life. I can not only adjust my eating, I can also give my life a completely new direction. While the boozy New Year's resolutions have already been forgotten by the end of the first week of January, the resolutions taken with a cup of tea or coffee will be kept for a long time even if they are not permanent.

I no longer needed to convince myself of all the things I could do. I had the concrete proof: the fact that I had lived for seven days without any food, that I had learned how to practice abstinence. Yes, I had the willpower to keep to resolutions. I had had the invaluable experience of knowing that I could withdraw from the world and that I could stay abstinent for a week. Freely. To achieve greater freedom.

And I had the confidence that I could keep my resolutions for a long time, that in seven days I had really been able to achieve a kind of new Creation within myself. It had not been in vain. I had gained something from it that would stay with me for the rest of my life. Reason told me that at some time I would probably return to my old habits, but I could fast again at any time I chose in order to experience once more that feeling of relief and healing.

Neither the fathers of the Church nor the monks had any illusions about the weaknesses of their fellow brothers, about the fallibility of human nature. The important dates in the liturgical cycle are geared to a continuous process of growth and decay. Indeed, each spring heralds the start of a new period of fasting — Lent — as the symbol of a new beginning.

The evidence is indisputable that we are not perfect and cannot be perfect, even though we sometimes pretend that is not the case. According to Christian tradition, the Kingdom of Heaven is the recovery of the paradise that is promised to everyone. Yes, it is innate, inborn in us, but human nature bears the stain of a fundamental error. The Bible explains this with the image of original sin, the sin that was transmitted to us through the fall of Adam and Eve.

This "original sin" comprises all sins, including the sin of eating. It consists in "not listening" to the truth but rather to the voice of the tempter, that is, the "father of lies." We all carry in us a small spiritual obstruction. It is a necessary part of the price of freedom. We cannot overcome this inner weakness for long by confiding in our own strength alone.

The right degree of moderation as a way of life

As is well-known, it is no use knowing that we are doing wrong, or what the psychological or environmental causes of our harmful lifestyle are, if we do not have the strength and determination to learn from our mistakes and follow the path of improvement. The practical implementation of this new approach requires patience and willpower, and setbacks are to be expected. But because it is so difficult, we often do not go beyond the simple realization. In the seven days of my fast I proved to myself that I could overcome inner resistances. During my fast I learned to take better care of myself. I

In the beer garden of the monastery of Andech

resolved to follow a course of moderation, especially in regard to eating. I would be aware of what I was eating and ask myself:

- What do I eat?
- How much do I eat?
- Why do I eat this or that food?
- Do I see eating as a comfort or a reward?

Father Rhabanus explained to the people on his course that our good resolutions did not mean that from that day forward we could no longer treat ourselves to anything enjoyable. Fasting and feasting go together. "It would be terrible if fasting made us despise the world, turning us into people who can no longer take pleasure in good things," he warned. "The question is simply: How free am I, how good is the good that I am treating myself to?"

"Actually, fasting has taught me to appreciate things," Father Rhabanus reported on his own experiences. "After I have finished fasting I eat less, because I have learned through fasting that my body does not need as much food as I used to eat in the past. But as a result I enjoy my food more." The true enjoyment of food does not consist of feeling as full as possible as quickly as possible.

A strict rule: fast each year

I have made another firm resolution. In future I will fast for a week twice a year: once before Christmas and then again before Easter. It is good to have such a rule. It will ensure that I undergo physical cleansing, spiritual purification, and mental strengthening. It will enable me to correct my inner and outer self and put me back "on track."

Fasting exercises the senses and helps us mature. This changes us so that our powers of judgment and decision-making also increase.

Brigitte Fabian, a healer from Munich with long experience of fasting treatments, says that two periods of fasting a year are ideal, one in spring and one in autumn. This "stabilizes our health and general well-being and increases our

Principles to bear in mind after we end our fast:

- What matters is not only what we eat but also how we eat.
- Eating properly is an expression of gratitude.
- Let us consciously concentrate on our food and eat it slowly, fully enjoying each mouthful. Eating in this way becomes a meditation.
- Let us experience each meal with all our senses.
- Let us avoid eating as a distraction or to comfort ourselves.
- Let us finally give up the struggle with calorie charts and let us no longer yield to the dictatorship of slimming diets.
- Let us experience joy in eating.

Feeding the poor is an extenion of fasting

inner contentment and freedom." She tells us that fasting leads to "strength and new self-awareness. You will acquire personal magnetism, and your eyes will shine and sparkle. Last but not least, fasting makes you more beautiful and keeps you young and fit." Dr. Hellmut Lützner has written in a guide to fasting: "I recommend that every healthy individual of thirty years of age and over fast occasionally... Because of our modern lifestyle, it is advisable and necessary to have a general overhaul if you are forty or over. This includes an 'oil-change' achieved through fasting, combined with fitness training. Prevention is the best cure."

After a course of fasting people often make a surprising discovery: they are more sensitive and alert. They are more perceptive of external conditions and react accordingly. Many no longer enjoy excessively loud music, others lose their taste for very spicy food, and many no longer rush around as much as before.

Do not add too much salt

I was worried about what would happen after I left the monastery. This fast should really herald a new beginning, coinciding with ending the fast in the right way. Father Rhabanus explained that on no account should we start to eat normally immediately after the end of our fast! Our digestive tract had first to readjust itself and become reaccustomed to what was

"Any fool can fast, but it takes a wise man to break a fast properly."
George Bernard Shaw

now an unusual amount of food. I ended my week of fasting with an apple. In the morning I broke my fast with an unpeeled apple — breakfast, the first meal of the day, is perfectly named. I had to eat it slowly, chewing each bite for a long time.

It was not until the evening of the first day after my fast that I had something more substantial — potato soup with vegetables and herbs, but without salt. At the beginning Father Rhabanus advised us to abstain from salt. Because salt is a binding agent, it would lessen the pleasant feeling of lightness that one gains while fasting and increase a feeling of heaviness. Those who added salt immediately put on a couple of pounds and felt — from a physical point of view — that it had all been for nothing. Therefore I was definitely not going to add salt to everything again!

There are various ways to increase food intake in the days following a fast:
- only fruit,
- only vegetarian,
- lacto-vegetarian (with cottage cheese and yogurt),
- or whole food

Basically, recovery time should be about half the length of the fast.

Meals after the fast

In order to spare the digestive system after fasting and to acquire a new attitude to eating, you should act as follows in the first few days after the end of your fast:

- Enjoy every mouthful and chew it thoroughly.
- Stop eating before you feel full.
- Eat only when you have an appetite.
- Eat plenty of roughage and easily digestible protein.
- Give up salt, because it retains water in the body.
- Rest after each meal.

Dinner in the priory of Jakobsberg

Having fasted for seven days, I had to plan on at least three days to reacclimate. Eating less after fasting will present few problems if you are aware of the basic principle: you can manage on little food and still be efficient. You can take the time to smell, taste, swallow, and enjoy.

"Think about the word 'mealtime,'" Father Rhabanus once said to me. What he meant was that the food should be ground like "meal," the milled edible part of a cereal grain, each mouthful being chewed at least ten times before swallowing, and that one should take the "time" to do so.

While everyone around me gobbled their food, I would have a "mealtime" in the literal sense of the word. "Make it a habit not to swallow 'tough morsels' without chewing, chewing, and more chewing." Also, I decided to briefly compose myself and say a short prayer of thanksgiving before meals, as I had seen the monks do. When performed deliberately, the traditional ritual of a short prayer of thanksgiving before meals is helpful in avoiding lapsing into bad habits.

Remaining faithful to new habits

We have not only lost the knowledge of how to eat properly but also of how to stop eating properly. Eating and not eating belong together like day and night. Fasting is one of the prerequisites for enjoying food properly. The bowl must be empty and washed out before it is filled with food. The stomach must be empty when you go to the table, otherwise you will not really enjoy eating. Fasting is part of the natural order. It is a time of expectation, a time for patience and strength.

Instead of falling back into bad habits, I would try to preserve some of the new habits from the days of my fast. I would find at least ten minutes in the day to relax and pray. I would make sure I had a lot of fresh air and went for a walk every day. I had noticed that fasting and the other exercises associated with it stimulated my powers of self-healing. While I was still healthy, I would seek to prevent possible illnesses by developing a new way of living.

Fasting had shown me a harmonious and healthy approach, and by overcoming the feeling of "having to eat" and avoiding everyday trivialities, my inner equilibrium had become stronger. I had discovered qualities and abilities in myself that I did not know I had. And the "enlightenment" of all this was literally plain to see.

Part of a way of life

At the end of my week of fasting, Father Rhabanus presciently warned me: "For all the praise of fasting, it is not a panacea." Of course, fasting for seven days cannot wipe out all our dietary 'sins' and those associated with our lifestyle. It is much more important to develop a new and lasting approach to eating and enjoyment.

All the well-meant moralizing advice — that you should not bolt your food — is utterly useless if you do not develop a real sensual enjoyment of food through regular fasting. A correct and lasting attitude to eating is more

Joy and laughter — everyday pleasures

important than a one-time fast. Those who fall back into their old eating habits should not be surprised at the see-saw effect on their weight and the imme-diate loss of the new feeling of freedom. Our spiritual renewal and healing is also threatened if we do not discipline ourselves. The monks know that no one has achieved saintliness through fasting alone.

Through fasting, monks teach us above all a lifestyle that improves human nature.

Our new attitude to life should not only include abstinence but also a warning against overdoing it. There is such a thing as an excess of "health," which is often more damaging than moderate consumption of "unhealthy things." One can overtax oneself, but one can also have too much care and treatment. This is true for the senses as well as for exercise.

Eating involves smelling and tasting and should be enjoyed as a gift. Today many people no longer eat what they like but only what is "healthy." They choose their meals on the basis of vitamin and fiber content, follow-ing the advice of questionable dieticians instead of listening to their own natural control, that is, their own senses. The Viennese doctor Rupert Klötzl has recommended organic food whenever possible, but says that a "purely scientific choice" cannot be good in the long term because it would be much too complicated: "In order not to become so dependent, I advise people to cook in such a way that they also enjoy what they are eating."

On his visit to the famous monastery on Mount Athos in Greece, Archbishop Roncalli, who later became Pope John XXIII, found the atmosphere very relaxed. As he was walking by, the fairly plump Don Angelo Roncalli heard two of the strictly ascetic monks whisper to each other: "How is it possible for this prelate with his round belly to enter paradise, since the gate is as narrow as the eye of a needle?" Roncalli turned round and quick-wittedly replied: "The kind Lord who has allowed this belly to get so round will make sure that it can also go through the eye of a needle."

Over 600 years ago, the great Dominican philosopher-monk, Thomas Aquinas, wrote about the little depressions of everyday life. He recommended laughing, drinking wine, sleeping, praying, bathing, friendship, and meditation to comfort us against the sorrows of life, constant worry, and despair. These natural means brighten up everyone's mood without pills or other medication. Fasting is one of the ways to make the arduousness of life bearable. While fasting I discovered many little things that you cannot buy and which are nonetheless — or perhaps for that reason — invaluable.

Spiritual ardor

"God wants to help people find the right path and to open up more and more to him," Father Rhabanus explained. This is why monastic fasting has a concrete, metaphysical goal, albeit one that can be interpreted in many ways. It is meant to lead to a kind of rebirth, to a resurrection, and more specifically, to the celebration of the Resurrection of Christ. It is the overcoming of death — the greatest celebration of all.

The monks see fasting and abstinence as a preparation for this celebration and a wonderful way of renewing themselves, overcoming any unwillingness to conquer life's problems. Those who fast will no longer fear the world around them because they know that they can endure periods of hunger, periods of solitude, and periods of emptiness. The monks and nuns know that God loves them, and that they do not need to add anything to avoid the reality of life. They can handle both abstinence and ecstatic celebration, as exemplified at the marriage at Cana. Both have their own season.

"Our fasting and our praying are a good, large camp fire."

Father Rhabanus

The right grand plan

The monks interpret the writings of the early fathers of the Church not as traditional historical documents but as timeless messages for people of all generations. Human nature has not changed. People long to immerse themselves in the presence of God. Fasting helps to guide us towards that which is

A new dawn for life's new beginning

essential. The great goal, our personal Easter, the resurrection as it were, from death into a strong, living person, is worth all the trouble and effort. "As soon as we understand that the aim of asceticism is to reach a goal perceived as full of life, we shall recognize it as a creative force," a wise orthodox monk from the Greek monastery on Mount Athos wrote about fasting.

Fasting is like applying a magnifying glass to one's whole life, the monks say. When fasting, people become concentrated on a goal that goes far beyond ordinary everyday life. One day an old monk was talking to a dynamic young man called Robert. The monk asked what plans he had for the future. "I want to read Law as soon as possible," the young man replied. "And then?" the monk asked. "Well, then I would like to set up a law firm, then marry and have a family." "And then, Robert?" "To be honest," the young continued, "I would like to earn a lot of money, retire as soon as possible, and travel all over the world. I have always wanted to do that." "And then?" the monk continued almost rudely. "I have no further plans for the moment," Robert replied. The monk looked at him and said: "Your plans are too limited. They only reach eighty years into the future. Your plans should be broad enough to include God and all of eternity."

When fasting we open up the windows of our heart

Many people fear God as they might a thief who is going to rob them of everything that gives them pleasure. But when monks make sacrifices during the Lenten fast as a preparation for Easter, God does not take anything away from them. Rather they are showered with gifts that make life worth living: awareness, fulfillment, freedom, and contentment. This may sound a little fantastic and exaggerated, but by fasting the monks open up their windows. They unlock the door and open up their hearts to a completely different reality, a higher power and force that they rediscover again and again in the man from Nazareth whose followers they are.

My final day with the monks of Jakobsberg coincided with the important yearly pilgrimage feast of the fourteen Auxiliary Saints. The sunny Sunday morning had attracted thousands of believers from the surrounding region. Already at the crack of dawn I could see lively groups, families, and staunch individuals from my fasting group climbing the steep hill of

Jakobsberg. It was a delightful end to my week of fasting. I had begun to notice how easy it now was for me to approach God. I found I had a lot more time for him. He offers me everything that I need and everything that makes my inner self warm, beautiful, and pleasant.

It was the seventh day. "And God," says Genesis simply, "blessed the seventh day and hallowed it, because on it God rested from all the work that he had done in Creation."

Exercise of the day: Guide to praying

The daily times of prayer during which the monks praised God, prayed to Him, and thanked Him raised them to a higher level.

When praying in this way the monks immersed themselves in a positive world of thought that little by little defined their life. The equation praising = living is reflected throughout the psalms that the monks sing. Only he who praises, lives, it is said. When you combine fasting with prayer you will experience an even stronger spiritual power. The wealth of prayers is great. For the last fasting day we can join in the fasting hymn sung by the monks:

> *Now it has come, the right time*
> *which gives us back God's favor,*
> *Now it has come, the day of Redemption,*
> *Filled with Christ's bright light.*
>
> *Now our whole heart must*
> *Renew itself through fasting and prayer*
> *And through abstinence he who is tired,*
> *and weak and sick becomes strong.*

Holy Days

The belfry at the monastery of Mount Athos, Greece

From appearance to reality

"*H*olidays" as Holy Days: my days of fasting with the monks were "holy days" or holidays for me. They made me feel more alive because they opened up my heart. And he who has a big heart is strong. Fasting prepares you for action, just as silence prepares you for speech. Being full makes you weak while fasting makes you strong.

The sacrifice you make when you fast consists of two phases. First it depresses you. At first sight, fasting seems like a change for the worse because it requires abstaining from something that we depend upon, something that we love dearly. But suddenly, we experience something indescribable. It is as if some Earthly disadvantage has been transformed into a divine advantage. What at first appeared to depress us seems in the end to give us new courage. Then after fasting, we finally look ahead to the future — because we have let go of our past and our sorrows, and because we have forgotten the suffering that was always on our mind.

When we fast we let everything go — all the things

that we dragged around with us, all the things that clung and stuck to us. The weight under which we were collapsing was our own. In the end fasting makes us lighter, free from false self-satisfaction. Fasting is a break with ourselves that makes us more mature. In this way we realize our true selves. After fasting we have a new self-confidence. We ourselves are aware of it and so are the people around us.

From seeming to being

Father Rhabanus told me that the person who fasts properly acquires self-knowledge. And the more you know yourself, the better it is for you. You are getting closer and closer to heaven. The early Christians spoke of each other as "blessed" (referring to the "blessed Peter" or the "blessed Dionysius"), while today we often call our friends "poor devil."

According to my fasting master, we too can become blessed when we fast. If we can break away from our set ways and distorted life, we will find it easier to discover our real life. We will sense something of that splendor that is within us but is buried and concealed. Then as we gain respect for ourselves, we become more respectful towards nature, towards God, and towards our fellow human beings. Father Rhabanus was right. I could feel how fasting sharpened the inner and the outer senses. The deliberate

Through fasting we regain our self-respect. abstinence from food, easier and more efficient than any diet, had led to conscious, more enjoyable eating. I could smell, taste, and feel again! And much more: for a minute, for an hour, the person fasting experiences something supernatural, something that reaches beyond Earthly life. At the end of the forty day fast of Lent comes the greatest happiness of all: Easter! No other celebration in the world is more magnificent, sumptuous, and powerful.

Healing
in the Monastery

Lucia Glahn

Preliminary

After a short time I felt the calming effects of the convent

"Happiness is the most important element in life."

Hildegard von Bingen

What interested me most at first were the herbs. What they looked like, what they could do for us, what illnesses they were for, and how they were prepared.

I was fascinated by the many colorful plants in Sister Leandra's famous herb garden in the convent of Oberzell. There was not a single medicinal herb you could not find in her flowery paradise. The cheerful "medicinal herb" sister had patiently shown me all her lovingly tended plants and explained their properties to help me in my research on medicinal plants. Yet my opinions changed during my stay with the Franciscan nuns in the convent of Oberzell at the Krumbad spa in Schwabia.

"Medicinal plants are not everything," Sister Leandra explained as she made posies of colorful flowers that she hung up to dry. She was strolling through the magnificent convent garden on a beautiful summer morning, her eyes shining after her meditation session. Later she brought me her CD player so that I too could try her meditation.

People who go to a monastery or convent to discover the secret of a healthy life will soon learn how many things are important for the health of the body, mind, and soul. There are behavior patterns and rules that at first sight appear utterly prosaic. But these rules serve as the center of gravity in the convent and each of the sisters experiences them in her own way. Their community reminds me of a kaleidoscope whose multicolored stones produce ever-changing patterns. The longer I looked, the more I discovered. Singing, praying, eating correctly, sleeping, taking breaks, working hard, having interesting conversations — all these tried and tested activities, drawn from the lived experience of our Christian monasteries and convents, exert a great healing power. And the openness and generous hospitality with which I was welcomed by the sisters in Oberzell and Krumbad soon revealed to me the remedial properties of their regularity and the rituals in their life.

The tradition of monastic life is almost as old as Christianity and has been developed by monks and nuns throughout the centuries. A way of life was created that helped the individual to look after the body, mind, and soul in such a way as to be in harmony as much as possible with the laws of the cosmos. The fact that monks and nuns are demonstrably healthier and live longer is an impressive testimony to their lifestyle, although health is not the primary concern or an end in itself for nuns and monks. That is not only the attraction, but also the secret of their art of healing. Much of the healing practices in monasteries can be applied in everyday life. Just try it; you'll find it is worth it.

Lucia Glahn

Welcome to the monastery

The Franciscan monastery of Oberzell near Würzburg

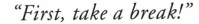

"First, take a break!"

"All the people who come to the cloister should be welcomed as if they were Christ because he once said: I was a stranger and you welcomed me."

From the Rule of St. Benedict

*T*he closer I came to my destination, the more uneasy I became. At the same time I was finding my forthcoming stay with the Franciscans in Oberzell more exciting than an adventurous vacation. It was the first time I had visited a monastery, and I had long wanted to try something of the kind. Why had I waited so long? Was it really true that for years I had had no time for it? No time for myself?

The bus stopped in a noisy main street on the outskirts of Würzburg. I walked away from the din and in just a few steps I passed through a tall Romanesque double gateway leading into a large inner courtyard. In front of me was the baroque façade of the old monastery, built to the plans of Balthasar Neumann, one of the most important rococo architects of the eighteenth century. I was immediately captivated by the ensemble of the monastery and the wonderful church. Here it was pleasantly quiet; I wondered where the noise had gone. There was the agreeable splashing of a fountain, and when I reported at the gate I was sent right away into the visitors' room. The heavy wooden door slammed shut behind me. Divine silence prevailed in the picturesque entrance hall. First, I noticed the artistic, colorful flower arrangements, in which the radiant orange of marigolds predominated. I learned later that they had been provided by "Herb Sister" Leandra. The sun shone through the windows, and through the open inner door there was a view of the long monk's walk flooded with light. It was like a picture from a book of meditation. Without being aware of it, I held my breath.

Sister Teresa came in from the refectory. It was twelve noon. Without meaning to, I had arrived in the middle of the meal. "No problem," she said kindly. "First I will take you to the Magdala convent, which is also where your room is."

Seeing my puzzled look, the sister explained that in the area next to the large monastery of fifty Franciscans was a smaller convent with eight more nuns affiliated with it. They live in a small modern house, right next to the main monastery building.

The entrance area and the terrace were idyllic, lined with flowers. Lavender and roses framed the picture. Another fountain bubbled away. Sister Lydia, who was responsible for receiving guests, immediately invited Sister Teresa and me to come in. "There is plenty there," she said, making an inviting gesture in the direction of the refectory, the convent's dining room. Normally the rule is that the sisters eat by themselves, but today the mother superior and another guest were coming too. Chairs were quickly pushed in between the others and more places were laid. We sat in a comfortable room, at a round wooden table lovingly decorated with ivy. In the center a candle burned. The atmosphere was calm and happy, and I began to feel really comfortable and at ease.

The homemade tomato soup with many fresh herbs and the cheese noodles tasted delicious. On the table was a carafe of fresh water. "We get this from our own spring," a sister explained. "The monastery lies in the middle of the water conservation area." The crisp cucumber, tomato, and lettuce salad, flavored with various herbs, was also from their garden. "There is borage in it," a nun pointed out, "which strengthens the immune system." "We are all healthy here," another nun laughed, "and many of us are already very old." While we talked about the way of life in the convent, Veridiana,

"Herb Sister" Leandra in the cloister garden

the mother superior, pointed out a study from a popular science magazine according to which the life expectancy of people in religious orders clearly exceeded that of the population as a whole. The mother superior smiled archly, then said: "So it is best for people to go into monasteries or convents." *Or to see for myself how things run differently in a convent in order to learn from their way of life,* I thought.

The health problems of a society that threatens to overtax more and more people with its increasing pace and confusion have become a central topic as we look into the future. There are trends that are worrying. For example, a growing number of people have a disturbed relationship with eating. Developments among teenagers are particularly alarming: studies have shown that as many as one schoolgirl in three have eating disorders. They show signs of anorexia, bulimia (overeating followed by vomiting), and other eating disorders. According to psychologists, this is the result of the mania for being skinny presented as fashionable by the media. But at the same time, the number of the overweight children and adults has leapt up. Experts warn that obesity is an unheeded catastrophe. In most Western countries people of normal weight long ago became a minority, and the number of overweight children has also doubled in the last twenty years. Among the consequences are diabetes, heart problems, and joint damage.

The alarm signals of a world that seems increasingly sick are becoming louder. Allergies are increasingly hard to control. Children and adults suffer more and more from food intolerances, hay fever, and neurodermatitis. Admittedly scientists are puzzled about the exact causes, but one thing is certain: stress can act as a trigger, explaining why we "go up the wall" more and more often, why we "have had enough" or "cannot stand it any longer." And in times of disturbance and rationalization, does not stress turn into a permanent feature? "One-fifth of all employees suffer permanently from anxiety and stress," the Karlsruhe Institute for Social Health has found.

In the opinion of scientists, one-third of all illnesses in industrialized countries are attributable to stress. People who are stressed are demonstrably far more susceptible to infection. They become angry at the drop of a hat, as evidenced by the phenomenon of road rage. "People react to the trivial details of daily life with the full force of a program that is really designed only for life-threatening emergencies," an American researcher found. Chronic strain over a long period leads to dizziness, diarrhea, gastritis, gastrointestinal ulcers, and in the worst case, heart attack. Headaches, loss of hearing, and tinnitus are also effects of overworking.

In industrialized countries health records are broken every year. Overcoming stress, escaping from problems, or looking for kicks leads to addiction. In Germany more than nine million people have problems with alcohol, and almost four million people are actually regarded as alcoholics. Almost 1.5 million Germans are dependent on medication, according to the German

Department against Dangers of Addiction. Especially worrying is that, in the opinion of experts, a growing number of children are already strongly in danger of addiction. For a long time, the first choice of many doctors and psychologists for treating hyperactive children, those suffering from relationship crises, or the divorce of their parents, has been the medication Ritalin. Disturbed biorhythms, chronic headaches and restlessness, and an increased sense of "psychological neglect" have been the consequences of overstressed, overextended families.

Too quick, too hectic, too noisy: secretly don't we want to apply the brakes more and more often? Do we not more and more often long for a different lifestyle: quieter, more relaxed, and more contented? What really makes us so sick and shattered? What can individual illnesses tell us? What should we do? How can we alter our everyday life? What do the nuns and monks know about it? Do they have the right tools for a healthier life? Do things like humility also belong to it? What about penance, remorse, and changing one's ways?

What about the task of discovering oneself? Not as an end in itself, as in some conventional therapeutic approaches where one concentrates on the self, takes it apart and then tries to put it back together again. How important is it to find oneself, one's spirit, one's soul? One's being. "Awake my soul," goes a prayer of St. Anthony of Padua, "and lead it away from all half-heartedness." In particular, how important is it to allow oneself to fall? Not into nothingness, but full of trust into the hands of a beloved higher power. Like the members of religious orders, who take the advice of Jesus seriously, we should calmly hand over our worries to Him.

I took a deep breath. The calm atmosphere prevailing during the meal had served me well. Lunch in the convent was over. Everyone waited quietly until the last plate was empty. Before the sisters ended their lunch hour, they sang the canon "Now thank we all our God." My "good spirit" Sister Teresa said to me tactfully: "First have a little rest and then I will pick you up again and show you everything." I needed to slow down. In the days to come she would say this to me again and again. I sensed an agreeable feeling of relaxation rising within me. I let myself stroll through the monastery garden and form a first impression of what a healthy life felt like.

The secrets of the monks

Christmas rose in the monastery garden at Oberzell

A brief history of the medical skills from the monasteries

A heavy scent hung in the dark vaults of the monastery cellars, a scent of herbs stored in numerous vessels in the medicine chamber. Next door were the gigantic copper vats in which monks were distilling healing tinctures from secret recipes, while outdoors in the herb garden a monk was carefully cutting medicinal herbs for treating the patients in the infirmary. Was it correct to picture the medical skills of the monks as having always been like this? Or did these scenes derive from pure make-believe or campy films?

Not at all. The activities of the nuns and monks in the Middle Ages, when their medical skills represented the only medical care for the entire population, probably looked very similar to this. The tradition has survived behind the monastery walls. For example, today in the Benedictine monastery of Ettal, Brother Vitalis still concocts his tinctures of arnica and liqueurs in the vaults of the monastery distillery, following ancient secret recipes. And still today, nuns and monks live according to the longstanding knowledge of holistic medical skills: a treasury of experiences and knowledge handed down from the traditional wisdom that forms the basis of Western culture, and that is only waiting to be used.

What monastic medicine has achieved

It is undeniable that nuns and monks built up and decisively shaped the development of European medicine and the whole of public health. From the fifth to the eleventh centuries they had an absolute monopoly on healing knowledge, until the creation of the modern style hospital through the special caring orders created for the purpose, such as the Sisters of Mercy, the Salesians, and the Sisters of Charity of St. Vincent de Paul.

Professor Gundolf Keil, the leader of the Würzburg Research Group into Monastic Medicine, judged their performance as follows: "Monastic medicine in the West was revolutionary and far more successful there than it was, for example, in Zen-Buddhist monasteries. The Christian monks of this period were much more effective in this field than they were even aware of. They made use of the prior knowledge of antiquity, supplemented by their experience of folk medicine, but they also developed new models of medical care. During the Carolingian period the practice of providing equally good medicine for anyone in need was first seen. A little later the monastic orders began founding hospitals. Here the theme of Caritas, charity, played an important role."

How it all began

How did monks' knowledge of healing come about? Why is there any connection at all between medicine and Christian monasteries and convents? What do members of religious orders actually have to do with illness and healing?

Essentially, it all began with Jesus and his disciples. Jesus was the redeemer and quintessential "doctor," *Christus medicus*. The word "savior" suggests this, being derived from the Latin word *salvator*, meaning "one who saves." In AD 110 Ignatius of Antioch was the first to identify Jesus as a doctor. Clement of Alexandria also praised Christ as savior and healer: "Therefore he is called by the name 'savior,' because he applied spiritual medicine to the well-being and salvation of the people. He protected health,

Library of the Premonstratensian monastery in Nova Rise, Bohemia

uncovered injuries, described the causes of the passions, amputated the roots of foolish desires, stipulated diet, and prescribed healing antidotes for the sick."

Jesus saw it as his essential task to make people sound and healthy, free from evil and from sickness. He also gave his disciples the power to heal the sick. (Paul even revived a man from the dead.)

Stories of miraculous healing play a key role in the New Testament. "Power came out from him and healed all of them," it is written in the Gospel of St. Luke (Luke 6:19). Jesus attracted people in droves: "Now more than ever the word about Jesus spread abroad; many crowds would gather to

Jesus, redeemer and physician

- In the case of healing achieved through God's help, the belief of the person healed was always crucial in the evangelists' descriptions of Jesus's divine power. So, Jesus said to a sick woman: "Your faith has made you well" (Luke 8:48). Conversely, the health that Christ gave people was always associated with a new view of things, with a new belief. He healed people fully, in both body and soul.

- The Capuchin father Guido Kreppold emphasized that healing through Jesus demanded complete commitment from the sick. Jesus was the last resort for people afflicted and disturbed by sorrow and in mortal danger. In the stories of the New Testament, they risked everything in order to be healed by him. So, two blind persons shouted out above the din and the opposition of the crowd to attract the attention of Jesus (Matthew 20:29–34). And to bring the paralyzed man to Jesus through the crowd, his friends even removed the roof of the house and lowered the sick man to him through the opening (Mark 2:1–12).

hear him and to be cured of their diseases" (Luke 5:15). He took pity on them; he cured the leper, he freed the possessed from their demons (which were regarded as the cause of many illnesses), he made the blind see, and he relieved the paralyzed from their afflictions.

Savior in the desert

Not as an escape from the world, but to follow Jesus, who himself had fasted in the desert for forty days in preparation for his mission, many Christians in

- The love of Christ was always a prerequisite for the development of health: love for its own sake which is the source of charity. Whoever did not assume and accept this had no love to give others.

- But Christ was not only a healer; he was also a sufferer (*Christus patiens*). The care of the sick was implicit in his commandment to love one's neighbor. Henceforth the suffering of Christ would be seen in everyone who was suffering. The example of the good Samaritan, who out of pity took care of someone who was suffering, formed the precedent. In this parable, Jesus introduced his program of charity and made clear what true pity really meant. The man from Samaria not only treated the wounds the man received from the robbers, he also took him to an inn and nursed him there. In addition, he made provision for the future of his protégé by giving the innkeeper money to go on looking after him. This parable is the source text from which the quintessentially Christian virtue of charity is derived.

the third century chose to retreat into solitude, first in Egypt, then in Asia Minor and Syria. The model of all hermits was the father of monasticism, St. Anthony (251/52–356), who lived to over one hundred years old in the Egyptian desert. Thousands followed his example, living in caves and devoting themselves to God alone.

These hermits developed principles that Benedict of Nursia would later adopt in a moderated form as his Rule for Western monks: for example, fasting to cleanse the body and soul, tranquility, and silence free from careless gossip. The desert hermits helped those seeking advice and healed the sick, who asked for their help.

St. Benedict, the founder of monastic medicine

The enormous medical knowledge of ancient scholarship was almost lost as a result of the fall of the Roman Empire, migration, and plague epidemics. Knowledge of most surgical practices vanished with the disintegration of the Roman Empire. That writings about healing herbs have survived is due to the founder of the Benedictine order, Benedict of Nursia, 480–547. With infinite diligence, his monks copied ancient medical texts about healing plants until their fingers and eyes hurt. At the time this approach was controversial; the criticism was repeatedly made that monastic doctors fell back on ancient knowledge. Hippocrates and Galen, the Greek personal physician of Emperor Marcus Aurelius, were after all pagans, whose wisdom the Christians treated with caution.

St. Benedict

Help for all

Unlike the Romans and Greeks, where only senior figures, kings, and emperors could benefit from medical skills, monks now treated all who sought help without exception, including the poor and homeless. This was new, and it was because Christian charity was a central requirement for members of religious orders.

In the most important Western monastic Rule, Benedict also emphasized nursing and with it laid the cornerstone for the medical care of the population. "Care for the sick must stand before and above everything: one should serve them, as one would Christ, because he said: 'I was sick and you took care of me,' and: 'Just as you did it to one of the least of these who are members of my family, you did it to me.'" Benedict was not only a seeker after God, the originator of the Benedictine order, and an inspired teacher; he was also a great doctor and healer, following in the footsteps of Jesus.

Monastic medicine — an integral program

The medical skills of the monasteries did not consist only of botany. They included loving care of the sick, fostering a positive view of things, and ultimately the healing energy that was set free by faith. Here health had a profound dimension. The concept covered the whole human being in his oneness in Creation and in relation to the Creator. Because Christian medical skill uses a particular concept of man as its basis and also includes other factors — for example, God's help — it differs fundamentally from modern high-tech medicine.

"Sick monks should be given a room of their own and a god-fearing nurse who serves them carefully and enthusiastically."
St. Benedict

With this approach comes the realization that in this life one has to be ready to take up one's cross. Not many people are spared this. We do not live in paradise. In this world, since the fall of humanity, there have been huge problems that we cannot solve. But we can face them. And we can try to live according to a structure that clearly reflects the Creation, that corresponds most closely to life on this planet.

In the monastery the sick were restored with meat, eggs, and wine infused with herbs. The abbot was simultaneously pastor, doctor, and psychologist. In the care of the sick, Benedict appealed for both doctor and patient to understand each other. Neither should create a burden for the other: "The sick too should consider that they are served to honor God; they should not impose on their brothers, who serve them, with exaggerated demands. But such patients must be uncomplainingly endured; then through this one will attain a greater reward."

The spiritual salvation of the sufferers was the most important aspect. Even before the healing herbs, spiritual therapy was applied in the form of confession and the Eucharist. Since it was believed that guilt also played an important part in causing illnesses, good health could be beneficially

Nuns preparing herbs

influenced by the Eucharist and forgiveness, a fact that until now has not been sufficiently appreciated. Forgiveness was requisite for every "healing" relationship.

What makes us healthy

- Orderly days, orderly rooms, orderly times, orderly tasks and roles — a life of moderation lived according to certain rules is an essential foundation stone of good health.
- The intrinsic secret of the healing treatment in monasteries and convents is that monks and nuns do what Jesus advised: they pass their worries onto Christ instead of being subjugated by them. This is not to become dependent, but to make themselves truly free. One must not do everything

oneself, nor could one do so. In the view of the religious orders, those who attempt this are arrogant and in their arrogance they are already sick. There is a charming story about this. A man met Jesus and asked him: "Where were you when I called upon you?" Jesus looked at him and said: "Do you see the footprints of your journey through life?" "Yes," the man said, "they have been made by two pairs of feet." "That is because I have always gone beside you," Jesus said. The man looked at the tracks and cried out: "But here suddenly there are only the marks of a single pair of feet to be seen, and I did so badly on this stretch. Where were you then?" Jesus smiled and said: "There I carried you."

- An unshakable faith in God supplies a healthy serenity, one of the most important remedies. Serenity means not desperately clinging to everything, but being able to let go. If one can no longer go any further, one asks God for help for a moment. Those who do this are not overcome so quickly, nor do they become sick so easily.

- Jesus said about mercy: "Just as you did it to one of the least of these who are members of my family, you did it to me." This tells us that we always receive back the help we give. Something that is divided becomes greater, not smaller. From this too comes the expression: "Shared joy is double joy. Shared sorrow is sorrow halved." When you help someone, you also help yourself; in healing another, you also are healed. At the same time it is important to look for help and to recognize that pride and arrogance only make people hard and unsympathetic.

- The saint and Carmelite nun Edith Stein said: "It is the duty of every human being to discover his or her self." To recognize one's own self, one's own being, is an important challenge. Be who you are!

- According to Hildegard von Bingen, repentance is one of the strongest methods that God has given humanity to become well again. One may commit many "sins" — and health disorders are also, so to speak, "sins" against the body and spirit — but there is always the possibility of change, not only to attain forgiveness but also to prepare oneself better for the road to recovery.

- Only those who accept and love themselves can achieve spiritual purity. This is a fundamental requirement in order to be able to love others and

The Lorscher pharmacopoeia: the first record of monastic medicine

help them. The expression of love is a work of mercy. If something is done without love, it is worth nothing, as St. Paul said in his passage in praise of love (1 Corinthians 13:1): "If I speak in the tongues of mortals and angels, but do not have love, I am a noisy gong or a clanging cymbal." And the Father of the Church St. Augustine once said that man is not what he eats or wears; man is "how he loves."

- Love includes happiness, which is an important means of preventing illnesses and of not slipping into a "negative" attitude. Why do the religious orders give so much space to the glorification of God and his Creation? Because it promotes positive thinking. Whoever praises God has a better, healthier attitude to the world. And in the end, he becomes a healing force, not a person of whom others will say: "you make me sick."

The monks' medicine books

The first surviving record of monastic medicine is the *Lorscher Arzneibuch* (*Liber Medicinalis* or "Book of Medicine"), a pharmacopoeia of very interesting herbal recipes that also contains numerous dietary recommendations. It was probably written in about 790 under the direction of Abbot Richbodo of the Lorsch monastery at Worms.

A lyrical masterpiece of botany and the first herbal ever written was *Hortulus* ("Little garden"), dating from 840. In twenty-seven chapters, Walafrid Strabo, abbot of the monastery of Reichenau and tutor to the Carolingian monarch, described the appearance and effects of twenty-four herbal plants,

The doctrine of the four cardinal humors

Monastic medicine in the Middle Ages was based on the ancient doctrine of the four cardinal humors (humoral pathology). This dates back to the most important doctors of antiquity: Hippocrates (fourth century BC) and Galen of Pergamon (second century BC). According to this doctrine, the body of a human being contains four fluids: blood, phlegm, yellow bile, and black bile. If the mixture of the fluids or humors is out of balance, illness occurs. Unbalanced nutrition or a poor lifestyle can also lead to an imbalance causing illness. The aim of the doctor was to even out the excess of a fluid using herbal remedies or bloodletting.

On the other hand, the relatively light and therefore harmless predominance of one fluid defines the temperament (mixture) of a human being: with a sanguine temperament, blood (*sanguis*) predominates; with a choleric temperament, yellow bile (*chole*); with a melancholic temperament, black bile (*chole melaina*); and with a phlegmatic temperament, phlegm (*phlegma*).

from lovage to the rose. In it he designed an ideal monastery garden.

The most widely distributed herbal in the Middle Ages was undoubtedly the *Macer floridus* from the eleventh century. In more than two thousand verses, Odo de Meung (from Meung-sur-Loire) recorded the appearance and healing qualities of some eighty plants. The summation of monastic medicine comes from Hildegard of Bingen. In her twelfth-century works on nature and medicine, the books *Physica* and *Causae et Curae*, she described healing plants and their effects in more than 200 chapters (see Reading for day 4).

The monastic reforms proposed in the eleventh and twelfth centuries, which spread from the monastery of Cluny in the Burgundy, put church services and contemplation at the center once more and curbed the monks' scientific curiosity. Gradually, the first Christian medical school at Salerno outpaced the monasteries. Then in the year 1130 the Council of Clermont prohibited religious orders from taking part in medical activities, although not all monks strictly complied with this ban. In response Christian hospital orders were set up and later adopted by established orders such as the Knights of St. John of Jerusalem, the Teutonic Order, and the Hospitallers of Mercy.

Today, the real monastery apothecaries that flourished in the seventeenth and eighteenth centuries until secularization are hard to find. But in many

Unusual recipes

Many recipes from the eighth-century *Lorscher pharmacopoeia* are still valid today, although some are admittedly unusual. For instance, in this ancient medical book a mixture consisting of sheep dung, cheese, and honey is recommended for treating wounds. This was to be spread on the injured part. The Monastic Medicine Research Group wanted to know exactly how it worked and discovered to its amazement that the cheese, a kind of Roquefort, stimulated the sheep dung to develop antibacterial material. So evidently the unappetizing compress served its purpose.

monasteries, healing herbal teas, salves, and tinctures are still produced from old, usually secret, monastic recipes. And in South America, church pharmacies are often still the only help available to the poor.

Nun with calf

The best preventative: holistic medicine

Those who live in harmony with nature are looking after their health

The basics of sickness and health

*I*t was five o'clock in the morning and the birds were giving a fantastic concert. I had woken up much too early, for fear of missing Lauds, the office of morning prayer. The first day in the convent was especially exciting and I really wanted to make good use of my precious time here. I immediately felt drawn to the monastery garden whose beautiful expanse I could see, with Sister Leandra raking her herb beds and pulling up the weeds. The plants were still wet from the dew and glistened in the sun.

I strolled through the monastery buildings, where every corner invited one to linger. Without noticing it, I had forgotten the time. When had that last happened to me? As the bells summoned me to Lauds I returned to reality. I hastened into the chapel where Sister Teresa was already waiting for me on a pew, smiling at me kindly. The clear chant of the Franciscan nuns transported me into another world.

In the opinion of the sisters a holistic lifestyle is the best medicine. For them this means that the essential things are to eat healthily, to have enough sleep, to work in moderation, to spare time for the community, and to have plenty of time for their relationship with God. Under this regime body, mind, and soul come together properly and in balance.

The sick may be healthy

Physical health is very important, but for monks and nuns it is not an end in itself. The Benedictine father Anselm Grün sees it as follows: "Health is not the criterion for whether our life is pleasing to God or not. Salvation is not the same as health."

So, too, Hildegard von Bingen presented the apparently paradoxical opinion that a healthy person was actually sick and a sick person could actually be healthy. In her view, people who had lost their balance and their relationship with God could not be healed, even if they were still physically fit. By contrast, those who were suffering from afflictions could live in peace with themselves and with God, and, according to Hildegard, they were therefore healthy.

Illness as a sign

In the monastery, illness is regarded as a sign that one's rhythm and proper equilibrium have been disturbed. Whether in eating and drinking, sleeping or waking, working or relaxing, intemperance makes one permanently sick. Those who live in harmony with their inner clock and the course of nature are already looking after their health. Illness may also be a sign of a disturbed relationship with God, oneself, and one's fellows, a sign of negative and self-destructive thoughts or actions.

For the Benedictine father Johannes Pausch, the increase in allergies, infections, depression, and addiction is also a sign of a spreading state of disorientation. The author offers an interesting explanation for it: the transition from the industrial age to the information age is a radical change, which has made old standards obsolete. "People often become sick in such transitional periods, because they cannot cope with the change. Their inner balance, the balance between body and soul, tilts, and this can lead to illness." As the psychotherapeutic leader of the monastic "Hildegard Center" in Upper Austria, Pausch also strongly recommends the pursuit of old values such as friendship, loyalty, charity, and religiousness again. He stresses the importance of finding a meaningful rhythm in life.

The Benedictine Anselm Grün advises listening carefully in order to discover what one's "illness wants to say." In Grün's words: "One person says: 'I have a stuffed-up nose' and is therefore overtaxed." The person who describes it as "catching cold" is perhaps also suffering from the coldness of others, while the person who is "infected" is probably looking to distance himself from others.

Illness as a challenge and ailments as opportunities

In the Bible, illness is also seen as an opportunity for repentance. Jesus healed innumerable people, and he healed them completely. They could not only see, hear, and walk, but they also received a new awareness.

Illness should not only be seen as a negative thing, Father Anselm believes. Often, it modifies hardened behavior, making a person softer and more understanding of the sorrows of others. Illnesses require us to interact with each other more sensitively. Anyone who has suffered problems can more easily share those of people who are disabled.

Illnesses may also be the consequence of repressed needs. A restless life, for example, may lack necessary restorative breaks. Sometimes an illness protects us from even more serious things. Grün believes that not being able to be ill may be an illness in itself, and after years of apparent health, a heart attack often occurs suddenly without any warning.

One can also emerge strengthened from surviving an illness. One notices again what is truly important, and one is grateful for things that were previously taken for granted. A woman who survived a serious liver disease once said in a newspaper interview: "I enjoy it so very much when I watch my child in the playground. Previously, this had always gotten on my nerves."

What monks and nuns recommend to remain healthy

To remain healthy, you should live according to a natural rhythm. St. Benedict recognized this long ago. Father Pausch recommends becoming more conscious of the changing seasons: "The experience of growing, maturing, and aging is good for human beings as well." For example, in the winter our

Candles as intercessions for recovery.

body has a greater need for silence. Someone who flies off to the tropics at this time "will have difficulty making the retreat necessary for arriving at inner peace."

- Use the healing powers of nature. According to research, people who keep plants in their offices feel more balanced than their colleagues in areas without plants. Patients who look at trees from their rooms recover more quickly than others who have only houses to look at out of the window. To cure eye problems, Hildegard von Bingen recommended gazing at a green meadow. For the medically knowledgeable Benedictine nuns of the Middle Ages, the strongest healing powers lay within God's Creation.
- Take time for healthy exercise, such as frequent walks or long bicycle rides.

- Think about relaxation and practice patience, one of the most important virtues of all. When sick, allow yourself enough recovery time in bed. Don't overtax yourself from fear of your employer or as a matter of personal pride. This will prevent worse illnesses from occurring.
- Do not reproach yourself for being sick. Self-love is part of convalescence. "Friends and relations should be careful with rash and possibly hurtful diagnoses," warns Father Anselm Grün. "The nearer I am to someone, the more strongly I forbid myself from giving a diagnosis of their illness, because I am not helping them by doing so. First I must endure the secret of their illness and mine. So initially I may cautiously wonder: What does the illness want to say to me? What does God want to tell me through the illness?" Despite all our healing powers, we are not supermen. Monks and nuns never forget: the help of God is always needed.
- Give serious thought to the topics of illness and death. Repressing these subjects simply means that fear of them will grow unconsciously with possible damage to health.

Monks at mass: What is sickness telling to me?

You can master anxiety

Anxiety is one of the central health problems in general and one of the main health problems of our time. Millions of people suffer from fear of failure, anxiety, concern about not being loved, worry about loss, fear of embarrassing themselves — and even from anxiety about missing something. Anxiety weakens the immune system; it can cause dizziness and heart problems, and it can be the trigger of many other illnesses.

Monks and nuns ease their anxieties in prayer, when singing the psalms, and in their meditations before God. This makes them calmer and gives them hope. They strengthen themselves in chapel services and in the Eucharist, and they do not allow worries to grow unchecked and thence become destructive anxieties. The members of religious orders follow the word of Jesus, as recommended in his parable: "Consider the ravens: they neither sow nor reap, they have neither storehouse nor barn, and yet God feeds them…. And can any of you by worrying add a single hour to your span of life?" (Luke 12:24–25)

Then, because the members of religious orders amass no riches but have committed themselves to poverty, they must, in theory at least, not worry about money. Because they have neither careers nor authority, they do not worry about losing their jobs or their power. Because they are committed to the truth, assuming they conform to it, they have no fear of being exposed as liars.

Practice relaxation

Serenity and relaxation are as important as vitamins. This relaxation practice is quite simple and practical. It can be done anywhere, even at the bus stop, or standing or sitting in the train, and during tiresome waits. First consciously tense each muscle and then relax it again. It is quite simple but very effective.

Behind many anxieties the fear of dying is concealed. By not fearing death we become like the Ettal monk who sees it as a "door into another world," and we can cope better with any health problems that may arise.

St. Benedict's recommendations

In his Rule, St. Benedict always provided fairly specific instructions to teach his brothers how to live. He never wanted to lump everyone together. "Everyone has his own offering to God," he said, "one this, another that." What is too much for one person may be too little for another. But most of the advice that he has identified as "useful tools" has an overriding validity:

- Love the Lord God with your whole heart, soul, and strength.
- Love your neighbor as yourself.
- Honor all persons. And do not do to another what you would not do to yourself.
- Discipline the body.
- Do not give yourself over to pleasure.
- Love fasting.
- Visit the sick.
- Help the oppressed.
- Comfort mourners.
- Do not let anger rule your actions.
- Carry no guile in your heart.
- Do not make false peace.
- Do not depart from love.
- Do not be proud or a grumbler.
- Be temperate with food and drink and guard against sloth.
- Remember daily that death may come at any time.
- Watch what you do and what you leave undone.

Body and soul

"The inner attitude is the most important thing. Medication is supplemental."

And how to bring the two into harmony

"Be friendly to your body so that the soul enjoys living in it."

St. Teresa of Ávila

*O*ften one brief moment will become engraved upon our memory and have a lasting effect on us. For example, as we strolled through the convent garden and Sister Teresa was telling me about the large convent, a nun appeared from somewhere and ran up to us. Asked her opinion about achieving good health, she immediately declared: "You know, what matters most is your mental attitude. Everything else, treatment and medication, that is just something supplemental."

The unity of body and soul

Every day there were little gestures of kindness for everyone at Oberzell, from the lovely floral decorations on the dining table to the helpful images and symbols at every corner, and the friendly attentiveness. Rarely had I received so many little gifts just in passing, whether a fragrant rose or a handful of freshly picked plums.

"Human beings exist as a unity of body and soul," Sister Veridiana explained in her cozy workroom. "This is reflected in our speech. For instance, we say that we are all tensed up, that our heads are spinning."

Here physical conditions are used to describe mental states. This is why the mother superior defines her task as much more "global" than most company managers do in the outside world. It is important for her "to be attentive. If someone has a problem I must detect it," she stressed. "I am not only the manageress but also the spiritual caregiver." Sister Veridiana knows how debilitating tensions between people can be: "I have noticed how relieved the sisters are and how it helps them when problems can be discussed and tackled."

Apologies and gestures of reconciliation for insults or disrespectfulness that can also make the body ill play an important part in the balance of body and soul. Kind words heal psychological injuries like a balm. St. Benedict also recommended another remedy, the "ointment of admonition" in order to "heal one's own wounds and those of others without exposing or revealing them." Thus Father Kneipp, an early theorist and practitioner of medicine based on holistic principles, suspected a mental problem when a patient just could not get better. In such cases the physician-priest offered the patient confession, because he knew from experience that the burden of a past fault can hinder recovery.

How you can heal the soul through the body

Just as the body can be healed through the soul, so can the soul be healed through the body. "There is a link between people's feelings and the organs in the body that is probably much closer than many believe," the monk Johannes Pausch explained. Metabolic diseases such as diabetes can seriously affect a person's psychological state. A patient with a low sugar level will have outbursts of rage when faced with the slightest irritation but will be all right again with the correct dose of insulin. A woman with thyroid problems will only find her equilibrium if the hormone level of the thyroid is brought back to normal through medical treatment.

The Benedictine monk also noted: "Thoughts alone are often not enough to help the mind; the body is always involved. That is why mental care also involves the care of the body.... Anyone who wants to do something for the soul must also do something for the body — and vice versa." The Father gave a very simple illustration of this: "When you offer someone a chair, you will help his mind as well as his body."

About the healing power of feelings and thoughts

It was not until recently that the concept of the unity of body and mind was perceived as a prerequisite for the general understanding of medicine. For the head of a monastery or convent, *cura animae*, the care of the soul, went naturally hand in hand with *cura corporis*, the care of the body. A body cannot be completely healthy if the mind and the soul are not purified. If one aspect is ignored, then the others will suffer too.

For Hildegard von Bingen, the soul had an effect on every part of the body and made it alive. "What the sap is to the tree, the soul is to the body. It develops its mental strength as the tree does its shape." Our feelings influence our health. We rack our brains about something and react to problems with migraine, and stress also affects the digestion. The negative effects of stress, anger, and grief on the body have been medically proven. Stress — which also includes anxiety and anger — seriously increases the risk of heart disease and circulatory problems.

Earlier still, St. Benedict of Nursia had warned the monks in his Rule: "We urge you above all: refrain from grumbling." As Father Anselm Grün explained: "People who constantly get angry will become ill at some point. On the other hand, consideration and friendliness will promote health. In his Rule, St. Benedict admonished the cellarer not to send away someone who was sad but at least to give him a kind word, because it is written that a good word is better than the best gift."

A miracle

One of the most famous physicians of the tenth century was Notker of St. Gallen, who ran a celebrated practice. The Bavarian Duke Henry was suspicious by nature, and he wanted to test the skills of this physician. He sent the Benedictine monk a little bottle of urine, but it had come from his chambermaid. The monk then diagnosed a miracle because the duke was pregnant. Duke Henry was convinced and agreed to be treated by Notker.

About the healing power of joy

Hildegard von Bingen believed that the best remedy was joy. In her opinion, pure joie de vivre and pleasure in creation came from God, who through his love made people glad in the truest sense of the word. It was no coincidence that St. Francis de Sales, whose faith was marked by great delight, frequently ended his letters with the words: "Live happily!"

The expression of cheerfulness is laughter, whose healing effect is often used in children's hospitals. When the clown comes and visits sick children in the hospital, they all feel much better. The company of cheerful people, a funny movie, or a comic story can help children, and adults as well.

There is now a branch of research, gelotology, studying the therapeutic effects of humor. One of its findings is that as well as reducing the threshold of pain, laughing can lower blood pressure, strengthen the heart, and normalize the rhythm of breathing.

About the healing power of music

Members of religious orders have many ways of caring for the body and soul. This is one reason why they love music so much. Music is one of the foundation stones of the universe (Christ as *summus musicus*), and plays an essential part in maintaining a healthy life. It has remarkable healing power. Certainly there is also music that makes people ill, but when music is good it brings joy and also creates a positive psychological mood that benefits and invigorates us. When we have problems, it also has genuine healing powers.

It is no coincidence that singing forms so great a part of the daily offices. Nor is it a coincidence that Gregorian chant in monasteries is the traditional music for celebrating the feast of the Eucharist. Music is not just of this world, it is divine and anticipates heavenly delights. It is something that flows through the body, doing us good, stimulating our breathing and massaging our organs. And it affects the mind as well as the body. Heavenly sounds lift us into another dimension, removing worries that might make us ill; we feel magnanimous about many things, including the little irritations that are not worth bothering about. We rightly speak of the power of music that it is

Hildegard von Bingen

like a balm on the soul and soothes it. The greatest composers have elevated it to the highest art in the wonderful *Marienlieder* ("Songs of Mary").

For Sister Judith at Oberzell, the healing effect of the psalms was one of the greatest mysteries in the Christian art of living. Sitting perfectly upright, she was listening to our conversation. She was concentrating on the subject, but she was completely relaxed. She explained that she had always been careful about her posture and that she never suffered from backache. Singing psalms had a healing effect that made a lot of medication superfluous. Sister Judith explained: "The psalms are our daily bread. They were baked in an old oven, so to speak, but the words have lost none of their power." At the start the text often involves an argument with God, and as a result it helps reduce our aggression. "Frequently a psalm starts with criticism but gradually its anger subsides. Then, like a fairy tale, it ends happily," the music-loving nun explained.

The psalms mirror the experiences of the people of Israel over the centuries; the subjects are flight, war, guilt, and the splendor and decline of cities. They deal with all the emotions and situations that occur in life, including love and hatred, happiness and sorrow, life and death, trust and hope in God. As the Benedictine monk Nikolaus Nonn explained: "This is why people in the psalms rejoice, flee, praise, lament, argue, and give thanks…"

"But the music of the psalms is also something very special," continued Sister Judith. "It has a lasting effect and involves the whole body in singing." The change in the body's posture, the bending forward and standing up straight, all have a beneficial effect on the individual organs. "The pause between each verse is also very important. It changes the rhythm of our breathing," the Franciscan nun explained. We breathe completely differently when singing. Sister Judith knows this from experience: "Its meditative effect gives a different structure to the day."

About the healing power of compassion

Monks and nuns ascribe special significance to the role of compassion in people's recovery. Friendly, sensitive dealings with the sick are essential to their recovery. This will be very clear to anyone who has seen how quickly a patient who is getting ever weaker and more miserable in the hospital will recover in a loving environment.

As Hildegard von Bingen said, compassion is "the king's best friend." Compassion suffers with those who are in a bad way (*miseriis compatiens*), behaves like the Good Samaritan (*imitans Samaritanum*), and embodies

Nuns playing music in the convent of Lichtental

pure humanity (*cooperiens hominem*). Without compassion, the hard-heartedness, coldness, and selfishness that are prevalent in the world would triumph. In Hildegard von Bingen's *Book of the Rewards of Life* (*Liber Vitae Meritorium*), the concept of compassion is celebrated: "My heart is overflowing with a desire to help everyone. I am considerate of every need. I want to help the frail and infirm and help them recover. I am like a balm for every sorrow and my words do good." For Hildegard, the "evil of all evils" is when "people no longer care about their neighbor's health and have no compassion for anyone any more."

The characteristic and particular attribute of monastic medicine was the caring love that saw the suffering Christ in every sick person. This was "an ethical principle of therapeutic application, through which the medicine of the Christian West developed far beyond the medicinal techniques of antiquity," as Heinrich Schipperges, an expert on Hildegard, wrote. It came before the application of herbs and medicine.

Love and affection do the heart good in the truest sense of the word. According to the World Heart Federation, positive social contacts contribute to a better chance of survival after a heart attack and are also important in preventing heart attacks.

How we can deal properly with suffering

It may be a rather unpopular idea, but no one can avoid suffering. Just as in Christianity, suffering and the overcoming of suffering also play a key part in Buddhism, although in Eastern religion the journey does not lead to redemption through a loving God but only helps to increase one's own spiritual strength. The Christian message is indeed paradoxical, through the cross to salvation and through darkness to light.

The imagery of the cross is inexhaustibly rich and difficult to grasp in its profundity. Christians see in suffering an opportunity to become stronger and discover new ways of looking at things. From this point of view, without suffering there is no health, nor purity of mind, body, or soul; suffering is like a fever that increases the body's powers of resistance. Often suffering has a cathartic effect, helping the body to rid itself of the poisons that it has absorbed, including the poisons in the mind, the garbage of civilization that has piled up around us and that occasionally almost suffocates us. It is a detoxification that we need badly from time to time and that is sometimes particularly needed by the soul, for instance after a breakdown.

Among monks there have been many who, like St. Ignatius of Loyola, only discovered their path through their own "passion," or suffering. In the case of the Spanish founder of the order of the Jesuits who started his career as a knight, it was his recovery from a serious wound that triggered his conversion. But St. Ignatius always spoke of the great comfort that he received from above during his suffering, which was so "sweet" that he sometimes gladly accepted it again.

Another example is that of the Carmelite nun Edith Stein. The daughter of Jewish parents who had converted to Catholicism after a period of agnosticism, she described the "cross and night" as the "road to heavenly light." Before Edith Stein and her sister Rosa were murdered in the concentration camp at Auschwitz, she sent a note with a last message from the Westerbork transit camp to her abbess. "*Scientia Crucis* ('Knowledge of the Cross') can only be achieved," she maintained, "if you really feel the cross deep down. From the very first moment I was convinced and from the bottom of my heart I said: *Ave, crux, spes unica* ('I greet thee, Cross, our only hope')!"

About the healing power of prayer

For monks and nuns, health without prayer is almost impossible. It is no coincidence that they "bless" or "heal" their day through the canonical hours, which they believe are indispensable for their balance and personal well-being, and for finding their places in the cosmos. St. Francis de Sales believed that praying was also "the most efficient remedy" against sadness. Finally, St. Jacob also advised: "Whoever of you is sad, should pray."

Prayer must be practiced, as the religious philosopher explained when he said: "Lord, teach us to pray. Teach me to see that without prayer my soul and my mind become stunted and my life loses support and strength." Throughout her life, Edith Stein, "who prayed constantly," also drew her energy and vitality from prayer: "Prayer is the line of communication with God." She considered prayer "the highest achievement the human mind is capable of."

Prayer is prophylactic. It prevents illness. When nothing else helps any longer "except praying," this was popularly known as "healing by prayer."

Exercise

Think whether your body and soul are really receiving the loving attention that they need. Here are a few suggestions:

- *Perhaps pause for a while, go and sit in a church and enjoy the pleasant, beneficial stillness and the devotional atmosphere.*
- *Pray with a rosary and feel the unexpectedly calming, healing effect on the soul of this mysterious prayer.*
- *Meditate in front of a candle, a picture, or while walking in the woods.*
- *Alternatively, include a visit to a convent or monastery in your plans and experience for yourself how pleasant a walk through a fragrant cloister garden can be.*

Abundance and balance

Nuns on their way to the refectory in the convent of Chamberaud

How to lead a balanced life

*I*t was a wonderful evening. A light wind was rustling through the leaves, the air was filled with the fragrance of herbs, and it was pleasantly warm. After the evening meal Sister Teresa and another nun were strolling with me through the convent garden. "Perhaps you would like to chat without me around," said Sister Teresa softly and was about to leave us. We protested, and Sister Teresa smiled and remained with us. The scene made me realize something. The Franciscan nun always anticipated what I might need — whether something was too much or too little. When she told me about her convent she paused regularly and asked me whether she should go on and whether I could still concentrate. She was always correct in her interpretation, and her questions made me think.

What was the right measure for me? When should the pauses come? When was a conversation too long? Was I asking too few or too many questions? Did I eat too much or too quickly? Rarely had I thought so often about equilibrium and I realized that the nuns were gentle and careful even in their choice of words.

"Nothing is less befitting a Christian than a lack of moderation."

St. Benedict

They thought calmly before they said anything and their answers matched your questions — no more and no less.

Moderation for St. Benedict

The rediscovery of moderation was the focal point of the Rule of St. Benedict, and it was undoubtedly the reason for the amazing success of his principles, which were subsequently adopted by all other religious orders. It was for good reason that the father of monasticism called moderation "the mother of all virtues." "Do everything in moderation," he urged; he was referring to eating, speaking, working, sleeping, relaxing, and moving — in fact, everything. Today it would be possible to add: moderate your speed, moderate the noise and pace of life, and use resources such as electricity and water in moderation.

Even if you feel that moderation cramps your lifestyle, without moderation there is no middle way and no way of your own, either. Moderation and the middle way are two sides of the same coin. They constitute the art of finding the right balance, the invisible center and crucial point in everything.

"Moderation is a capital virtue, a fundamental attitude around which everything is centered," the mother superior elaborated. And it should be applied in every area of life. "For us it means, for instance, not stuffing ourselves when it is our favorite food and not skimping when we do not like what is served," Sister Veridiana explained. She believed moderation was even more far-reaching: "We belong to the one-third of people who live in affluence, and it is important to me not to forget the rest of the world."

It is important to be grateful that we have what we need, but also to help others who have nothing. "The overall balance must be reestablished throughout the world," Sister Veridiana pointed out.

When moderation and the middle way are disrupted

"A moderate, balanced way of life seems to have become discredited in our society. It is important to rediscover moderation," Father Pausch observed. The consequences of lack of balance make us ill and can destroy us and the world around us. Whether climatic catastrophe, environmental pollution, food scandals, terrorism, or war — all are the health-endangering and life-threatening consequences of a disturbed equilibrium. Eating disorders,

Nuns baking bread in the convent of Oberschönenfeld

addictions, and stress-related illnesses are all symptoms of being out of balance. For the monks, this starts with little things, with individuals, with their feelings and their thoughts. Greed for money, the pursuit of pleasure, recognition, and career advancement lead to inconsiderate actions towards oneself and others. Too much on one side is balanced by too little on the other: we have too much information but too little real knowledge. There is too much time for work, too little time for oneself, one's partner, one's children, or one's parents. The list is endless. Only through illness and suffering do we become aware of this imbalance in our way of living.

Rules for moderation and the middle way

With his Rule, St. Benedict wanted to help monks find the middle way:

- The seven canonical hours protected them from unremitting work and a hectic pace of life. These occasions for prayer were inspired by the psalm: "Seven times a day I praise you for your righteous ordinances." St. Benedict used this as the basis for the prayers said at the canonical hours that are still observed today. There are seven breathing spaces in the day, seven opportunities to relax, to step back, and to reflect on God and oneself.
- To ensure that their work, including spiritual activities, did not become too one-sided, all brothers had to help in the kitchen or garden. Manual

work was as highly valued as mental work. No one should look down on another because of their work or position.

- Moderation in eating — including the consumption of alcohol — was also an important criterion. It is the case that St. Benedict was very careful with his instructions. He knew that people have very different needs. Each monk had to decide for himself whether he heaped too much food on his plate or not. The founder was also lenient when advising a degree of moderation in drinking. He wrote: "Admittedly, we read that wine is not an appropriate drink for monks, but because the monks today no longer accept this, we should come to an agreement that we not drink to excess but sparingly." But one thing was incontestable for St. Benedict: "The monks must avoid any kind of immoderation and a monk should never show any sign of repletion."

- Gluttony was scorned, but so were excessive asceticism and excessive fasting. In some monasteries the monks presented a document to the abbot, the so-called *schedula*, containing their proposals for Lent. The abbot checked that they were not overdoing things — or not doing enough — and then initialed it.

- Moderation in work was extremely important. In order that work did not become an end in itself, it was carefully limited with regard to time and subordinate to religious services. Prayer was more important than work. Nevertheless, the monks were self-sufficient and ever mindful of St. Benedict's injunction: "Idleness is the enemy of the soul."

- He also recommended moderation in speech and silence, insisting that talkativeness was incompatible with true conversation. Monks always had to listen carefully before they said anything and had to take good care not to say anything hurtful or rash.

- For St. Benedict, moderation in sleep meant waking up and going to bed early. Everyone should have enough sleep but no one should be "addicted to sleep."

- He also enjoined the monks to observe moderation in thoughts and feelings. Excessive curiosity, destructive ambition, greed, jealousy, and envy had to be controlled. On the other hand, community, team work, and consideration were be encouraged.

Gothic cloister in the convent of Poblet in Spain

- St. Benedict also said that the superior of a community, the abbot, had to be a "wise physician" to everyone, always concentrating on the middle way: "So he runs everything in complete moderation, so that strong people can achieve what they want, and the weak will not give up."

A structured day

Exercising moderation means creating a structure. Plan your whole day purposefully and include breaks for meditation. As a suggestion, here is the timetable of a day at the Abbey of St. Hildegard in Eibingen:

5:30 A.M.: Lauds (morning prayer)
"From sunrise to sunset the name of the Lord is praised" (Psalms). After Lauds, breakfast. In the refectory no one speaks. Afterwards, time for praying and spiritual reading.

7:30 A.M.: Terce and convent chores
In accordance with ancient tradition, members of holy orders are to spend time at prayer at set times during the day. Of these, the liturgy has retained Terce, Sext, and Nones. Gregorian chant, with its austere beauty and deep spiritual meaning, plays an important part in these prayers.

8:30 A.M.: Start of the working day
Work is a fundamental part of the life of Benedictine nuns and monks. With it the monastic community will contribute in a responsible manner to the shaping of God's Creation. It protects against lethargy and leads to spiritual development. No work was considered too lowly.

Humility, the cornerstone of moderation

For Christians, the true middle way is God. Love and charity are what determines moderation. An exaggerated opinion of oneself, megalomania, and excessive perfectionism rock the foundations of moderation, as do feelings of inferiority. Father Pausch describes humility and self-confidence as the cornerstones of moderation. For him, moderation is not slavish submission but "the conviction that all good qualities come from God and belong to him, that people are the tools of God and made in the image of God." Humility is the opposite of arrogance. People who are humble remain unassuming and friendly in spite of all their success.

11:30 A.M.: Sext
After the midday meal. "There must be reading at the table. The meal is taken in absolute stillness. No sound or whisper can be heard, only the voice of the reader" (the Rule of St. Benedict).

12:30 P.M.: Common rest time

1:15 P.M.: Nones

2:30 P.M.: Working time
Areas of work in which the convent of Eibingen is active: research into the life and work of St. Hildegard, care of the elderly, vegetable growing, working with gold, and wine making.

5:30 P.M.: Vespers (evening prayer)

6:00 P.M.: Evening meal

7:15 P.M.: Compline (night prayer)
Time for the nuns to immerse themselves in the sphere of silence and practice stillness, the way to find God and peace of mind.

The oldest serving Benedictine abbot in the world, Odilo Lechner, said this about humility: "It is not about man rising ever higher, but about God who has descended from heaven and come down to us. It is the same in human life, where one must become small in order to grow." Humility includes serving like Christ did, who even washed the feet of his disciples. Service protects one from arrogance and turns the picture of a merciless God upside down. It does not destroy but rather helps and heals. This is what nuns and monks understand to be their task: serving other people. In his Rule, St. Benedict wrote about caring for the sick. He said we should serve the sick as if they were really Christ. Serving also includes taking in strangers, respect, and love.

Remedies from
the cloister garden

Historic apothecary in Cloister Reutberg in Upper Bavaria

On the use of herbs and medicinal plants

"The whole world is at man's disposal and entrusts him with its goods in loving service."

Hildegard von Bingen

*F*or the treatment of suffering and the prevention of various ailments, monks and nuns would almost exclusively use healing herbs. Monastic medicine was herbal medicine. There were several reasons for this. St. Benedict of Nursia established his order in Italy, a country with a highly developed knowledge of horticulture. The monasteries were to be self-sufficient. So growing their own vegetables and herbs already played an important role, and the herbs were used not only to add flavor to food but also as therapeutic remedies.

Monks and nuns acquired their knowledge of the effects of individual plants from their study of ancient writings and through their own careful observations. Monasteries and convents exchanged their knowledge and experience as well as hard-to-find seeds and plants. Many Mediterranean plants, such as rosemary, lavender, and lemon balm, were brought to Northern Europe and established there by monks, who carried seeds as well as precious objects on their backs when they crossed the Alps.

Angelica *(Angelica archangelica)*

According to legend, the archangel Raphael brought angelica to humanity in the fourteenth century as a cure for the plague. The monastic doctors presumably used it against bacterial illnesses. The bitter angelica tea also was drunk as a treatment for stomach and intestinal problems, for instance as a stomach stimulant. It is helpful for treating loss of appetite, flatulence, and bloated stomach. Benedictine and Carthusian monks still flavor their liqueurs (Benedictine and Chartreuse) with aromatic angelica oil.

Aniseed *(Pimpinella anisum)*

Aniseed is the distinctive flavor of ouzo, pastis, and some Christmas pastries. In the monasteries the white-flowering plant is used both as a seasoning and a remedy at the same time. When chewed, aniseed overcomes troublesome bad breath. Aniseed tea is helpful for coughs and diseases of the respiratory system. The plant is also effective for digestive problems and flatulence, and it strengthens the stomach.

INSTRUCTIONS To make aniseed tea, pour one cup of boiling water over a heaped teaspoon of ground aniseed. Steep for ten minutes, then strain the infusion.

Arnica *(Arnica montana)*

This Alpine plant with yellow flowers grows in the wild. It was known to ancient peoples as one of the most important healing plants. Its popular name today is Leopard's Bane. It is the supreme healing plant of folk medicine. Hildegard von Bingen recommended it as an external treatment for ulcers. The priest Sebastien Kneipp believed it was the best treatment for wounds, since its anti-inflammatory bitter substances have healing properties. The latest medical research has found that the constituents of arnica can stop the growth of tumors. Thanks to its strong healing power, many troubles can be eased with arnica: acne, hematoma, hypertension, burning feet and heaviness in the legs, problems with staunching bleeding, bad circulation, phlebitis, inflammation of the neck and pharynx, sore throats, hemorrhoids, cardiovascular disorders, stomach and intestinal troubles, abdominal cramps and premenstrual syndrome, joint injuries, wounds, and muscle pains.

An arnica tincture diluted with water is helpful for injuries, inflammation, stiff muscles, and muscle tension. Brother Vitalis produces this in the Benedictine monastery of Ettal. For inflammations, a cold compress is recommended, or for serious injuries, a hot compress. Hip baths with arnica tincture help treat hemorrhoids. Diluted arnica tincture or arnica tea is effective against inflammations of the throat: gargle with it several times a day, but do not swallow the tea because arnica contains poisonous substances. Daily application of an arnica cream makes troublesome pimples vanish.

INSTRUCTIONS Dilute one to two tablespoons of tincture of arnica and add about two cups of water. For application by rubbing, mix the tincture with an equal quantity of water.

Quick recipe for an infusion of arnica: Chop one to two tablespoons of dried arnica flowers and put them in a small bowl. Cover completely with one cup of boiling water. Steep for ten to fifteen minutes, then strain. The cooled infusion is suitable for use in moist compresses for treating injuries.

Caraway *(Carum carvi)*

Still popular today, this spice was used by monks as a digestive remedy for flatulence and a bloated stomach, and against nausea. Caraway tea is also used as a means of stimulating the formation of mother's milk. Caraway oil massaged into the skin promotes the circulation and eases rheumatic problems. Chewing caraway seeds cures bad breath.

INSTRUCTIONS To make a tea to treat flatulence or problems with the stomach or intestines, crush two teaspoons of caraway seeds and pour a cup of hot water over them. Strain the liquid after ten minutes. A mixture of caraway and fennel seeds may be used for this tea.

Carrot, wild *(Daucus carota)*

The carrot was already valued in antiquity as both a vegetable and as a healing plant. The standard work of monastic medicine, *Macer floridus*, valued the carrot for its medicinal effect, for example as a remedy for problems of the liver and spleen, asthma, and diarrhea: "Cook this root in milk, the decoction will help asthmatics, even if they have been suffering for a long time, and it also treats diarrhea." Today, it is recognized that carrots are particularly beneficial for eating disorders and lack of vitamin A. Eaten regularly, they should promote the ability to learn.

Chamomile *(Matricaria recutita)*

Chamomile has been highly regarded by monks and nuns since ancient times and it even came to be seen as a "plant doctor." In Germany this widely dispersed healing plant is used for healing sores, as an analgesic, and as an antispasmodic. Chamomile tea eases pains of the stomach and abdomen. Gargling with chamomile was used by religious orders in the Middle Ages to treat inflammations of the gums. Hip baths with chamomile have proven effective against inflammations in the genital area. This healing plant also eases dermatitis and menstruation troubles.

INSTRUCTIONS To make chamomile tea, pour one cup of hot water over one to two teaspoons of chamomile flowers and steep for ten minutes.

Chicory *(Cichorium intybus)*

Hildegard von Bingen discovered the properties of this unassuming plant with blue flowers, recommending it for hoarseness and digestive problems. Chicory was also recognized as a remedy for treating hemorrhoids and disorders of the stomach, liver, and skin. Today the leaves and roots of chicory are used to treat loss of appetite, flatulence, and for stomach and digestive problems.

Comfrey *(Symphytum officinale)*

This well-known healing herb is good for the health of the legs. Up to three feet high, the hairy-leafed plant contains a cell-increasing, bone-forming substance. The monk physicians used this healing plant particularly for treating sores and broken bones. Covering with comfrey salve accelerates the healing process in the case of broken bones, bruises, or burns. Comfrey is also a good treatment for muscle and other strains, and for hematoma.

Elder *(Sambucus nigra)*

In monastic medicine this was highly regarded as a universal remedy. It is effective for reducing fever and relieving pain. The flowers and berries of the shrub induce perspiration and are therefore drunk in cases of colds and flu, often in combination with lime flowers. As a precaution against colds, the juice of boiled elderberries may also be drunk. "Because the extremely useful services provided by the elder tree are no longer remembered, this loyal and formerly well-respected friend of the family has been rejected many times. But the old friend deserves to be highly regarded again," Sebastian Kneipp declared.

INSTRUCTIONS To make elderflower tea, pour hot water over two spoonfuls of flowers and steep for ten minutes.

Fennel *(Foeniculum vulgare)*

This is among the oldest known healing plants. Hildegard von Bingen praised the benefits of her favorite vegetable: "However it is eaten, it makes people cheerful, brings about agreeable warmth and good perspiration, and promises good digestion." The tea from fennel seeds is effective against indigestion, flatulence, and stomach colic. Mothers can quite safely give fennel tea to their babies and small children.

Flax *(Linum usitatissiumum)*

Flax is one of the oldest cultivated plants and was first used for making textiles. Later the healing power of the plant was also recognized. Hildegard von Bingen recommended it, saying: "Anyone who has burned some part of the body with fire should boil flaxseeds (linseed) in water on a high heat and dip a flax cloth into the water and place it while still hot on the burn, and the cloth will draw out the burn." The saint also recommended a flax compress for treating pneumonia. In monastic medicine it was originally applied externally, but later the recipes of antiquity were also adopted, in which flaxseeds were recommended as a laxative and as a remedy for ulcers. Today, it has been scientifically demonstrated that flax seeds help with gastritis, intestinal irritation, constipation, and dermatitis. It is even suspected that flaxseeds taken internally may offer protection against breast cancer.

INSTRUCTIONS For constipation, eat one to two tablespoons of freshly crushed flax seeds and then drink two glasses of water two or three times a day.

Warning: Do not use this remedy if there is any risk of intestinal obstruction or a restricted esophagus!

Garlic *(Allium sativum)*

You should never tire of this little bulb. It is not only a natural antibiotic but also an anti-aging vegetable without side effects. Hildegard von Bingen recommended eating small quantities of raw garlic. According to the *Handbook of Monastic Medicine*, this kitchen flavoring gives protection against changes in blood vessels caused by aging and can reduce cholesterol levels by up to ten percent. Through it, dangerous arteriosclerosis may be prevented. Garlic also reduces hypertension.

INSTRUCTIONS To increase powers of resistance, crush one ounce of garlic and boil the juice in four cups of water. Drink the decoction during the course of the day.

Ginger *(Zingiber officinale Roscoe)*

Ginger from Asia was already highly valued in Europe in ancient times. Scientifically, it is still regarded as the most important herbal remedy for motion sickness and the nausea associated with it. Monastic medicine also valued the powerful spice as an aid to digestion and for treating coughs and other respiratory problems.

INSTRUCTIONS To make ginger tea for digestive problems and against nausea, peel a piece of fresh ginger root and chop into very small pieces. Take a spoonful of the chopped ginger, pour hot water over it and let steep for ten minutes.

Hop *(Humulus lupulus)*

Hops are not only used in brewing beer. Because of its calming effect, hop tea made from hop flowers is a good sleeping draft and reduces nervous tension. Hop compresses are effective for wounds and eczema because of their antibacterial properties.

While at first monks mainly used hops for making beer, Hildegard von Bingen in particular recognized their medicinal effect. She pointed out, however, that while hops were soothing, they could also make people sad.
INSTRUCTIONS Put two teaspoons of hop flowers in one cup of boiling water and leave for fifteen minutes. Strain to remove the flowers and drink the tea half an hour before going to bed.

Lavender *(Lavandula officinalis)*

Monks brought this fragrant blue plant with its calming effect across the Alps into their cloister gardens. A little bag of lavender flowers under the pillow helps against insomnia. Lavender oil eases burns and stings and drives away ticks. Lavender tea is good for headaches and colds, has a calming effect, and gives freedom from flatulence.
INSTRUCTIONS Steep one to two teaspoons of lavender flowers in a cup of hot water for ten minutes. For a relaxing bath, add four ounces of lavender flowers to eight cups of water and bring to the boil. Strain the liquid and pour it into the bath water.

Lemon balm *(Melissa officinalis)*

Benedictine monks also introduced lemon balm from the Mediterranean region. Hildegard von Bingen declared that this plant, with its agreeable lemon scent, had "the strength of fifteen other herbs in itself." The monastic doctors used it for creating a brighter mood, promoting calm, and for achieving a beneficial deep sleep. Today lemon balm extract is recommended for nervousness, heart problems, gastritis, flatulence, and, applied locally, for lip herpes. Still made today is the high-proof spirit of lemon balm

At a glance: What helps when?

Abdominal problems, period pains arnica, chamomile, peppermint, yarrow

Acne arnica

Bad breath anise, caraway

Broken bones comfrey

Burns St. John's Wort, lavender, flax

Circulation problems arnica, spelt, rosemary

Colds, flu elderberries, mullein, yarrow, onion

Concentration wild carrot

Coughs, bronchitis mullein, thyme

Depression, melancholia St. John's Wort, lemon balm, fennel

Earache mullein, onion

Exhaustion valerian, rosemary, lemon balm

Flatulence aniseed, angelica, fennel, caraway, lavender, lemon balm

Gastrointestinal disturbances aniseed, angelica, fennel, chamomile, caraway, flaxseeds, lemon balm, peppermint, rosemary, chicory, wormwood, onion

Headache valerian, peppermint

Hemorrhoids arnica, chicory

Hypertension, high cholesterol levels arnica, garlic

Indigestion ginger

Inflamed gums arnica, chamomile

Inflammation, strains, stiff muscles arnica, comfrey, marigold, chamomile

Insomnia, nervousness, stress valerian, hops, lavender, lemon balm

Kidneys, urinary infections nettle

Lip herpes lemon balm

Loss of appetite angelica, chicory, onion

Motion sickness ginger tea or tincture

Nausea ginger, caraway

Resistance garlic, nasturtium, onion

Rheumatism stinging nettle, rosemary, caraway

Skin problems, eczema arnica, hops, redcurrant, chamomile, marigold, flax

Stings lavender, narrowleaf or broadleaf plantain, onion

Throat inflammation arnica, marigold, sage, thyme, chicory

Urinary tract problems nettle, parsley, thyme

Wounds arnica, St. John's Wort, chamomile, narrowleaf plantain, onion that the Carmelite nuns have been producing since the seventeenth century, a popular panacea.

Instructions The priest and herbalist Anton Weidinger recommends a lemon balm bath for nervousness and insomnia, as well as for menopausal women and girls with problems in puberty. Cover four ounces of lemon balm leaves with hot water and steep for fifteen minutes. Strain the leaves from the liquid and add the lemon balm infusion to the bath water.

Marigold (*Calendula officinalis*)

The bright yellow or orange petals of marigolds adorn Sister Leandra's herb garden and enhance her salads. With inflammations of the mouth and throat, it is helpful to gargle with marigold flower tea. A salve or tincture made from marigold flowers is beneficial for rashes, sprains, and inflammations.

Instructions For a marigold flower salve, heat eight ounces of Vaseline, stir in a handful of flowers, and bring to a boil. Strain through a cloth and pour the salve into a jar. To make marigold tea, pour boiling water over one to two teaspoons of marigold flowers. Let it steep for ten minutes.

Mullein (*Verbascum densiflorum Bertol*)

This plant with bright yellow flowers grows to a height of six feet. It was already highly valued in antiquity for its healing properties. While the leaves are poisonous, the flowers have curative powers. Hildegard von Bingen advised: "Mullein is warming and dry and at the same time somewhat cold, and anyone who has a weak and miserable heart should cook mullein with meat or with fish or with pastries, or with other herbs, and eat it often. It will strengthen the heart and make it happy." Mullein flowers contain an anti-inflammatory mucilage and are helpful for head colds and coughs. Steeped in hot water, the dried blooms yield a golden yellow, expectorant tea for coughs. Sister Leandra often adds some petals to her tea blend. Mullein oil has proved effective against earache.

INSTRUCTIONS To make mullein oil, put a handful of flowers in a bottle with half a cup of olive oil. Leave the bottle in the sun for three to four weeks, shaking it regularly. Then strain the oil.

Nasturtium *(Tropaeolum majus)*

The bright yellow to orange-red flowers of nasturtiums grow along part of the cloister wall at Oberzell. Both the pretty flowers and the leaves can be eaten raw or used to give piquancy to a salad. They taste of horseradish. With a high vitamin C content, nasturtium is also a natural antibiotic and strengthens the body's resistance. Sister Leandra not only decorates salads with it but also eats the flowers from time to time in passing, or strews them on bread and butter with other herbs: "If possible I mix some flowers into food every day, and since doing so I have had no more colds."

Nettle *(Urtica dioica and Urtica urens)*

"When it is newly sprouted from the earth, it is useful cooked for people to eat because it cleanses the stomach." Hildegard von Bingen was full of praise for the often underestimated "weed" of today. Nettle tea purges and helps with urinary infections, kidney problems, and rheumatism. The root is rec-

ognized as good for treating prostate ailments. But Sister Monika of Spa Krumbad warns that "one should not exaggerate its use. Too much nettle tea may also wash away mineral substances from the body."

INSTRUCTIONS For nettle tea, pour a large cup of hot water over two teaspoons of nettle leaves. Steep for ten minutes.

Onion *(Allium cepa)*

The onion was the medicine of the poor. In monasteries, it was regarded as a popular remedy for the digestion and as a stimulant for the appetite. With its antibacterial constituents, it is helpful for colds.

INSTRUCTIONS To treat earache, cut a small onion in

half, wrap it in a cloth, and put it in the affected ear. Its healing vapors will reduce the pain. This method is only suitable for people who are not too sensitive to smells. Onion also helps with insect bites and minor abrasions. Take a halved onion and apply the cut side to the injured part. The juice stops itching and pain, and also disinfects.

Parsley *(Petraselinum crispum)*

The monks planted parsley as a vegetable as well as in their beds of healing herbs. They used it as a diuretic and treated ulcers and gnat stings with a purée of freshly mashed parsley. Today it is recognized as excellent for flushing out problems of the urinary tract, gastro-intestinal troubles and promoting good digestion.

Peppermint *(Mentha piperita)*

This herb is appreciated for more than the pleasant sensation of its refreshing menthol smell. Peppermint oil trickled on the forehead noticeably helps with headaches. Caution: Do not use the oil on the faces of babies or toddlers, since there is a danger of asphyxia!
Peppermint tea is useful for nausea and gastrointestinal problems. It is also excellent for treating diarrhea and constipation. It eases strong period pains.
INSTRUCTIONS Pour one cup of hot water over two to three teaspoons of peppermint leaves and let it steep for ten minutes. Tea made from fresh leaves tastes best.

Plantain, *Narrowleaf (Plantago lanceolata)*

Monks and nuns valued the broad or narrowleaf plantain particularly in the summer because the juice of this unpretentious plant that grows in meadows or by the roadside is excellent for insect bites. The plant juice also makes sores heal more quickly. "If farmers injure themselves while working, they immediately look for leaves of the narrowleaf plantain. They then press and knead them continuously until some drops of juice are forced out of the rather stubborn leaves," the priest Sebastien Kneipp wrote. Sometimes the leaves are applied directly to the injury: "This forms the first, and sometimes the best, emergency dressing."

INSTRUCTIONS For insect bites or injuries: crush the leaves of the narrowleaf plantain and rub the juice on the affected part of the skin. This stops itching and accelerates healing.

Redcurrants and blackcurrants *(Ribes nigrum and Ribes rubrum)*

Monastic medicine recommended redcurrants and blackcurrants for skin problems, sickness, heart problems, and for stimulating the circulation. The oil from the pips helps treat rashes and eczema, as the scientists of the Würzburg research project into monastic medicine have demonstrated. It is therefore also suitable for neurodermatitis. The juice of these currants stimulates the immune system through its high vitamin C content and thus protects against colds.

Rosemary *(Rosmarinus officinalis)*

It was monks who discovered the healing properties of rosemary. Popular in the Middle Ages, it was used to strengthen and stimulate, for treating indigestion or stomach cramps and rheumatism. This effect has been demonstrated scientifically today. The priest Sebastien Kneipp also swore by the strongly fragrant plant: "Rosemary is priceless as a healing herb, and there are probably few herbs that can equal it."

INSTRUCTIONS For exhaustion and as a stimulant, pour a cup of boiling water over one teaspoon of rosemary leaves and let the tea steep for ten minutes.

Take a rosemary bath as a stimulant and against rheumatism, preferably in the early morning. Prepare an infusion of two ounces of rosemary leaves. Let it steep for a quarter of an hour and then pour the filtered infusion into the bath water.

Rosemary wine is a stimulating remedy for older people and helps with poor circulation. To make it, add one ounce of rosemary leaves to four cups of white wine and let it stand for a week.

Warning: Do not use rosemary during pregnancy!

Sage *(Salvia officinalis)*

Since antiquity sage has been regarded as a symbol of eternal life. This cure-all of monastic medicine and favorite herb of the priest Sebastien Kneipp will be found in every cloister garden. It is no coincidence that its Latin name comes from the word *salvare*, meaning "to save." It has antiperspirant and anti-inflammatory properties. Today sage is gargled to treat sore throats and drunk as a tea for coughs and colds. Hildegard von Bingen believed that sage drew evil fluids from the body and recommended eating it either raw or cooked. She also saw it as helpful in cases of bedwetting: "If someone cannot retain urine because of cold in the stomach, boil sage in water and strain it through a cloth, and drink it hot often, and the problem will be cured."

INSTRUCTIONS To make sage tea, pour boiling water over two teaspoons of sage leaves and steep for ten to fifteen minutes. To prepare a tea to reduce perspiration, use three teaspoons of sage leaves for the infusion.

Spelt *(Triticum spelta)*

Admittedly this is not a healing herb, but for Hildegard von Bingen this grain full of minerals was almost a wonder food, particularly effective against feebleness, weakness, and problems of circulation. The medically skilled nun recommended that spelt should be eaten every day in any form: "Spelt is the best grain, and it is warming, fat, and nourishing, and it is milder than other kinds of grain, and it is good for the flesh and blood of the person who eats it, and it brings a feeling of contentment and joy to the nature of the human being.... And if someone is so sick that illness prevents him from eating, take whole grain spelt and cook it in water with the addition of fat or an egg yolk, to make it taste better, and give it to the patient to eat, and it will heal him internally like a good, healthy salve." Through the frequent consumption of spelt, diabetics can reduce the use of insulin.

St. John's Wort *(Hypericum perforatum)*

The name of this famous healing plant with yellow flowers comes from John the Baptist. Legend has it that the dark-red juice produced when the flowers are crushed comes from the blood of the beheaded saint. Monks and nuns valued the herb for the treatment of wounds, rheumatism, and problems of menstruation. The *Lorscher Pharmacopoeia* mentioned St. John's Wort particularly as a medicine for melancholia. Today it is a recognized treatment for depression.

Instructions For St. John's Wort tea, add two teaspoons of St. John's Wort to one cup of water, bring to a boil and strain.

In addition, St. John's Wort oil helps to heal cuts and burns. Put one ounce of crushed flowers in one cup of vegetable oil and leave the mixture in the sun for five to six weeks. Strain to remove the flowers.

Caution: St. John's Wort can sometimes reduce the effect of other medications!

Thyme *(Thymus vulgaris)*

This Mediterranean plant with an aromatic sweet flavor is not only a popular seasoning. Monastic medicine was also aware of the herb's healing powers. Hildegard von Bingen recommended it against whooping cough, for example, an application that is scientifically recognized today. As a tea, thyme is used to treat coughs, throat inflammation, and bronchitis. It also assists the digestion and appetite and helps flush away infections of the urinary tract.

Instructions Pour one cup of boiling water over two teaspoons of thyme and steep for ten minutes.

Valerian *(Valeriana officinalis)*

The monks considered this pinkish-white flowering plant to be a universal remedy. The *Lorscher Pharmacopoeia* recommended this "divine remedy" that "replaces excessive insomnia with corresponding sleep and frees from exhaustion." Valerian calms the nervous system. It eases nervous tensions, insomnia, headaches, and exhaustion, reduces stress, and helps with stomach cramps.

Instructions Against insomnia, a cold extract is recommended. Shred two teaspoons of valerian roots and pour one cup of cold water over them. Let stand for twelve hours. Drink one cup two to three times daily.

Warning: Do not take valerian with prescription tranquilizers or sleeping pills!

Wormwood *(Artemisia absinthium)*

The Franciscans of the Krumbad spa like to put some crumbs of dried wormwood into their soup. "It is good for the digestion," says Sister Monika, the abbess. "But one must be careful not to use too much, or everything tastes very bitter." By the Middle Ages monks valued wormwood for its ability to improve digestion and appetite, and as a treatment for worms. It is also effective for treating bloated stomach and flatulence.

Yarrow *(Achillea millefolium)*

Many people swear by this modest white plant that usually flowers by the roadside. Sick sheep eat it instinctively. In the Middle Ages, it was regarded as a remedy for the plague. A tea made from its flowers stimulates the metabolism, cures flu and colds, and helps with abdominal problems. Hildegard von Bingen also prescribed it for ulcers and sores. Sister Leandra likes to mix the healing plant into her tea.

Digression: The Holy Medicine of Hildegard von Bingen

Anyone who devotes time to monastic medicine will inevitably come across St. Hildegard von Bingen (1098–1179) and her *Sancta Medicina*, her "Holy Medicine." She wrote the final work on monastic medicine of the Middle Ages and enriched it with details of many new plants. Hildegard von Bingen is regarded as a founder of scientific natural history and as one of the most important women of the Middle Ages. The abbess of the Rhineland Benedictine convent of Rupertsberg was a prophet, visionary, author, composer, natural scientist, and therapist. Her work was lost for a long time but today, nine hundred years after her birth, her medicine is as interesting and topical as it was in her own day. The *prophetissa teutonica*, the German prophetess, as her contemporaries called her, has been adopted by New Age and commercial interests, and sometimes remedies are offered under the label of Hildegard medicine; these should be treated with caution.

As an author, Hildegard surpassed all women and most men of her period with her extensive writing. She corresponded with popes, archbishops, kings, and abbesses, and fearlessly conversed with the Emperor Barbarossa. Her reputation as a prophetess extended beyond the boundaries of Europe.

The convent of Rupertsberg became the "consulting room of Europe."

The "Sybil of the Rhine" published her divine visions in Latin in the three books *Scivias, Liber divinorum operum*, and *Liber vitae meritorum*. In her own words, her visions were "not dreaming, not intoxicated" but "wide-awake" experiences. Although she saw the "divine light" as a child, she first published her visions only after she was forty. At that time this was a risky undertaking for a woman, who called herself the "mouthpiece of God." The trigger and impulse for publication was an illness, which Hildegard interpreted as the result of keeping silent. Only as she dictated her first book did she become healthy. This pattern continued throughout her life. Before each major, new step the saint became badly ill: for instance, when setting up a new convent or before her travels preaching, an activity that women of the time were not permitted to engage in. Between 1150 and 1160, Hildegard von Bingen showed that she was not only a mystic but also a natural scientist and a doctor. In those ten years, she wrote extensively on monastic medicine: a "nature study" and pharmacology, *Physica*, and a "medicine book," *Causae et Curae,* in which healing treatments were described. These were based on the most important plant healing books of antiquity and the Middle Ages, and on her own precise observations and experiences. They interwove spirituality and practical instructions in a new, integrated kind of therapy.

In her nature studies, Hildegard described the effect of healing plants in over two hundred chapters and also provided comprehensive instructions for the treatment of illnesses. There were about two thousand remedies and pieces of advice in all. It is important to realize that these must be seen against the background of the understanding of the medieval world. The saint's treatments were based on the doctrine of the four cardinal humors that was current at that time (see page 147).

Heinrich Schipperges, a doctor and expert on Hildegard, warns: "Most of the recipes have not been transferred directly into the repertoire of a modern pharmacy or into the doctor's consulting room." Nevertheless, Hildegard's work was groundbreaking in many respects. Many of her findings, such as those concerning arnica, mullein, fennel, and spelt, are still convincing today.

Hildegard had a full understanding of her medicine and associated it more than anyone else with the Christian teaching of the Creation:

- To the holy nun, health meant the harmony of the human being with God, the environment, and the whole order of the cosmos. "The reason for Hildegard's medicine goes back — completely in accordance with the theory of creation and redemption — to the Creation of the world, emphasizing the special position of mankind in the cosmos and his healing mission," wrote Sister Philippa Rath, the cellarer of St. Hildegard Abbey. According to Hildegard, human beings are inseparably connected with the cosmos and have the task of protecting it. But because we behave like "rebels," the elements may become out of balance and also make us sick.

- Sometimes illness for Hildegard was, however, just a burden that a human being must carry, one that if it is accepted can make a person more open, gentler, and stronger.

- For the Benedictine nun, health presupposed a healthy way of life, completely in accordance with the doctrine of the founder of the order that moderation would bring joy and stability in life.

- The best remedy of all is the compassion of the doctor and the care given in the face of suffering. In the end, it is God's own healing strength that comes to help the human being, and without it all medical skill and attention is ineffective.

Eating and drinking

Cistercian monk in the monastery of Zwettl, Austria

Lessons from the monastery kitchen

*I*n monasteries and convents, mealtimes are something special. The table lovingly covered and decorated with ivy, with a burning candle in the middle, already lifted my mood on my arrival in the little Magdala convent. The grace sung together lent the meal a solemn character. The atmosphere was quiet and cheerful. Argument had no place at the table; it would lead only to stomach aches. Any problems could be tackled later. The meal was simple but delicious and, whenever possible, from the nuns' own gardens.

I found it calmed me to be able to look at where the lettuces, tomatoes, zucchini, pumpkins, and herbs grew. Chemical sprays are taboo. Sister Leandra and her assistants are organic gardeners. Even the honey comes from the apiary belonging to the convent. I could watch the bees on one of the cloister's meadows when they swarmed out. And one thing particularly fascinated me: I could even get my own drinking water from the spring.

Nevertheless: paradise on Earth does not exist in the

Liqueur manufacture in the monastery of Ettal

cloister, either. Meat, vegetables, and fish are all purchased. "The problem of contaminated meat and grain involves us everyone," said Sister Teresa, dampening my high spirits. The Oberzeller Franciscans insist on seasonal vegetables and are careful in what they buy. But there is no hysteria. In the end, serenity wins. "Everything lies in God's hand," says a sister. This sense of basic trust is not only better for the nerves but also for the whole health of a human being. Anxiety before eating causes additional harm, because it noticeably weakens the immune system.

Food and drink are fundamental

Eating right keeps us healthy and helps recovery from illness. The dietary laws in various religions elevate the importance of eating far above the mere intake of food. Also the choice and the amount of food and drink, always strictly regulated in the monastic communities of the West, were determined by spiritual practices and the alternation of religious periods of fasting and feast days. Too much or too little in one or the other direction was an indicator of an imbalance in the overall condition of a monastic society, including its spiritual level.

How important the topic was to the religious orders in the Middle Ages is also evident from the fact that there were repeated, profound arguments about the quality and observance of dietary laws. The number and sequence of the dishes were not regarded as insignificant matters, any more than were the rules about refraining from meat or the question of whether eggs and cheese were allowed in Lent.

Warning against gluttony

Overindulgence in food, which was considered a sin, was consistently frowned upon, even though it is well known that not all members of religious orders avoided it at all times. The early Christian church father Clement of Alexandria declared: "One must avoid many kinds of foods because they have numerous evil consequences. Physical discomfort and upset stomachs occur if the palate is spoiled by the diabolical culinary arts or the empty, bravura performances of the kitchen." And St. Jerome used classical learning to support his warning against eating and drinking too much: "Hippocrates in his aphorisms taught that fat, portly bodies would certainly suffer from gout and other bad illnesses if moderation was not adhered to."

St. Benedict too warned of gluttony, but the founder of monasticism, who was himself probably vegetarian, was moderate in his rules about meals. He intuitively knew what studies confirm today: everyone has different needs. He refrained from insisting on hard and fast rules for diet or fitness. Accordingly, he allowed a "modest amount of food" for the main meal consisting of "two kinds of cooked food for each table with consideration for the weak individual." And although his rule forbids eating the "meat of four-footed animals," it allows exceptions for sick people and also for the aged.

Eating right for health

The Austrian herbalist, priest, and Dominican monk, Josef Weidinger, emphasizes the importance of the correct composition of a meal. For him a "good housewife is at the same time a doctor." He mentions the healing

Convent kitchen at Oberschönenfeld

effect of the parsley root for diabetics and the use of basil to fortify the stomach.

Some vegetables have just as many healing properties as herbs. Hildegard of Bingen recommended fennel for brightening a patient's mood and helping against flatulence, and she praised the digestive benefits of spelt. Anyone who devotes the time can do without many medications simply by choosing the right kinds and amounts of food. Studies point out that about one-third of all cancers are associated with incorrect nutritional habits. Research has shown that the best diet for protecting against cancer consists of plenty of vegetables and fruit, whole wheat products, and a low level of fat. For the priest Sebastien Kneipp, nutrition is a therapy. In his treatments, he has switched many patients to adequate, simple food and achieved remarkable success.

Because many monasteries and convents grow their own vegetables and fruit, the food arrives at the table only when it is truly ripe. You will never be served strawberries in winter. Seasonal meals are not only healthier but give one a feeling for the rhythm of nature. Josef Weidinger recommends buying less expensive vegetables and fruit. Overripe produce is no good. "Vegetables in season are cheapest." Local seasonal produce does not have to be shipped or stored. Indeed, eating a lot of apples, peaches, pears, or grapes while they are in season will do no harm. On the contrary, it is good to stay with one type of food for a period of time. It will help stimulate the digestion.

Mealtimes in the convent

In large convents mealtimes in the refectory follow very clear rules. The abbess of the Benedictine abbey of St. Hildegard in Rüdesheim describes it as follows: "The refectory of a convent is not just a bare dining room. Here is where the shared celebration of Communion continues into everyday life. The meals are taken silently, and a table reader recites the latest news from the press

Father Kilian

Father Kilian ate well and enjoyed it. In accordance with his inclinations he became "Coquus," and therefore responsible for the kitchen. The importance of the kitchen in old monastic wisdom is undeniable: *Bona coquina, bona disciplina* ("With a good kitchen, good discipline"). The monks of Maria Laach, who were later associated with Beuron, reported that he called them to one side and every year he asked: "Well, are you still sensible? Do you still drink beer? Do you still have the yard-long sausages?" Father Kilian remained plainspoken throughout his long life and his remarks were always original. He explained one day: "The most beautiful gospel for me is the divine wedding meal, which the Lord himself prepares and serves at the table. Enough to eat at last!"

Drutmar Cremer, *What Would Benedict Say about It?*

Monks as connoisseurs

Whoever works properly can also relax properly, and whoever fasts properly can also celebrate and indulge. We owe many culinary treasures of the kitchen to monks. "Friends, come quickly, I am drinking stars!" the Benedictine monk Dom Perignon cried out, as he tried Champagne for the first time in the eighteenth century. The blind vintner from the Epernay region of France had invented the definitive method of making Champagne, and he also invented a suitable stopper for the bottle: a cork fixed with steel wire.

The monastic orders spread their knowledge as they traveled: without the monks of Grottaferrata, for example, there would be no Frascati, and without the monks of Cluny there would be no Burgundy. The art of brewing beer still attracts the devout and the less devout to the famous monastic breweries today, such as the monastery of Andech above Lake Ammersee in Bavaria. Many monasteries and convents have their own specialties, such as fine lavender honey from the French Benedictines, handmade milk chocolate, fruit lozenges without artificial coloring or preservatives, and the licorice pastilles with mint made by the Dominicans at Lourdes.

at noon. In the evening, there is continuous reading from a book. At midday the table-reading is introduced with a section from the scriptures while in the evening, the reader finishes with a section from the Rule of St. Benedict."

On Sundays the midday meal with the Franciscans in Oberzell is marked by an impressive ceremony. It is a ritual that is a century old. After Mass the sisters sing a psalm as they walk through the convent to the festive baroque dining room (during the week, on the other hand, they leave the chapel of the sacrament in silence) and sit down at the long tables laid there. Then, after grace, Sister Leandra arranges music and gives a short introduction to it. This time she has chosen St. Francis of Assisi's "Song of the Sun," a very happy piece.

Meanwhile, the soup is passed around. The sisters wait until the person facing them has been served before they begin eating. Respect for others is a just as salutary as the composition of the meal itself.

Table manners: a monastic tradition

At Oberzell, each sister has her own fabric napkin. It belongs as much to the culture of the table as saying grace at the beginning and end of the meal. The custom that everyone waits until her neighbor is served before beginning is firmly established. Consideration for others and concern for one's own health is seen in the careful way that the sisters chew each bite. They know that digestion begins in the mouth. Everyone takes time to enjoy each mouthful as a sign of respect for the food that God has allowed to grow and that the cook has prepared with love and effort.

Table manners have their origin in monasteries, even the use of napkins. The association with the celebration of a meal together at the Lord's table lifted meals into a quite another category. Early on, monasteries distanced themselves from prevailing habits, where it was customary not only to eat with the hands but also to burp and break wind without inhibition.

At the end of the meal, nothing should be left behind on any plate. The obligation to eat everything means that each sister takes only as much as she really wants and can eat. Nothing is thrown away. Anything left over is put in the refrigerator.

Dietary advice from the monasteries

- Always eat meals at the same times. Regular meals not only structure the day, they are also important for the digestion. "Anyone who always eats at different times cannot expect the body to have a regular rhythm and may have digestive problems," Father Pausch points out. For instance, breakfast at Oberzell is at 7:00 A.M. after Lauds. Lunch is at 12 midday after prayers and earlier on Sundays at 11:30 A.M., while dinner is after Vespers at 6:00 P.M.

- Fortify yourself in the morning with a nourishing, healthy breakfast and hold back from eating and drinking too much in the evening. Monks and nuns today still follow the old saying: eat breakfast like a king, lunch like a princess, and dinner like a pauper. There is also the fact that one sleeps badly at night if too much undigested food weighs upon the stomach and intestine, because the digestive organs also need a break in the late evening.

- Therefore do not eat meals too late or you will tax your body unnecessarily and may be bothered by nightmares. At night the body is meant to rest.

- Give yourself enough time for each meal. Create an agreeable atmosphere at the table; even a single candle gives a meal a ceremonial air. In the monastery, the candlelight reminds one of the middle way of life, and of God. Avoid heated discussions at table and chew everything thoroughly. Proper chewing eases the digestion and makes you feel full more quickly. Furthermore, you become more aware of what you are eating. Anyone who gobbles food risks heartburn and essentially spoils their enjoyment of food.

- Prepare your meal with love and imagination. This is not only as a mark of affection for your own family; cooking is very relaxing and counteracts the hectic rush of life. Be sparing with salt, replacing it with the strength of fresh herbs.

- Eat in moderation, taking only as much as you really can eat. In this way you will avoid having to throw away what is left or eating when you are already full. The sisters in Oberzell only help themselves to more if they are really hungry. This way of conscious eating is better than any diet.

- Give up snacks. The digestion of anyone who is continually eating can never rest. There is no junk food or unhealthy snacks in monasteries.

- Pay attention to what you drink and exercise restraint not only with alcohol but also with strong coffee and tea, which do not quench the thirst but deplete the body's supply of water and calcium. In the monastery everyone drinks mineral water, spring water, or juice, and of course also herbal teas. Try for yourself how pleasant a tea made from a mixture of different herbs can be.

- And finally: if it is no longer an established part of your meals, introduce the old tradition of saying grace again. It gives a meal quite a different meaning, increases respect, and "sanctifies" the food, investing it with positive meaning.

Omelet with sage

The following dish is recommended by the cellarer of the monastery of Andechs, Father Anselm Bilgri:

Ingredients: 1 teaspoon pine nuts, 6 eggs, 6 tablespoons milk, 2 tablespoons freshly grated Parmesan, salt, newly ground pepper. 8 leaves fresh sage, 1 teaspoon olive oil, butter.

Toast the pine nuts lightly in a pan and remove again. Whisk the milk and eggs together. Stir in one tablespoon of Parmesan, salt, and pepper. Fry the sage leaves in hot olive oil until crisp. Remove half the leaves from the pan and set aside. Melt the butter in the pan and add the egg and milk mixture. Put a lid on the pan and let the omelet cook over a low heat for about five minutes. Turn the omelet over and cook the second side for a further five minutes over low heat. Sprinkle the omelet with the rest of the Parmesan, the sage leaves, and the pine nuts.

Fasting

"Abstinence bestows strength."

How to purify the body and regain strength

*I*t may sound like a paradox, but fasting is not only a universal remedy in the monastic tradition but also a means of achieving of happiness. Men and women who have fasted for a least a week give glowing reports of their experiences. "I am happier, more active, more organized and more disciplined. My skin is cleansed and more luminous. It is wonderful," reported the participant in a fasting seminar excitedly. Another explained: "Fasting helps me to meditate better. As a result I feel more centered and able to discover God in myself."

Less is more. Getting rid of ballast is extremely liberating and sharpens the feeling for what is essential. This is experienced by everyone who fasts for a certain length of time. Fasting is neither a beauty treatment or a slimming cure. It is an age-old tradition; the belief that fasting has a healing effect on both the body and the mind is accepted by all the great religions of the world.

Fasting: cleansing the body and soul

According to tradition, Christians fast to prepare themselves for holidays and feast days, and for spiritual strengthening. For Anselm Grün, fasting is "praying with your body and soul." "When I think about it," observed Father Anselm Bilgri, cellarer of Andech, "it is precisely the practice of fasting and abstinence that gives monastic life its distinctive profile." One of the fundamental effects of fasting is cleansing, not only from a physical but also from a spiritual point of view. Renunciation and abstinence in the widest sense should rid the body and also the mind of sick-making poisons, bad thoughts, negative feelings, habits, and addictions. Renunciation is for monks and nuns the ideal way of self-strengthening, a purifying medicine. It is no coincidence that there are special "fasting sermons" that support fasting with "spiritual nourishment," providing the participants with ideas to think about.

Those who refrain from eating will become clearly aware of their own dependencies. Fasting is like a "kind of spring-cleaning of the soul," as Sister Adelhilde of Oberzell explained. Now and again one must sort oneself out thoroughly, cleansing and clearing out, whether getting rid of extra pounds or bad living habits. As nuns and monks know very well, fasting not only makes one feel much lighter physically but also provides powerful feelings of relief and liberation.

About the origin of fasting

The practice of fasting is as old as Christianity itself, and it played a fundamental part in the development of monastic life. The word "monk" is derived from the Greek *monos,* meaning "alone." In the eyes of the founding fathers of monasticism, the search for God was quite impossible without fasting. Bishop Athanasius of Alexandria wrote: "See what fasting does! It heals illnesses, dries excess fluids in the body, drives out evil spirits, chases away bad thoughts, gives the mind greater clarity, makes the heart pure, cleanses the body, and finally leads the person to God. Fasting is a great force and achieves great success."

Many desert monks ate on only two days of the week. Their diet consisted of herbs and raw fruit and vegetables. Others lived off bread, water, salt, leguminous plants, berries, and a few vegetables. This ascetic life soon took on extreme forms that St. Benedict quite rightly condemned, a fact reflected in his Rule for the Benedictine order in which he always urged the monks

Fasting dries out excess fluids

towards a life of moderation. In his instructions he recommended that during Lent the monks should reduce their food and drink intake a little, sleep less, and abstain from unimportant talk and foolishness. Every brother had "a volume of the Bible and must read it from beginning to end." This would help them wipe out all their "previous careless mistakes." Again St. Benedict proved himself a great psychologist. Because he recognized the dangers of going hungry, he emphasized the "happiness" that the monks would derive from fasting. He believed that grumbling and bad moods were in contradiction with the meaning of this religious exercise, as was exaggerated asceticism.

The whole dimension of fasting was revealed to the desert monks by the prophets of the Old Testament and finally by the arrival of the Lord whom they wanted to follow. After all, Moses had to fast for forty days and forty nights before he was pure enough to approach God and receive the Ten Commandments. The prophet Jonah could only save the inhabitants of Nineveh from God's wrath by persuading them to fast in order to atone for their sins. Elijah and Jesus also fasted for forty days to prepare themselves for their respective missions.

Indeed, fasting is kind of "basic washing cycle," a process that brings up all the rubbish and garbage accumulated by the person fasting. There is a further benefit: the internal seducers that flatter and tempt us, the false whisperers that we usually gladly tolerate are now recognized for what they are. Those who do not defeat them will not only lose the fasting battle but will also return to their old bad habits and idleness.

Renunciation and suffering are already in themselves the beginning of a new course that, as with all new beginnings, must be adjusted from time to time. In addition, fasting produces the "fuel" necessary to help us drive our sometimes rather battered vehicle more efficiently along the road of life.

Fasting: an effective medicine

The physician Otto Buchinger, a Protestant who had converted to Catholicism, rediscovered the preventive and healing properties of fasting in the 1920s. He wanted to make this type of cure accessible to a wider public. "Health fasting" lasts several weeks and can be supervised either by monks or doctors in fasting clinics. Health fasting and religious fasting are "fundamentally the same," according to Buchinger. He believed that the welfare of the body and the welfare of the mind were closely intertwined. In his work he discovered that long-term abstinence from food could prevent health problems from occurring as well as heal existing ones:

- A fasting cure is a particularly effective alternative in the case of chronic illnesses. Quite amazing results have been achieved in the case of long-term illnesses such as rheumatism, arthritis, arteriosclerosis, and skin problems. Depression — and this too has been medically proven — can be alleviated by abstinence from food, because the withdrawal of food triggers the release of hormones that lift one's spirits.

- Fasting is also an extremely efficient method of reducing fat and high cholesterol levels. Drugs used to lower cholesterol levels are also used to treat Alzheimer's disease because doctors suspect a connection between them.

- The internist and physiotherapist Helmut Lützner, who made "fasting for healthy people" a popular treatment, believed that abstaining from food can speed up the healing process. By "sending the digestion on holiday," the body saves thirty percent of its overall energy expenditure, and can use this new energy for healing purposes. Indeed, we fast every night in order to regenerate ourselves. The first meal of the day is rightly named "breakfast."

- Fasting strengthens, not weakens. No mountaineer or sportsman eats immediately before a climb or a strenuous effort. During a fast the energy reserves in the body are more quickly accessible than when energy is released through the lengthy and enervating process of digestion.

- Fasting sharpens the mind and increases creativity. Helmut Lützner explained: "An Austrian philosopher said that he had written his best things while he was fasting. I know from painters that they experience a wealth of impressions of color and form, which they then translate into images; people from other walks of life also experience extraordinarily productive phases."

- Fasting sharpens one's sense of appreciation: someone who has endured all those days of abstinence comes to enjoy and celebrate life quite differently. "I have never eaten vegetable soup with such relish as I did at the end of a fasting period," one participant wrote after completing a fasting cure, "I really celebrated this first meal."

- It is important to find the right time for your fast. If you are under pressure in your life or work, it is best to postpone it. You must have enough time to be able to make a retreat. (See also Part I: "Fasting in the Monastery.")

Work and relaxation

Breaks for sitting down and relaxing are indispensable for well-being

How to avoid becoming overwhelmed

*A*t first glance it appeared to be a small matter but the meaning behind it impressed me enormously. When I handed over the money for a postcard at the Oberzeller convent gate, I noticed with interest that the nun, who was working at her computer, had put a burning candle on her desk. It was a symbol of the presence of God that was giving her strength in her work. The atmosphere was one of calmness and serenity, and the calm cheerfulness of the nun soon infected me too.

"Where are you running to? Stay where you are, heaven is within you. If you look elsewhere you will never find it."

Angelus Silesius

Ora et labora

A convent or monastery offers an important alternative to our very stressful working life, in which pressure, anxiety, and professional ambition affect an ever larger number of people, often making them ill. We can learn a lot of things from the members of religious orders and adapt them to our daily life. *Ora et labora* was St. Benedict's motto: "Pray and work."

Prayer occupies a place of honor in the monks' lives. Work is considered of secondary importance, less important than one's relationship with God, religious services, and meditation — an almost revolutionary thought nowadays. The salvation of the soul is more important than work. No one is allowed to forget this in a monastery or convent, because daily life is organized around prayers and choral singing. These occasions are pauses for breathing during which everyone puts thoughts of work aside and reflects on completely different things in life.

Monks and nuns live in the knowledge that they don't have to do everything on their own, and in fact they could not do so anyway. A short prayer when you feel you cannot go on is often enough to make you more relaxed. As a result, anxiety and stress are reduced, and work becomes easier and more bearable. Those in holy orders consider it a sign of false pride and arrogance not to offer one's cares up to God, not to ask Him for help, or to fail to ask the other brothers and sisters for their support. This helps them discover new solutions to their problems and prevents work from causing too much stress and ruling their lives.

"If it is only a matter of results, then something is wrong," Peter Pausch warns us. The real value of work lies in the opportunity to develop our creative skills and in social interaction through collaborating with colleagues. Pausch added: "Those who properly understand work realize that the reward of work is not just a salary and holiday."

Work: every task counts

Work is not an end in itself but must serve the community and be a homage to God and his Creation. In the monastery no one has to toil away through life, driven by a craving for prestige and career advancement. Edith Stein once said that in the end it is all the same whether one peels potatoes or writes. When she joined the Carmelite order, this gifted academic, like all other novices, was first assigned to the kitchen, where she felt very much out of place. Later she admitted to a former school friend that it had been a good school for teaching humility, since in her whole life until then she had been admired only for her academic work.

All tasks are equal in the convent. Manual work is valued as highly as spiritual achievement. At Oberzell the sisters are assigned to different tasks

Nuns and beehives: harvesting honey is valuable manual labor

in turn: laying the table, serving the food, clearing the table, washing up and drying. "Equality for all" is the motto.

Happiness and love: the prerequisites for working successfully.

One of the great innovations of the Rule of St. Benedict was its emphasis on the dignity of labor. Times of mass migration, vandalism, and war called for a recultivation of the land. Work that had been despised as the preserve of slaves and servants was now elevated in status, which helped to create the foundations of a new culture and increasing prosperity.

What mattered most, according to the Rule of St. Benedict, was less what was done than how it was done. Work done with joy and love naturally goes better, but those who work reluctantly often make a mess of it and even become ill as a result. Father Anselm Grün advised everyone to recognize their bodies' warning signs: if we are always nervous and distracted in our work,

Celebrating the Eucharist: Sunday as a gift from God

it may be that we are running away from ourselves. People who are always tired when they work, even when they have had enough sleep, may be unconsciously defending themselves against problems.

On the Sabbath and meditation

Silence, breaks, and, in particular, prayer are the pillars of everyday life in a monastery. For instance, Sister Teresa loves to withdraw to her favorite place in a corner of the convent garden. From there, behind the vegetable patch, you can see the picturesque monastery complex while looking out towards the river Main. As we were sitting there, enjoying the sun and the atmosphere, she said: "When I do not have time to meditate, I feel it. I get confused more easily, and I make rash decisions in my work that are not the right ones."

Sister Veridiana, the mother superior, cannot imagine how she could face the challenge of her responsibilities without her daily meditation: "In the convent we all reserve half an hour every day to meditate," she declared. One can just let "the thoughts come into your head." Or the nuns meditate on a word or text from the Bible: "When I have periods of silence, I feel quite differently during the day." After the midday meal, Sister Veridiana looks again for a quiet spot, and this is often the chapel. "This gives me a certain perspective. Usually I have a piece of paper with me and note down the thoughts I consider important to make sure that I do not forget them. Many things come to the surface in a silent environment, and it does you good."

One of the rules of the convent is to honor and celebrate Sunday, because it is a special source of strength. Sunday is a day of rest in the literal meaning of the word. Free of the noise of construction and traffic, it is also free of hustle, bustle, and stress, a means of rediscovering the pleasures of a carefree day. It is a day for the senses and for the contemplation that is indispensable for the equilibrium of body and soul, as well as an excellent boost to health. It is a day in which church services will allow you not only to find peace within yourself but also to turn towards God.

Father Pausch is convinced that having the seventh day as a day of rest is not a concept plucked from the air but is part of the fundamental order of life. According to St. Benedict, humanity has evolved on a rhythm based on seven. Relaxation on the seventh day is very important for the body and soul. Christians "fill up with soul fuel" when they go to church on Sunday, and all who feel rested and have found their "middle way" will discover that they enjoy their work more and have more energy.

Breaks matching the body's biorhythms

Long before all the medicinal tips and alternative cures of today, the art of healing practiced by the monks also explained how by following a rhythm matching human biorhythms, you can achieve much more and preserve your equilibrium. St. Benedict drew most of his knowledge from the Holy Scriptures, and this included the division of the day into seven units, the seven canonical hours. When doctors later recommended taking a five-minute pause every hour when working, this too corresponded to the striking of the monastery clock calling everyone to silent prayer on the hour.

It has subsequently been scientifically demonstrated that the monastic rhythm of praying actually corresponds to human biorhythms. Nuns and monks may also become stressed, but in accordance with the Rule they work when they feel fit and rest when their body requires it. A walk through the flowering garden at Oberzell does much to revive the senses and promote cheerfulness and peace.

Sleeping and waking in the right way

Premonstratensian monks of Strahov at evening prayers, with Prague in the background

Living in harmony with the rhythm of day and night

"When I have problems sleeping I drink tea made from cowslip, lemon balm, lavender, and St. John's Wort." Sister Leandra has herself experienced the beneficial effects of her herbal teas. Also she sleeps better since she has taken up gardening.

Many people can only dream of sleeping well. Those who toss and turn during the night will suffer the following day. They will not have the necessary energy at work and will feel tired and moody. According to medical research, in cases of serious sleep problems productivity at work is reduced by forty percent and social contact is reduced by twenty percent.

The consequences of a sleepless society

The "sleepless society" is one of the greatest problems of our times. The constant lack of sleep leads to nervousness, aggression, irritability, inhumane behavior, and a wide range of health problems. It is no coincidence that sleep deprivation is used as a means of torture in dictatorial regimes.

Even those without sleep disorders tend to confuse

night and day. Many young people do not go to bed before 11:00 P.M. Sleep is generally considered a necessary evil. Nowadays working late into the night is considered normal. The consequences are general overtiredness, traffic accidents, accidents in the workplace, and carelessness in doing work. For example, the fault in the atomic reactor in Chernobyl in 1986 was the result of mistakes made by an overtired inspection staff.

If you are deprived of sleep over a long period, the problems are not restricted to lack of concentration, aggressiveness, or irritability; the entire immune system is weakened. It is also a scientifically recognized fact that lack of sleep leads to high blood pressure, stomach and bowel disorders, and depression.

The sleep rhythm of the monks

Sufficient sleep is the best way to promote both physical and mental health. It is also the best way to achieve calmness and strength. Nuns and monks have known this for a long time. They know that if they obey the rules of their order they will live in harmony with the rhythm of nature. So it is only logical that they go to bed early and get up very early — in many monasteries and convents at 4:00 or 4:30 A.M. Many monks and nuns "go to bed with the chickens and get up with the chickens."

The ancient monastic rules create the best conditions for restorative sleep and confirm the findings of scientific research on the subject:

- Do not eat too late or too much in the evening. St. Benedict's advice to his monks to eat during daylight hours was well-founded. An overfull stomach leads to nightmares and insomnia. St. Benedict also pointed out the importance of enough sleep and absolute silence during the night. He recommended at least eight hours sleep for most of the year.
- Wine or beer may help you to fall asleep but then it can wake you up in the middle of the night. Whether it is too much alcohol, coffee, black tea, or cigarettes that you consume, you will pay for your excesses. Instead try drinking a refreshing, calming herbal tea before going to bed.
- In order to protect his brothers from worrying dreams, St. Benedict recommended that "they made peace before sunset if they had quarreled." Father Pausch advises everyone to reconcile with everyone else at least for

that day before going to bed, and to put off all outstanding discussions to the following day. He emphasizes that this is not taking the easy way out. It really does you good and will ensure that you have pleasant dreams.

- To ensure a healthy sleep routine, it is important to consciously bring the day to an end. In the convent or monastery this conclusion takes the form of Compline, which closes the day in a positive manner and gives thanks to God for it. Often the nuns of Oberzell go for a short walk in the evening. They stroll past bubbling springs, flower beds with lavender and roses, past fragrant herb gardens, and under overhanging plum trees, or past the stations of the Cross up in the convent wood.

- Review the day without any bitterness, either with relaxing music, or during a short walk, or sitting quietly in an armchair. The brief looking back will ensure that the day does not end in an arbitrary fashion. The nuns often combine this with a short period of contemplation or meditation on a passage from the Bible. The feeling of security this provides makes sleep really beneficial. For monks and nuns, this time also includes the beneficial ritual of evening prayer.

Dreams: God's forgotten language

Dreams can tell us a lot about our perceptions and our subconscious. They are another side of life, a kind of encounter with our innermost feelings. Thus they provide the opportunity for us to learn more about ourselves. A decision is often different when you "sleep on it," as the popular advice goes.

In one of his lectures, the dream therapist Helmut Hark described these nocturnal images as "God's forgotten language" that deserved more consideration. Dreaming is not only natural but necessary in order to process all of the experiences of the day. In addition, there are spiritually induced, beneficial dreams of special significance. Hark went on to say that since in both the Old and the New Testaments dreams always pointed the way at a "crossroads of history," the nocturnal messages contained in dreams and the directions of the word of God belong together.

Father Pausch also recommended that we should pay attention to our dreams in order to enrich our everyday life. We can train our memory to remember dreams. We should plan to do so before we fall asleep. According to Father Pausch, the desire to fall asleep with a particular dream is a "wonderful possibility." Therapists have worked real wonders with this. His advice: when we have a problem we should ask, before falling asleep, to dream of the solution. "Often this person will get up the following morning knowing what he or she must do."

Cloister in the monastery of Bebenhausen

The night follows from the day

- Take breaks in order to develop a better relationship towards night and day. According to the observation of the sleep expert Jürgen Zulley, it is especially the "young professionals under great pressure who forget to take breaks, and they are then unable to unwind in the evening. Therefore people should consider how their day can contribute to healthy sleep. In the past we always used to ask: did you sleep well? Now we ask: how was your day?"

- Take your time getting ready in the morning. As Father Pausch put it, "The kind of morning you have can influence the rest of your day, and unfortunately people often rush in the morning." He recommended stretching vigorously first thing in the morning instead of tumbling sleepily out of bed: "The morning prayer is a wonderful opportunity to connect with God and the world and to join in the great scheme of the Creation."

Wide-awake people are more aware of their surroundings. This might seem obvious but nevertheless it is something that people often forget. The truly alert are rested and well-balanced. They take in the world around them with all their senses, they are in a good mood, calm and relaxed, and as a result they have the necessary strength to tackle all the challenges of work and family.

Sebastian Kneipp, confessor and hydrotherapist

The pioneer of modern physiotherapy, the great naturopath Sebastian Kneipp, was born in 1821. He was expected to become a weaver like his father but felt called to the priesthood. After studying theology at university, he became ill with tuberculosis. When his

Tips for a good sleep

- Only go to bed when you are really tired. If you are not asleep within fifteen minutes, get up and only go back to bed when you have the feeling that you really can go to sleep.

- Try and establish a "going to sleep" ritual. Choose a relaxation exercise, say a prayer, read a book, talk to your partner, or do anything else that works for you.

- It is important to have plenty of fresh air in the bedroom. Sebastian Kneipp believed that there was nothing worse than a stuffy bedroom. Stuffiness in the bedroom causes bad dreams and may also make you ill.

- If you have problems going to sleep or waking during the night, you should not work or watch television in bed. Put a little bag of lavender under your pillow. It will have a calming effect.

- Kneipp also believed that the following method was very reliable. Wash yourself with a cold washcloth and go to bed without drying yourself (with or without pajamas).

- A short walk in the evening will help you sleep.

- Structure your day carefully and be well aware of it when you begin the day. Plan enough time for breakfast and getting ready in the morning. Stress in the morning can spoil your sleep that night.

- Not every sleep problem ought to be a cause for concern. After the age of forty, one should be aware that frequent waking through the night is linked to the reduction of deep sleep, a byproduct of the aging process. It is therefore normal to sleep more lightly and wake more frequently during the night than before. Your doctor can provide you with more information about this. Sleeping problems can also be caused by physical pain or depression.

doctors decided that they could do nothing for him, Kneipp discovered a little booklet on hydrotherapy by Dr. Siegmund Hahn. Bravely, he tried it on himself. In the middle of winter he threw himself into the icy Danube for a few seconds three times each week and then rushed home. The cure was successful. His appetite increased and his weakness disappeared.

Sebastien Kneipp

Kneipp started as a father confessor in a Dominican monastery and then worked as a priest in St. Justina from 1881 onwards. In the course of this he discovered something very important: medical treatment, which was still based mostly on the theory of the four humors, must be holistic. In an age of industrialization Kneipp fought against the prevalent idea that man was simply a robot designed to work. He believed that the harmony of body, mind, and soul was a prerequisite for health. The rejection of religious obligations, disordered habits, and excesses such as unbridled sexuality or addiction to drink and pleasure made people ill. The hydrotherapist believed it was the duty of all individuals to look after their health and mobilize all the positive forces in their body to achieve this. Sebastian Kneipp's therapy is based on five pillars:

- The use of water,
- Medicinal herbs,
- Stretching and movement,
- Wholesome, healthy nourishment,
- Spiritual harmony or "order" (the so-called therapy of emotional order).

Kneipp also believed that an orderly life contributed to a healthy body. This meant a regular rhythm of sleep and wakefulness, plenty of movement, regular meals, and relaxation.

He also recommended preventive care to maintain good health: hardening oneself through plenty of fresh, cold air, moderation in alcohol consumption, and plain, wholesome, mainly vegetarian food.

In addition, the physician-priest recommended "dry, simple, hearty, unsophisticated, plain cooking, not spoiled by hot spices" and very little salt.

Naturally, Kneipp recommended water as the best drink. He held that coffee, black tea, and chocolate were drinks without any nourishing properties. Kneipp recommended going barefoot as often as possible and advised against overheated, airless rooms, especially the bedroom. He warned against soft mattresses and thick quilts that make one sweat at night.

Sebastian Kneipp's restorative soup

"If this restorative soup were known and used, a large number of unhappy people would be made happy," Sebastian Kneipp firmly believed. Cut black rye bread into slices, dry them on the stove, and grind to a powder in a mortar. Take two or three spoonfuls, stir them into boiling milk, and season lightly. The soup is ready after two minutes. You can also use fresh wheat grains instead of rye bread. This nourishing, invigorating soup is easy to digest and remarkably full of nutrients.

Thigh affusion and running in the dew

Like all therapies, Kneipp treatments "do not help each and every person in the same way," explains Sister Monika, the mother superior of the Krumbad spa, who is an expert in Kneipp therapy. "You should not always do the same exercises but vary them." (Important! The Kneipp treatment is not suitable for people with heart problems or debilitating diseases such as cancer).

Thigh affusion

Thigh affusions are very good for cases of cold feet, bad circulation, colds, rheumatism, sciatica, and paralysis of the lower limbs. Start with a warm water jet from a hose. Direct it along the front of the right leg from the bottom to the top. Repeat the operation at the back of the right leg and on the left leg. Repeat this process again but with cold water. The difference between the hot and cold water should be at least fifty degrees Fahrenheit.

Important: do not dry yourself afterwards. Just brush the water off your legs and put your clothes on. Then make sure you move about.

Running in the dew

This is a wonderful way of starting the day. Go out early in the morning and run barefoot through the wet grass, then brush the water off your feet. Then put your socks on and continue moving for about fifteen minutes. This will make you very alert and protect you from colds. Those who prefer can create their own Kneipp-pool in their bath. Run the cold water up to your calves and walk up and down gingerly like a stork for two minutes. In summer you can use a paddling pool filled with icy water in order to get yourself going. However, it is important that the feet should be warm beforehand.

Solitude and fellowship

Andech Benedictine monks playing cards

Finding oneself and finding others

*D*uring a very special evening in Oberzell, I came to fully understand the meaning of the community of a religious order. A middle-aged woman had returned to the community of the Church, and the ceremony of readmittance was marked with a solemn service in the convent chapel. As a former pupil of two Oberzell Franciscan nuns, she wanted to celebrate joining the convent, so she cooked and served the food to the nuns in the Magdala convent. The small party was very merry and harmonious — in fact, it somehow reminded me of the biblical story of the return of the prodigal son. What a difference from our fragmented society where people muddle through life on their own, I thought. I felt as if I were part of a great family — and I enjoyed the wonderful warmth that permeated the atmosphere.

The convent community: an alternative model of living

Even in convents and monasteries there are arguments, jealousy, and selfishness. Nevertheless, monastic communities are an impressive alternative to society outside the cloister, with its staggering array of therapies intended to cushion pervading loneliness. In accordance with their philosophy, the sustaining routines of monastic life form a kind of safety net. Everyone is to be a physician to his neighbor. In contrast, people in modern society have just recently discovered the negative effects of isolation. "Isolation leads to a disruption of the natural rhythm of life," Father Johannes Pausch warned, "since there is no one else who needs to be taken into consideration."

Irregular mealtimes, irregular sleeping times, and a lack of emotional nourishment damage our health in the long term. In contrast, sharing happiness and fun make up for injuries and quarrels. In order to ensure that communal living works and is beneficial, St. Benedict devised some ingenious rules that can also help us — who are not monks or nuns — live together more happily:

- Listen to each other! The word "listen" is very important to St. Benedict and is therefore mentioned very early on in his Rule. "Listen, my son, to the instructions of the master, listen with your heart." St. Benedict does not mean listening vaguely but being attentive to others with all one's senses. In order to listen, we must also be able to be silent. "When we really listen we take others into our hearts. An encounter takes place," the Benedictine abbot Odilo Lechner explained. Listening also means obedience. Together with poverty and chastity, obedience is one of the three vows to which monks and nuns commit themselves. Obedience means listening to the advice of the abbot and to God. But it also implies respect for others and listening to what they have to say. This is a challenge that we find extremely difficult to face today.

- Be there for others! Monks and nuns devote their life to the service of others. For them, serving means caring about each other, helping each other, regardless of how demanding or time-consuming it is — and without thinking about what's in it for them. People who care about others feel happier and more contented. St. Benedict saw serving others as essential for the smooth functioning of a community.

- Remain modest; beware of arrogance! In a convent or monastery, humility is the most important virtue. Humility does not means submitting slavishly. Modest people are open to criticism, admit their own weaknesses, and are not afraid of asking for help. But they also know their own strengths, and as a result they do not suffer from a lack of self-esteem. Humility makes people more easygoing, so they do not become stressed as easily, and are more sensitive and helpful. It also creates closeness. People who cannot find humility are always worried about losing face. They try to protect themselves by putting up defensive barriers, thus barring their way to real health.

- Have compassion! Like the compassionate Samaritan who looked after the wounded stranger, we must care for the needy. Loving care of the old, the sick, and the desperate is one of the most important aspects of St. Benedict's Rule. Compassion and sympathy for others can also bring a new quality to our lives at work, with our families, and our partners, and make us more human.
- Share yourself — and also your time! The willingness to share and to give is necessary for successful communal living. "Relationships thrive on sharing. Relationships grow as a result of sharing. Only those who are willing to share can grow and develop," Father Johannes Pausch explained.

The vows made by nuns and monks

Those who decide to join religious orders promise to live in accordance with the evangelical precepts of chastity, poverty, and obedience. The evangelical precepts, recommended in the Gospel, are so called because Jesus mentioned these virtues as prerequisites for those who truly wanted to follow him. In his Rule, St. Benedict therefore demanded the following from the monks: "No one should own anything, nothing at all, not a book, not a desk, not a pencil — absolutely nothing. Everything should be held in common as it says in the Scriptures, so that no one can call anything their own and claim it as their own."

The perfect exemplar of this rejection of material possessions was Jesus himself: "Though he was rich, yet for your sakes he became poor, so that by his poverty you might become rich" (2 Corinthians 8:9). Further, Jesus told a man: "Go, sell your possessions, and give the money to the poor, and you will have a treasure in heaven." Through their rejection of money and possessions the monks wanted to be free from financial worries. In the end what matters most is "that nothing should take precedence over our love of Christ." Poverty also meant rejection of pathological claims to power and prestige, and the rejection of luxury and vice — a prerequisite for the good operation of a community.

Another vow made by monks and nuns is that of chastity, the voluntary abstention from sexual intercourse. This concept can be extended to include fidelity, temperance, reserve, and purity of thoughts and feelings. The promotion of fidelity can be applied outside the convent or monastery to marriage partners. The important thing is to work on a relationship instead of moving on to another one at the first sign of trouble.

Solitude

What is so important about the example of solitude set by monks and nuns? What does it say to us? In a positive sense, we understand that solitude also

A monk in the convent of Ettal

has a restorative effect: those who want to be alone in the "proper manner" retreat of their own free will for a certain period in order to gain new strength and energy, zest for life, peace, and cheerfulness. This retreat from everyday life helps improve their equilibrium and leads to the rediscovery of the middle way. In addition, stress-related conditions such as allergies, susceptibility to infection, and sleep disorders will be ameliorated.

In monasteries and convents, retreats are a matter of course, and rarely have I seen so many solitary people — in the positive sense of the word — as in Oberzell. The nuns walk through the garden, deep in thought, picking flowers here and there, meditating in front of a statue of the Madonna, or simply going about their business in silence.

Beneficial solitude: the desert lives

It was no coincidence that hermits (from the Greek *eremos,* meaning solitary) withdrew to the solitude of the desert in order to devote themselves entirely to God. The desert was the symbol of absolute interiorization, the most extreme form of solitary living. There was nothing to distract the hermit: no people, no buildings, no animals and plants, no noise. He was completely on his own. There was only the beauty of the endless expanse, of the sky, and the rhythm of day and night, extreme heat and great cold. The hermit had to concentrate on himself, his inner images, thoughts, feelings, and memories. He could no longer run away from himself.

Such a retreat was also an enormous challenge, accompanied by terrible temptations, which St. Benedict described. He had fled Roman society, spending three long years as a hermit in a cave near Subiaco in the Sabine mountains before he founded his order. But after overcoming crises and abstinence, such a retreat also offered him the chance to see things in a new light, to make discoveries about himself and start afresh.

The opportunity given by a crisis

It can be extremely demanding to come to terms with oneself. Quieting down is not easy, as I found at Oberzell. It was as if I had suddenly fallen outside of space and time into another world with another rhythm. At the beginning I noticed how now and again my happiness and peace could turn into their opposites. Suddenly, when out walking, sitting in my room or on a bench, I was overtaken by restlessness, almost panic. Like an addict "going cold turkey," I was dying to get my cell phone and talk to my family and friends, although there was nothing to discuss. I was wondering why I had left my book behind and was considering whether I should quickly drive to the nearest town before Vespers in order to buy something that I probably did not even need. I felt like a hamster whose wheel had been taken away. *Just try to hold out,* I told myself, and after a while I was filled with a feeling of peace and contentment — and I was very happy that I had stayed.

After each retreat, however short, my encounters with the nuns became increasingly valuable to me. Each subsequent meeting became more important and meaningful, and its influence longer lasting. Those who withdraw from the tumult and noise of everyday life in order to discover their own "middle way" will feel more at ease with others and more accepting of responsibility. The theologian Dietrich Bonhoeffer wrote: "It is only when we are part of the community that we can be alone. Community and solitude are two sides of the same coin."

A meeting with oneself

- In your diary, make an appointment with yourself for an hour, a day, or even a whole weekend. You may be amazed at how happy and invigorated you feel after your private meeting with yourself. Abbot Odilo Lechner recommended that we build periods into our life when we are deliberately silent: "When I go into a corner of my room and light a candle there, then I have created a place that invites me to be silent."

- Plan periods in your life devoted to silence and peace, about which the religious philosopher, Romano Guardini, wrote: "It is silence that opens the ear to the sound present in all things, in animals and trees, mountains and clouds."

- Be respectful in your dealings with others. Resentments can make you really ill in the long term. Check whether you let others finish what they have to say and whether you are really listening to what they are saying. Usually we are already thinking of a reply or planning our next move before the other person has even finished speaking.

- But above all be loving and patient with yourself as well. It is only then that you will be able to be loving and patient with others.

God heals us

"What is it about the invisible power of faith?"

Turning for help to a higher power

Some places in the convent have such an intense atmosphere that they sometimes took my breath away. For example, the convent chapel. In order not to be late I would arrive twenty minutes before the beginning of Lauds. A few nuns were already there deep in contemplation. The sun shone through the window near the high altar, illuminating the solemn nave of the church. The atmosphere was wonderful and soothing, while the stillness was "holy" and had a calming effect that made one feel supported. With its size and height, the church was open and receptive to the divine. This is where the Oberzell nuns come and draw their energy as well as their impressive calm and composure.

Is not the entire convent a source of energy? "All the visitors who come here experience its positive and beneficial effects. This is probably because people have prayed and sung here for decades. Something like that is quite tangible."

What is it about the invisible power of faith? Is it really true that people can be healed by prayers alone? Can one become healthier and happier through a good

> *"Nothing is more powerful than prayer, and nothing can be compared with it."*
>
> St. John Chrysostom

relationship with God? Scientific research has recently turned its attention to the often phenomenal healing power of faith.

Believers are healthier

A study of four thousand old people in North Carolina produced some very interesting results:

- Regular churchgoers are visibly healthier and suffer less from depression and anxiety-related neuroses than those who do not go to church.
- Those who attended at least one religious service a week had lower blood pressure and their risk of dying from circulatory diseases was reduced by half compared to people who did not attend religious services once a week.

According to the findings of researchers at Harvard University, praying — with a rosary, for instance — has the same calming effect as meditation. Heartbeat and breathing become slower, the muscles relax, and the production of stress hormones is reduced.

One of the studies commissioned by the U.S. millionaire John Templeton that was completed in 2001 also revealed churchgoers live seven years longer than non-churchgoers, spend twenty-five percent less time in the hospital, and come home twenty-five percent earlier.

The psychiatrist leading the study, Harold G. König of Duke University, explained the results of the Templeton study as follows: believers are more likely to avoid excessive eating, drinking, and drug abuse. "But that is not all. People who believe in God have the feeling that someone cares for them. They feel uplifted even when life does not make much sense." Also interesting is the fact that people who only watched religious services on television or prayed at home fared worse than actual churchgoers. König continued: "The community gives you a distance from your familiar, circumscribed surroundings, and you do not feel as lonely. If you concentrate less on yourself and more on God, the Church, and your community, then your own problems will recede into the background."

According to an article in the magazine *Public Forum*, Herbert Benson, director of a Catholic Hospital in Boston, confirmed the following trends: "Faith in a medical treatment probably contributes to between sixty and ninety percent of all cures, but the faith in an invincible, almighty Being produces an incomparably greater healing power." Because "just as anxiety, fear, and depression can be as dangerous as disease-causing agents, so calmness, love and faith can affect the physiology of the body like medicine."

John Templeton, mentioned above, has created a foundation that provides financial support for research projects dealing with the subject of faith. One of the first positive results was from studies looking at the effects of distance praying on AIDS sufferers. Relatives or strangers prayed for the patients without their being aware of it. Result: after six months, the patients in the "distance healing group" had fewer and less serious relapses than the patients in the control group. They spent considerably fewer days in hospital and were in better spirits than those in the control group.

Templeton's first wife died at a very young age. When questioned whether he ever doubted his faith, he replied: "No, I tried to be humble and said to myself: no one knows why these things happen. Why should I question why God allows a disease like cancer? Humility means that he knows better than I do."

Transcendence in everyday life

In the convent everything has a meaning that transcends its everyday function. The lovingly tended garden behind the convent walls reflects the original harmony of Creation. The herb garden in the convent, a living work of art, mirrors the delights of the garden of Eden. In the center is a small stone plaque partly concealed by plants. On it is written: "In the silence of our garden we can speak with God. Our souls can open up to heaven in order to see things in the right perspective."

It is clear that the belief in an orderly Creation, filled with the presence of God, is perceived as a powerful healing force. It is a foundation and basis for all other therapies. A community in which one only fulfils a function works differently from a group in which everyone is treated as a brother or sister.

Healers in the West

"Healing through the word of God is an old story," Peter Seewald writes in his book *Die Schule der Mönche* ("The School of Monks"). "The only thing that is new is that we have forgotten it." Indeed, for centuries it had been a very natural thing for people in good times and bad times to call for the help of God,

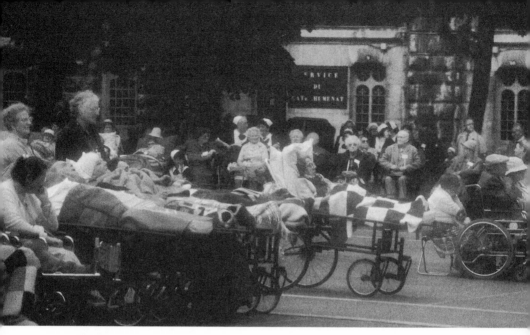

Pilgrimage at Lourdes

identified in Jesus Christ as a force of love. A transcendental awareness, celebrated by the young people of the "New Age" in a purely egocentric way, was an essential component of the teaching that, like the religion of love in the "Old Age," was also very practical in its application. There was an awareness of connections between heaven and Earth that the mind could not grasp and yet were entirely real. No one doubted that God existed and gave signs of his existence. No one doubted that the great saints who were close to God after their death could intercede with God and help people.

Charismatic people could and can help people in spiritual or physical need through their gift of perceiving the innermost being of a person. Believers such as the Capuchin brother Konrad von Altötting or Father Pio were and still are healers blessed by God. Their canonization presupposes a definite miracle, a force that has a supernatural origin. And it is still official Catholic teaching that God gives each person companions in the form of angels to protect his or her most essential being. "You are not alone," the great scholar Romano Guardini said. "Your self is in the hands of one who sees you and sees God, who sees the face of God and you in his light."

It is said that nothing is impossible for God. The Church not only has holy places that possess special, almost tangible, healing powers but also a vast number of rituals, practices, sacraments, and prayers that are aimed at direct healing — in the here and now, as it were — in the form of holistic healing therapies (with the help of priests). This healing deals not only with physical afflictions; it is also an inner healing, a release from anxieties and complexes as well as the problems that stem from familiar sources. Trust in God is the only prerequisite for this road. "Few people realize what God will make of them if they surrender unreservedly to the guidance of grace," said St. Ignatius of Loyola, founder of the Jesuit order.

How to experience God's healing power

Pilgrimages

For many people, pilgrimages are a way of supporting the healing process. For years, millions of people with a wide range of ailments have traveled to Lourdes in the hope of being cured by the healing power of the mother of God. The criticism aimed at all the commerce surrounding Lourdes is understandable, but it is not entirely fair since there is much more to Lourdes than that. Over six thousand unexplained cures have been reported in Lourdes in the past 140 years. Sixty-six of them have been recognized by the Church. These include a Frenchman, a sufferer from multiple sclerosis who had tried all treatments and was completely paralyzed. He went home completely cured.

Prayer

Monks believe that physical and spiritual health are impossible without prayers. Praying is a prophylaxis; it prevents disease — even if it is only a quick, short prayer asking for support. "Prayer is like talking to a friend whom you love to see and chat with because you are certain that he loves you," St. Teresa of Ávila once said. Prayers are like first aid for minor health problems but also for serious diseases. It is no coincidence that people say, "All we can do now is pray." The visitors' books in hospital chapels show how often people go there to pray: they are full of expressions of thanks and prayers for health.

Bible reading

Special healing power is also ascribed to the Bible. It contains straightforward health advice. (For instance, St. Paul told his companion Timothy,

"No longer drink only water, but take a little wine for the sake of your stomach and your frequent ailments.") But it also has many rules of conduct set by the "Savior," that is, the physician Jesus who promoted the health of the entire person. He recommended loving oneself and one's neighbor, not to be anxious, and not to worry, as well as not to sin anymore. His precepts also included forgiveness for our mistakes and reconciliation both with others and ourselves. The monks and nuns say that regular reading of the Bible has a calming, broadening effect on the soul. It makes people more modest and also more content. For monks and nuns, the *Lectio divina*, the regular reading from the Holy Scriptures that is prescribed in the same way as contemplation, is an immersion in the presence of Christ in order to cleanse the mind of disturbing images and thoughts that can make one ill.

Symbols and signs

It is no accident that special attention is paid to the importance of loving care in the retirement home of the Oberzell convent. Thus the fountain on the first floor is shaped like a opened Bible made of glass. The holy signs and symbols of faith with which people have surrounded themselves for centuries give a feeling of security and confidence in Christ's support, providing strength and peace.

Blessings

In contrast to a curse, a blessing aims to keep people healthy. A blessing is a kind of promise and plea for protection that may take the form of a blessing for a journey, the blessing of a parent given to a child, the blessing of a priest during Mass, or the blessing of the sick. And naturally in monasteries and convents, the grace or blessing (*benedicere*) is invariably said before each meal.

Positive vibrations

Monks and nuns strive to think good thoughts and have a positive attitude as a result. On the other hand, negative thoughts, images, and lies make us ill. Indeed, St. Benedict recommended in his Rule: "Turn away from evil and do good! Search for peace and pursue it." Here the founder of the order is referring to the healing power of positive thinking, which is not based on selfishness and is an end in itself. It strengthens the person with the positive thoughts, and has a beneficial effect on others as well.

The Eucharist promotes good health

The Eucharist provides heavenly refreshment and divine strength through the body and blood of Christ. The host has an unmistakable healing aspect, and it is no coincidence that the words spoken by the faithful are aimed directly at the health of the individual: "Lord, only say one word and my soul will be healed." In the liturgy, Romano Guardini wrote, it is "not a matter of thought, but of reality."

Intercession

People who believe in God see that intercession for the sick, accident victims, and others who are suffering is as natural a phenomenon as their daily bread. Many monastic orders, including the Franciscan nuns at Oberzell, pray for intercession for the sick. Requests for special prayers can be sent anonymously to the convent by e-mail. Every day there is another intercession on a lectern at the entrance of the Sacrament chapel, which is then included in the nuns' prayers.

Spiritual exercises

As well as the main spiritual exercises of fasting and praying, there are also practices such as days for taking stock and recharging one's energies in a holy place, religious and spiritual exercises, contemplation, confession, asceticism, and worship. Even apparently minor actions such as making the sign of the cross or crossing yourself with holy water have healing properties.

Prayer for healing

Be awake, O Lord,
With those who are awake
Or cry in the night.
Take care of the sick,
Let the weary rest,
Bless the dying,

Comfort the suffering
Have pity on the depressed,
And be happy with the joyful.

From a blackboard in the intensive care unit in a Munich hospital

Help through saints and patron saints

My grandmother told me that whenever she was ill as a child she was given a big book to read about the lives of the saints. These stories were not only great fun, but they were also thought to be very therapeutic.

Saints are still seen by many believers as important comforters, helpers, and advocates with God. Countless votive gifts and reports in books of miracles mention the curing of serious diseases, achieved to a certain extent with the help of saints.

Saints are like beacons of light in life. For the Capuchin monk Guido Kreppold they were "models of Christian self-realization." "They are like good friends," explained Sister Monika, the mother superior at Bad Krumbad, adding as she smiled quietly: "You do not always run to the big boss for every little thing."

How do the saints actually work, according to Christian belief? It is true that they are not in the visible world, but one can ask for their help. This can be done through pilgrimages, processions, and prayers for intercession. St. Teresa of Lisieux once said that saints can help people much better from heaven than during their life on Earth (and indeed many miracles have been verified). Holy places and places of pilgrimage such as the basilica of St. Anthony of Padua are full of testimonies from people who say that they have been helped by the Virgin Mary or a particular saint. Miracles have already been ascribed to Mother Teresa of Calcutta, for instance the healing of a tumor.

In the Middle Ages, abbots were also astronomers and physicians. Monks developed the Western medical science of antiquity, thus creating the foundation of the general health care of today. The history of monasticism is punctuated by the emergence of brilliant, holy individuals who developed complete healing systems. In addition, each region of each country had its "own" saints with whom it had a special relationship.

One of the best-known saints in the tradition of popular devotion is St. Blaise. Every year on February 3rd, priests give the blessing of St. Blaise in front of two crossed candles. This is believed to give protection against throat infections, choking, and similar disorders. St. Blaise was bishop of Sebastea (in Armenia), one of the fourteen auxiliary saints, and a physician

Praying for intercession: saints as comforters and helpers

by profession. According to legend, through his prayers while in prison he saved a young boy from dying from suffocation. Before his death as a martyr in the third century under the Emperor Diocletian, he asked God to help all those who prayed in his name for the healing of afflictions of the throat and other diseases.

Brother death

That monks and nuns are not afraid when death knocks on the door is quite evident in their death notices, which often describes death as "going home to God's eternal happiness and calm." The accompanying rituals also reflect their positive attitude towards death. When a Carthusian monk dies, the other monks gather in the refectory after the funeral to eat together in celebration of the fact that one of them has reached his goal.

The Cistercians have developed a wide range of rules to ensure that every monk dies a good death. According to one of these: "When a sick brother approaches death, the community gathers together in a spirit of brotherly love to support him with their prayers. The monks kneel round his deathbed

The fourteen auxiliary saints

For the Oberzell nuns there is only one answer to the question of which saint to invoke for support for particular illnesses: the fourteen auxiliary saints. The auxiliary saints were honored and invoked for help as early as the ninth century. According to legend, before dying these saints prayed to God for the grace of intercession, which God granted them:

- Achatius, against the fear of death and doubt
- Egidius, for a good confession
- Barbara, as the patron saint of the dying
- Blaise, invoked in cases of throat problems, against fear of death and doubt

- Christopher, against unexpected death
- Cyriacus, against temptation at the hour of death
- Dionysios, against headache
- Erasmus, against abdominal pain
- Eustace, in difficult situations in life
- George, against epidemic diseases in domestic animals
- Catherine, against ailments of the tongue and for easy speech
- Margaret, as patron saint of women giving birth
- Pantaleon, as patron saint of physicians
- Vitus, against epilepsy

and respond to the litanies and prayers that the abbot recites. The abbot chooses a few monks who will pray at the bed of the dying monk and a priest to say comforting words to him." The rules assume that the soul is immortal. The abbot must ensure that the body is never alone and that there is always a candle burning near it. The monks remember the dead monk for thirty days after the burial, the so-called Tricenarium. They place a cross at his empty place and also put his lunch and supper there so that the "poor can eat it."

For Christians, death is not the end but the beginning of a new life. Therefore Sister Adelhilde in Oberzell found it quite natural to say: "The day is always so short. I too must now prepare myself for death." With her friendly smile, the eighty-five-year-old gives the impression that she still has many years in front of her. Sister Adelhilde has a personality and charisma that impress the nurses and the sisters equally. "When you fight an illness it always becomes worse," she said thoughtfully as she sat on the terrace of the convent's retirement home. Some time ago she had broken a leg. For Sister Adelhilde, the important thing was not the broken leg but "a divine providence," as she explained. "That was how I discovered my new role in life, namely to help here." So now she is staying in the retirement home of her own free will. She was given a room with a nun suffering from senile dementia to whom she often sings. And she added emphatically: "You should always see Christ in your neighbor. It strengthens you, making you happy and free. I would not want to exchange my life with anyone, however rich they might be. I am always happy, and today I am even happier than I was yesterday."

Sacred space within ourselves

Try to find a very soothing place, such as a church. Enjoy the beneficial peace and tranquility, and the encounter with God. The Capuchin monk Guido Kreppold recommended: "It makes you feel very good to go into a church and immerse yourself in the silence. Close your eyes and take some deep breaths; continue this for a while and just allow the surrounding space to work on you. You may find what you are looking for in your inner self: tranquility, peace, a feeling of home, security, depth, and the vastness of the soul; you may even discover a little of what is greater and more powerful than ourselves and can save us from our inner confusion and emptiness. You might even come to the realization that the treasures found in holy places are in fact within yourself. Or you could read the Bible, whose tales and stories also have a beneficial, soothing effect." The Capuchin monk explained why this is so: "It is the experience of countless people who have encountered 'holiness;' they felt a fascinating force that touched their innermost selves and healed them."

Silence
in the Monastery

Simone Kosog

Preliminary

Learning to be alone is the first step to inner peace

W hen I told people that I wanted to go and spend a few days in a convent in search of silence, they all reacted quite differently. "Is everyone allowed in?" a neighbor asked me. "I hope you won't convert!" my mother said, rather worried. A physiotherapist friend told me about an abbess who regularly went to sleep while being treated. And many thought that I was already quiet enough. (They did not know about my pounding heart!) Another friend, who was always in search of new spiritual inspiration, was very excited at the thought of finding that stimulation in Christianity almost on her doorstep and not somewhere in the mountains of Tibet.

The yearning for silence, for moments when we succeed in slowing down the pace of our life and making time to pause, is great. I was astounded how much the convent here had to offer.

For instance, I had not known that meditation in Christianity was a tradition that dated back to the third century. Or that saying a rosary had a lot in common with meditation. That the Lord's Prayer can be a real adventure. That nuns and monks are constantly striving to achieve silence and have developed a whole array of methods to help them.

Sister Annunziata, who recounted her entire life story to me during our conversations, knows that many of the spiritual experiences that were common knowledge in the past have been forgotten. Naturally she thinks it is a shame that a growing number of Christians are leaving the Church, although she can often understand why. "How can someone who attends a church service anonymously in a large city find a way to the Church?" People today need suitable places for those experiences and for meeting good communicators, teachers like Jesus who set an example in the way he lived. "Apart from the feeding of the five thousand, Jesus never dealt with large crowds but worked in small, manageable circles. He always preferred direct contact." She never asked me about my faith or made me feel that she considered herself better than me. She pointed out all the "treasures" that Christianity has to offer. And through her example she showed that in convents and monasteries there are people who know how to find them.

Simone Kosog

Welcome to the convent

The Cistercian abbey of Oberschönenfeld

"You have given me the best room!"

With short, quick steps and holding a very fragrant baby, we crossed the forecourt leading to the convent gate. It was cold and windy, it was drizzling — and we were half an hour late.

It was one of those mornings. Of course, I hadn't managed to pack the day before, so I just collected all my things together early that morning. I showered and hugged the baby. He was only ten months old and this was going to be our first long separation. Anyway, reasonably punctually, our family — my husband, my older son, our baby, and I — were in the car traveling towards the oldest German convent of Cistercian nuns, the abbey of Oberschönenfeld, where I was expected at midday. We had not been traveling for more than ten minutes when little Paul began to go red in the face and started to cry. Shortly afterwards a very distinct smell started to spread through the car. We had forgotten to pack some clean diapers, so we had to make a detour to go and buy some. We had also forgotten the map, and we left the highway much too early. Country roads and yet more country roads;

I kept checking the time on the digital clock in front of me. Today of all days I wished I had been on time.

Sister Annunziata greeted us wearing a blue and white apron over her nun's habit. "Here you are!" "I'm really sorry…" I said. I wanted to add that I was usually punctual. I didn't want her to get the wrong impression! But Sister Annunziata just smiled. "It doesn't matter. Shall I keep your soup hot so that you have time to say goodbye?" I was happy that she could not hear my dramatic inner monologue.

Strength comes from peace.

Popular saying

According to legend, in the twelfth century Count Mangold IV discovered a hermit on the site of the present convent. This man had traveled on a pilgrimage to the Holy Land to atone for the transgressions of his father and himself, and he wanted to spend the rest of his life as a solitary penitent. After the hermit's death, the count's wife built a chapel on the site where the hermit had lived. Then, when her husband died, she herself withdrew with other women into solitude. This community joined the Cistercian order in about 1220.

Today about thirty nuns live at Oberschönenfeld. Over the centuries the little chapel developed first into a small, then into a larger wooden building, and finally into a convent built of stone. It is a friendly establishment with a chapel, main building, and numerous outbuildings, grouped around a large inner courtyard and surrounded by a wall.

Sister Annunziata was a woman of forty with a friendly face, a look of determination, and slightly flushed cheeks, as if she had just returned from a brisk walk. She opened the door to my room. It had a high ceiling and was very spacious, like everything else in this convent. White-plastered walls, floorboards, a

Sister Annunziata

table and chairs, a large old wardrobe, a wing chair near the window, a pendulum clock, and a gigantic bed with thick quilts, white covers, and a cushion with a crease in the middle. There was everything one could need, no more: a spacious simplicity, giving a pleasant, unobtrusive welcome. My husband's six-year-old son Jonathan looked around and examined my new lodgings. He then went to the window: "You've been given the best room! You can see the woods and a mountain. Perhaps you will be lucky, and they may even have cats. In fact, we could all stay here."

Then they went off, leaving behind a full diaper. Slightly at a loss, I looked around. I was supposed to be relaxed here. For weeks I had been yearning for this silence, for the feeling of not being rushed and distracted. But after tearing about like a dervish, my mind was still spinning round and round. I thought I had better discuss my program with Sister Annunziata as soon as possible. There was so much to talk about: the silence, the rules, humility, the architecture of the convent. It seemed strange that the chapel was so lavishly decorated, since it clashed with the frugality of the Cistercians. I would have to ask her about this. And when was the next choral service? Maybe I should start writing things down. Hardly an hour had passed and already I was banging away on my laptop. Stop!

"The wise are recognized by their few words."

From the Rule of St. Benedict

It is never possible to become completely relaxed immediately when you switch off from the everyday rush. "Almost two-thirds of all professionals are unable to relax after work," one commentator has written. "Conditions around us make it difficult for us to relax completely. With its endless demands for greater productivity, our everyday life makes it hard to find time for peace and quiet. "As a result we live our life at the speed of light," says the American sociologist Jeremy Rifkin. The term "24/7" needed to be coined to describe a lifestyle that takes place round the clock, twenty-four hours a day, seven days a week.

The International Labor Organization is predicting a dramatic increase in stress-related disorders, caused by ever faster technologies and growing globalization. It is therefore not surprising that stress-related illnesses such as depression, heart problems, strokes, cancer, diabetes, and burnout

Guests in repose at Himmerod monastery

syndrome have become the main diseases of our society. In Germany the working days lost in industry as a result of stress-related illnesses and psychological problems cost several billion euros a year.

Adults and especially children are increasingly diagnosed with attention deficit hyperactivity disorder (ADHD), associated with hyperactivity and the inability to concentrate on a particular thing for any length of time. For quite a while now hardness of hearing caused by noise has become the number one disease of the sixty-eight recognized occupational diseases. At the same time, acute hearing loss and tinnitus have become widespread: the ear gives up since it can no longer cope. It requires a silence that it no longer has, which is why it rejects all further noise. When the mind is unable to stop the noise, the body must do it, and it does so quite radically.

So the call to slow down is becoming increasingly relevant. The question now is, what must we do and what can we do? Are there any traditions, such as those here at Oberschönenfeld, that could tell us something?

I looked around the convent and walked along the long stone corridors whose coldness was all-pervasive and soon penetrated even through my clothes. The place was completely deserted; the only sound I could hear was that of my own footsteps. There were no clattering noises and no voices. I walked past numerous closed wooden doors, many of them painted with the words: "Private. Please do not enter." I imagined nuns sitting behind these closed doors. Some perhaps were deep in conversation while others alone in their cells were concentrating on their tasks. Suddenly I felt great sympathy with what they were doing, with their seriousness, with the strength that seemed to emanate from these heavy doors.

"Nature is a very good tranquilizer."
Anton Chekhov

Many people have their own special story about Christianity, and if someone had told me ten years ago that I would seek the secret of life in a convent, I would have thought it quite ridiculous. After a euphoric Catholic youth during which I was a server in church and a member of the choir, I began to feel disappointed. Even today I still do not know exactly why. I believe it was partly because I no longer believed in a judge in heaven who decided what was good and evil. There were also those overzealous, moralizing churchgoers. With absolute doggedness they were determined to pray themselves into heaven.

I felt so angry with the Church that on holiday I even refused to visit

The whole life

One day St. Dominic visited St. Francis of Assisi. They greeted each other by embracing but it is said that they did not say a single word to each other during the whole time they were together. But when they parted company, one had communicated his life to the other.

The solitude of the cell

"Go to your cell, stay there, and the cell will teach you everything," was one of the recommendations of early Christian monasticism. This sentence could mean several things because the cell can also be interpreted as the "I" or self, the cell of one's own being. Solitude is necessary from time to time so we do not sink into meaningless activity. There is a famous saying by Blaise Pascal on this theme: "All misfortunes happen because people cannot stay in their room." The author Maurice Sachs described his monastic experience as follows: "In the solitude of the cell, the self gathers itself together and finds itself; virtues return and the reenergized person feels safe and happy. Peace, peace, and the contentment of peace. Monasteries have a magic of their own. For those who believe, and even for those who do not believe, it is the presence of God. Everything reflects this divine presence. This explains the slow ambling in the silence of the cloister, the half open lips, the whispered prayers… and the moving mystery of any place where man collects himself and reflects. Because when man becomes aware of himself, 'the spirit moves.'"

churches that were well worth looking at. Then I became interested in Zen Buddhism and yoga. I pushed Christianity aside. As time passed, however, I mellowed a bit and and found my curiosity about Christianity somewhat rekindled.

I started browsing through a few books on Christianity in order to prepare for my visit to the convent, and I suddenly became very excited at the prospect of finally starting a long overdue study of the subject. And the more I read, the more I found out, much of which was actually acceptable and also unbelievably practical. The old concepts suddenly acquired a completely new meaning.

When I returned to my room I was grateful for the warmth. I looked out of the window and saw an old nun who was progressing slowly and ponderously through the garden, tottering first to one side of the path where she looked under a fir tree, then to the other side where she looked under the bushes until a ginger cat suddenly appeared. She bent down and stroked the cat. Then she went back to the convent with the cat following her. Would I ever be so happy?

There was knock at the door. Sister Annunziata. No, she could not spend any more time with me today because she was looking after another group. But tomorrow, yes. Then she added that the bakery was closed at the weekend and so was the bookshop. "I'll see you at the canonical hours, if you like."

Exhausted, I sat down in the armchair. I had never imagined so much silence.

The long road to peace and happiness

A place of meditation: the cloister in the monastery of Weingarten

*A brief introduction
to life in the cloister*

*"I was lost in earthly
existence and darkness;
there I heard your
voice behind me, but I
did not understand it
because of the noise of
those who have no
peace."*

St. Augustine

One of my friends had a curious habit: every time he went on holiday he looked for a place that was really quiet, where he would be surrounded by complete silence. He was absolutely obsessed by this. He thought that a place where there was no noise reminding him of civilization would offer him the greatest, most mysterious, and most intense experience of his life. For years he looked for such a place, but in vain. He climbed the highest mountains, but there he could hear the noise of airplanes. He walked through forests but there he could still hear the noise of cars in the distance. He traveled to wide-open plains, but he could hear the humming of power cables and wind turbines. Then he journeyed into the Namibian desert, a hundred miles across. He climbed a dune in the midst of endless other dunes. All that he could see was sand, and all that he could hear was the faint rushing of the wind. Had he finally found his "silent" place?

What is so important about silence? Does the body need such peace to reenergize itself? Or is it merely an image invented by the Romantic movement, or by

"Peace and silence bring the whole world back into the proper balance."
Lao-Tzu

the German middle class that promotes silence as a civic duty? Or are places of silence merely an excuse for the idle, for the lazy, slow-moving individuals who find no pleasure in work or life? Perhaps silence is a refuge for people who deep down hate the world, for the angst-ridden and the failures, who do not enjoy the animated bustle of life and spoil everyone else's fun. In any case, why have these idle, world-hating people spent so much to accomplish this? Why have convents and monasteries been built all over the world to achieve this?

Silence creates space

For those in religious orders, silence is the very foundation of their lives, an indisputable "must" that forms the very basis of their existence as members of these orders. This silence ranges from the restriction of noise to deliberately refraining from speaking, which creates inner peace, a state of mind that promotes happiness and knowledge through deep harmony. The reason is very simple: truth lies in silence and God is found in solitude. In silence and solitude the soul is able to get a glimpse of eternity.

In the world of monks everything is geared to silence. Their traditional habit screens them from the world. Their buildings have thick walls insulating them from noise. The purpose of the cloisters in the inner courtyards is to ensure that the noise of people moving about their business does not disturb the surroundings. They are places of peace, tranquility, contemplation, and the flowing interaction between movement and mind in a place of meditation. There you can walk, pace up and down, and speak through your movements and gestures, which are your way of communicating. The daily routine of rest, reflection, inner spiritual work, and solitude begins in silence and — quite unlike the world outside — ends in silence with an early night.

Silence creates space. It is a vital prerequisite for relaxation, recuperation, and recharging our batteries. Monks and nuns believe that it is only in silence that human beings can live in harmony with themselves and the world. It is what gives them their confidence, their power of judgment, and, last but not least, their cheerfulness. Even God himself sought peace. According to the Bible, after creating the world God decreed that: "The seventh day is a Sabbath to the Lord your God; you shall not do any work — you, your son or your daughter, your male or female slave, your livestock, or the alien resident in your towns" (Exodus 20:10).

According to monastic tradition, silence is indispensable for establishing a link with God, with the divine, the mysterious, the origin, the energy, and the strength — or whatever one wants to call it, since it is something that cannot really be expressed in words because it transcends the world. It is not only in Christianity that the atmosphere of silence and tranquility is a prerequisite for deep contemplation and enlightenment; it is also a tradition in many other religions. In Zen Buddhism, remaining in *zazen* is the basic exercise for achieving enlightenment. *Zazen* means "sitting in deep contemplation," and is practiced by meditating in the lotus or half-lotus position or on a chair. It describes a state free of thoughts, with a highly alert attentiveness that is, however, not directed at any particular object or attached to any content.

In the same way that silence and tranquility heal people and make them complete, so noise and agitation make people ill. St. Francis de Sales described noise as the "worst evil after sin." The founder of the Salesian order said: "Just as civil wars can destroy and weaken a country so that it is unable to resist an enemy from outside, so the soul is weakened by confusion and noise." The problem of noise is extremely serious. It has its source in the depths of the soul, and according to St. Francis de Sales, it often occurs because of our own "deep desire to possess things."

The experience of the desert

When the first hermits left the settlements of their communities, they did so in order to escape from a world that was in danger of falling into chaos around them. They wanted to save themselves, and by moving into the desert they also wanted to show the way to others. These people were convinced that silence held the key to a mystery, and possibly to the secret of life.

The first of a long line of desert fathers was St. Anthony. The son of a prosperous family, the Egyptian-born hermit was only twenty years old when during a religious service he heard the call of the Holy Scriptures, and felt that it was addressed to him personally. What struck him so forcefully was a passage from St. Matthew's gospel, telling the story of a rich young man who

Hermitage near Saalfelden in the region of Salzburg

asked Jesus how he could achieve perfection. Jesus said to him: "If you wish to be perfect, go, sell all your possessions, and give the money to the poor, and you will have treasure in heaven; then come, follow me" (Matthew 19:21). Anthony heard the story, turned round, gave away his possessions and his inheritance, and traveled to the outskirts of the town. Following the example of Jesus, he began fasting and gradually increased the severity of his asceticism. From the outskirts of town he moved to a rock tomb and from there he moved deeper and deeper into the desert. "He remained awake so long that he often did not sleep at all during the night," Bishop Athanasius wrote in his *Life of St. Anthony*, and this was "not just once but often. He ate once a day after sunset; occasionally he only ate every two or even every four days. He lived entirely off bread, salt, and water."

For hermits, the desert represented the recognition of truth, it symbolized contentment, and it connected them with God — but also with the constant danger of temptation. All the great prophets had followed this path; for instance, Elijah, who spent forty days in the desert, and St. John the Baptist, who went to the desert to prepare himself for his mission as forerunner of Christ. Moses spent forty days in solitude where he heard God in the rustling of the wind and also received from him the Ten Commandments, the Magna Carta of human life. Jesus, too, in emulation of the hermits, was transported to the wilderness by the Holy Spirit before his public appearance in order to collect himself and concentrate on the task before him.

Withdrawing into the desert had been part of spiritual tradition for a long time, especially for those who dedicated their lives to God and yearned for him. In doing so they hoped to achieve inner purification and existential encounters with the many temptations and tempters that are an essential part of every change of direction and new beginning.

The man who slept on the hardest boards

Today St. Anthony would be considered a pioneering extreme sportsman who wanted to set records for others: a winner in the field of fasting, a world master of endurance wakefulness, and the man who slept on the hardest boards. Indeed, there were a large number of hermits whose asceticism took extreme forms and developed into false dynamics through their egocentricity and arrogance. Self-castigation was taken to such an extreme that it led to chronic illnesses and even death. These extreme forms of asceticism lasted for several centuries. Through severe fasting, Bernard of Clairvaux developed a stomach complaint at an early age that plagued him throughout life.

"That man is richest whose pleasures are cheapest."
Henry David Thoreau

For St. Anthony and the other serious desert monks, solitude and abstinence were not ends in themselves. In the knowledge that there was a deeper truth, it was the way to overcome one's own personality, to get rid of it, and return to the essence of life, to God.

The greater the solitude of the hermit, the stronger his personality became. His voice rang out into the world from the desert where he was no longer distracted by everyday activities. More and more people went on pilgrimages to visit hermits, seek their advice, and emulate their way of life.

When hermits themselves were at their wit's end, they went up a mountain and prayed — and found the answers to their questions. In the tranquility and peace of the desert, Anthony learned not to speak and how to listen. Listening — to one's own inner voice, but also to the voice of God.

The dance of demons

The desert is a metaphor for internalization and overcoming difficulties, the most radical way of achieving tranquility and silence. Work on oneself starts in the desert. "To desert" means to let oneself go. To distance oneself from the noise of everyday life; from the false whispers, the constant bombardment of what to do and what to think. The desert helps people to abandon false goals and find a new direction. This form of inner purification brings up to the surface all the mess, all the seductive temptations that have accumulated within us and that we must fight off as if they were wild animals.

We all have our own demons. They are part of our life on Earth. They represent temptations that would rob us of our tranquility. There are also the demons that tempt us to overindulgence in food, for example, and those that turn us into workaholics and tempt us into arrogance and pomposity. St. Anthony — and later also St. Benedict — described the real struggles that had to be endured when they arose. "The devil put dirty thoughts into his mind and tried to arouse him sexually," the *Life of St. Anthony* declares. But because the man of the desert held his ground the demons were really challenged. "In those days the demons raged at night in such a way that the whole place seemed to shake," it was said, "and they turned into wild beasts and reptiles; the place was filled with terrifying apparitions of lions, bears, leopards, and bulls as well as snakes, asps, scorpions, and wolves." The

"You will see that happiness follows contemplation."

St. Teresa of Lisieux

The maxims of the ancient fathers

The wise old monks of the Egyptian desert were called *'abbas,* or patriarchs. The English word *abbot,* meaning the superior of a monastery, is derived from it. When such an *'abba* uttered an inspired or illuminating thought, his words were handed down (as *apophthegmata,* or maxims). The monks saw this as knowledge born from silence, as advice that admittedly was given in a concrete situation but whose validity went far beyond the moment itself. We know some of the words of wisdom of the desert fathers from the writings of John Cassian, who lived with the monks in Egypt for over ten years. He also recorded the following

story. A few visitors had come to see a solitary monk. They asked him: "What is the meaning of your life of silence?" The monk was busy drawing water from a deep well. He spoke to the visitors: "Look into the well! What do you see?" The people looked into the well. "We see nothing." After a short while the hermit asked the visitors again: "Look into the well! What do you see?" The visitors looked into the well again. "Yes, now we can see ourselves!" The monk explained: "You see, when I was drawing the water, the surface of the water was moving. Now the water is calm. That is the experience of silence: you can see yourself!"

din produced by all these apparitions was "terrifying and their rage horrible." But in the end, with God's help, the saint won the fight: "St. Anthony, bruised and tortured within, also experienced serious physical pain; but he lay down without trembling and wide awake within his soul."

The first monasteries

After St. Anthony there were many men, including saints such as Pachomius and Basil, who devoted themselves to the pursuit of silence and tranquility in order to practice the art of *hesychia,* the art of divine silence that facilitated the encounter between the divine and one's own soul (see page 268). Hermitages, originally each with a single occupant, were increasingly forming groups, and the buildings were then surrounded by walls. The only reason for living alone had been to satisfy the "requirements of the individual," St. Basil realized, and he therefore founded a monastery in Capadocia whose Rule was based on the original Christian community in Jerusalem. "All who believed were together and had all things in common; they would sell their possessions and distribute the proceeds to all as any had need. Day by day, as they spent much time together in the temple, they broke bread at home and ate their food with glad and generous hearts, praising God and having the goodwill of all the people" (Acts of the Apostles 2:44–47). Basil saw togetherness as a very important element in the community but solitude was equally important. "It is good for novices to practice silence," he

Guided movement: the staircase in Himmerod Abbey

prescribed in his instructions. "They will learn to forget the past, because it will be silenced, and they will have the leisure to learn goodness."

The mystery of Monte Cassino

After St. Basil, other monks wrote down their Rules, but none was as important as the Benedictine Rule, written in about 530 in Monte Cassino in Southern Italy. In fact, St. Benedict of Nursia wrote down his instructions only for his brother monks. However, his Rule proved to be so prudent, intelligent, devout, and above all, successful, that in the ninth century it became binding for all Christian monasteries. Fifteen hundred years later it remains topical and is still followed by hundreds of thousands in monasteries and convents. Today, people outside the orders are becoming increasingly interested in what it says.

"Inner peace can only be achieved if you ignore the unessential and concentrate on the essential."

Bernard of Clairvaux

The wise monk of Monte Cassino knew people. He knew what was easy for them and what they found difficult, and he wrote down instructions to guide them through life, based on his profound knowledge of the basic elements of human life and behavior. Following these instructions required a certain rigor and determination, but at the same time they took the various talents and personality of each individual into account.

Anyone who wants to achieve true peace and tranquility will find here firm instructions for every step:

1. *Obsculta*, "listen." This is the first word of St. Benedict's Rule that changed the world. Listening properly is the prerequisite for change and further development. It requires openness and willingness to hear both the voices within us and the advice and needs of others. It demands attentiveness to the surroundings in which we find ourselves, to life itself, and to God. Listening properly is not only a task for the head. St. Benedict also recommended: "Use the ear of your heart."

2. The basic principle of moderation and the middle way plays a decisive part in every area of life. It is present throughout the Rule and applies to work, eating, drinking, and clothes as well as to praying and fasting. People should not be tempted to extremes but go through life in a measured manner. Moderation and the middle way create order and rhythm

and prevent chaos. The main rule is: "Excess must be avoided above all."

3. The practice of silence is essential for achieving inner peace. This is why St. Benedict said: "The monks must always be eager to strive towards silence." Silence is not something to be pursued just for a day or so; it is a lifelong challenge. St. Benedict indicates how difficult it is in the eleventh of the twelve stages of humility: "When talking, the monk speaks quietly without laughing, humbly and with dignity, using few and sensible words.

Hesychia: divine silence

Hesychia is a special experience in the history of Christian monasticism, a form of spiritual collection and composure. The word is derived from the Greek word meaning "silence" or "stillness." It implies solitude, isolation, quietness, and being at peace, as well as not speaking. A person seeking hesychia in order to be at one with God is a Hesychast: a man such as the desert father St. Basil, who considered silence a prerequisite for the sanctification of man. It had to be so quiet and peaceful around him that he could feel the trembling of the air, allowing all mental excitement to subside. In one of his sermons, St. Gregory Palamas described hesychia as follows: "Hesychia is the state of tranquility of the mind and world, the forgetting of the vile and lowly, the mysterious recognition of the supernatural, the abandonment of ourselves to thoughts of something better than we are. So those who have purified their heart in this manner through silence and who have become united in an inexpressible manner with the thought and recognition of transcendent light will look at God in themselves as if in a mirror." "Only the collected mind is truly alert," wrote the philosopher Dietrich von Hildebrand (1889–1977), "and only the alert mind lives in the truest and fullest sense of the word."

He does not make a lot of noise, because it is written: "The wise man is recognized by his few words."

4. The individual can only find tranquility and peace if the community in which he lives exists in harmony. Therefore he must not only look after his own good but also that of others: "The followers should therefore respect older people, and the older people should love the younger ones."

5. People can discover their true essence only by striving towards the divine. This contact with the divine can be achieved through prayer, examination of one's conscience, penitence, religious services, contemplation, and above all, through charitable works. For monks it is not work that is most important but the delight in God: "Nothing should be given preference over religious services."

6. Each person should perceive and follow the path set out for him or her by God. This does not mean slavish service. Instead it is a matter of discovering one's own path and as a result finding not only Christ but also one's personal happiness in life.

You can also meditate about the furrows in a field

Detail from a window in the Cistercian monastery of Maulbronn

7. In order to follow this path with greater ease, St. Benedict recommended finding peace in a particular way, and not only peace with fellow human beings but also with ourselves. The saint made this clear when he withdrew to his cave near Subiaco. To find himself, he wanted "to live there on his own," as Pope Gregory noted. We should be silent, listening, letting things suppressed within us for a long time come to the surface, and questioning our own cravings. "Pursue peace!" St. Benedict urged, and he quoted a promise made by God: "Then you shall call, and the Lord will answer; you shall cry for help, and he will say: 'Here I am'" (Isaiah 58:9).

Again and again in his Rule, St. Benedict refers to the Bible, which is for him the most important rule. In the last chapter of the Rule he asks: "What page or saying ascribed to God in the Old and New Testaments is not an exact rule for human life?" St. Benedict himself saw his Rule as an interpretation, an elaboration of the Bible applied to monastic life. From today's point of view, many of St. Benedict's instructions may appear rather laborious and rigorous in their practical application. Following the Rule, monks spend most of their time in silence and prayer. A strict daily routine divides the day into periods without much variety. In fact from the beginning, the solitude of the desert was replicated in many ways in Western monasteries. A call to monastic life cannot be compared with worldly life; rather it could be described as something extraordinary and daring; some might even say impossible. It is not a road that many can follow, but its radical demands can show the way to those who have faith.

St. Benedict also begged his fellow brothers for forbearance. He admonished them: "You should for carefully considered reasons be a little stricter and mend your ways and treasure love; do not let yourself be confused by anxiety and do not flee from the path of salvation. The beginning of it cannot be other than narrow." This is a reference to Christ himself, who had said the same thing: "For the gate is narrow and the road is hard that leads to life, and there are few who find it."

Today monasteries and convents are still oases of peace and tranquility in a noisy, hectic world. At a time when everything around us is becoming faster and noisier, when we speak of stress-related diseases, and when hearing disorders have spread like an epidemic, these foundations all over the world, like lights on a mountain, are a memorial to peacefulness, reflection, and turning back, to order amidst chaos, and to certainty in a world of irritations. And as a tribute to a perfect peace that can properly be described as almost divine.

The pole sitter

Some hermits chose a secluded valley in the desert, or lived in a cave or on a remote mountain, but Simeon the Stylite chose a pillar on which he lived his ascetic life. Thus in the fifth century he became the founder of an extraordinary movement in Syria — stylitism — that spread throughout the Byzantine empire. Simeon's column was initially ten feet and ultimately sixty-six feet high. Thus isolated from the world, he lived without any protection from the sun or the rain until his death, while still managing to take part in public life. The saint, who must have been a friendly man and a peacemaker, preached twice a day to pilgrims who came to him in ever-increasing numbers.

About the daily routine

Traveling in order to arrive: still life on the island of Lesbos

How to find the correct rhythm

*T*his refectory, or dining room, where usually only nuns ate, was enormous, and when I joined them at the table I felt like an intruder. If it had been a restaurant it would easily have seated two hundred people. But the nuns sat far apart not facing each other. They ate in silence, gazing only directly at their plates. No one looked at the paintings on the walls, depicting stories from the Bible, or at the large cross, or at the other nuns. The nun who had been a sister of the order for the longest time sat farthest away. The abbess, Mother Ancilla, sat at the head, flanked by her two deputies. Next to her table, in the corner near the window, was a wooden pulpit from which the sisters took turns reading.

Sister Hildegard, who sold bread in the monastery bakery, adjusted the microphone to her height. She was somebody one would describe as typical — a rather large woman with an equally large heart. Now, up there in the pulpit, Sister Hildegard was no longer just a typical nun; she was the reader, and only that. While the four nuns who were on table duty carried the soup onto a large steel counter, she read from the Old Testament, The First Book of the Kings, speaking slowly in a North German accent.

The main course was served. Today it was pasta. Here and there the clattering of silverware could be heard, steel against steel. "Did you hear how the sisters were scraping with their cutlery?" Sister Hildegard asked later, amused. Silence is relative; even snow can make a noise. According to research carried out at Johns Hopkins University, snowflakes falling on water are noise pollution for many aquatic creatures.

Sister Hildegard then read from a treatise on the Rule of St. Benedict. "He who thinks he is better because of his clothes endangers the freedom of his heart…" There was a banana for desert. "…to allow the origins of monastic life to bubble up…" The nuns then cleared the table, taking away all the empty dishes and gathering up the leftovers. Every movement was measured and orderly.

Sister Hildegard switched off the sound system, causing a crackling in the loudspeaker. The abbess stood up, and the sisters left in the same order as they had been sitting at the table. They crossed the cloister and went towards the outside door where there was a coat stand. The abbess threw a shawl over her shoulders, the Brazilian nun put on a thick purple jacket, and we went to the cemetery to pray for the dead.

"As long as you do not see into my heart and I do not look into yours, night will reign."

St. Augustine

Then the abbess put an end to the silence with the word "Benedicite." The nuns reacted immediately. Just a second ago they had been gazing inwards towards God and concentrating on praying. Now their faces opened up, and they looked outwards with equal intensity. They offered me friendly smiles. "All this must be very strange for you… It is excellent that you have come…" Then we looked together at a blackbird in its nest in a tree close to the graves and afterwards went on our way.

Living according to Rules

Sister Annunziata came to Oberschönenfeld for her novitiate on April 10, 1988, at precisely 11:25 in the morning, just before the soup was served. She had given her notice as a nurse, sold her car, and given up her apartment. Six months later she joined the convent. At the time she thought that every-

Bell ringing in the enclosed convent of Oberschönenfeld

thing would sort itself out of its own accord. Instead she faced some difficult and demanding times. "I still remember how after the evening meal I
would sit in my cell and think: Shall I now go to bed? Is this going to be my
life?" There were some very stressful months until she became accustomed
to the completely different rhythm of the convent. Sister Annunziata had to
learn like a child; nothing was like anything that she had known before.

In Oberschönenfeld the first bells ring at five o'clock in the morning.
This is not merely to convey the time, indicating that those who want to
can now rouse themselves; rather it is an order to get up. This is the start of
a day that continues until evening, following strict rules and punctuated by
six occasions for communal prayer. The other events of the day, such as meals,
spiritual reading, work, personal prayer, and leisure time are all arranged
around these times of prayer. Many things are less strict than they were in

About time and eternity

Christianity gave the world a new concept of time. This does not only refer to the division of history into the time before the birth of Christ and the time after it, or even to the Gregorian calendar, but to a new understanding of time. The basis of this new understanding was the linear representation of time. It had a starting point: the Creation of the world by God. It also had an end: the Second Coming of Jesus Christ, when the passage of time would stop and life on Earth would be replaced by paradise. In ancient times, philosophers had another representation of time. Plato had a static view of reality, which he saw as the realm of eternal ideas. In Hinduism, time was divided into self-repeating cycles. Like Christians and Muslims, Hindus and Buddhists also believe that time is finite and that after it comes eternity. But this will not be by the hand of a personified God but by the actions of humanity itself, which as a result can transcend the cycle of birth and rebirth.

According to the philosopher Boethius, who lived in the sixth century, eternity is "the perfect possession of a limitless life in a single, all-enveloping present." But Christ already participated in this eternity during his life on Earth. The evangelist Luke wrote: "The kingdom of God is not coming with things that can be observed; nor will they say, 'Look, here it is! or: There it is!' For, in fact, the kingdom of God is [already] among you" (Luke 17:20).

the Middle Ages — for instance, for some years now the Cistercian nuns at Obenschönenfeld have been wearing lighter, smaller veils that reveal more of their faces. But they still have to follow the rules of St. Benedict: when to speak, when to be silent, when to work, when to pray, who sits where in the choir, and also which psalms are sung in the morning and which in the evening.

A question of time

Ora et labora, pray and work. By this iron maxim, St. Benedict was not recommending eternal exultation or unending work for his followers. He was encouraging them to make better use of their time, to develop a new economy and culture after decades of devastation resulting from war and deprivation.

He also intended to recast the concept of work, which until then had been seen as something completely inferior, an occupation for slaves. Time was to be measured. Here too is further evidence of St. Benedict's religious genius; neither prayer or work were to be taken to extremes, but both were to follow the way of moderation. The fixed prayers said at the canonical hours later spread to the clergy of the Church all over the world, and by these prayers monks created a completely new awareness of time.

It is therefore no coincidence that the first mechanical clocks in Europe were found in monasteries. Nor is it surprising that the oldest clock adorns a church tower, the Cathedral of St. Pierre in Beauvais, France.

Observance of a canonical hour in the convent of Kellenried

The awareness of time was and still is an essential component of monastic life. It almost has a poetic dimension:

- in Vigils, evening prayer: "I lie down and go to sleep, I wake up again because the Lord protects me…"
- in Lauds, the first of the morning's acts of praise: "From Zion, the crown of beauty, God goes forth radiant…"
- in Compline, which ends the day: "With his wings the Lord protects you; you need not fear the terrors of the night."

The seven canonical hours were not based on an arbitrary standard; St. Benedict derived this regimen from the biblical division of the week into seven days. Subsequently several attempts have been made to change this weekly rhythm. In France, revolutionary Jacobins thought by altering it they could draw the population away from Christianity. In Russia, the communist government hoped to increase industrial production by creating a ten-day week. But sooner or later all these attempts failed. First animals became ill, then people. "The message of saying prayers at the canonical hours is to live every day in the actual rhythm of the day," the Benedictine monk David Steindl-Rast believes. In it he sees the "core of the monastic message." Nowhere else can one better appreciate "the extraordinary meaning of time" than in a monastery or convent, and also appreciate "the importance of how we use it." The monks' division of time therefore corresponds to a very special rhythm, to particular oscillations, an inner order predetermined by Creation.

Outer and inner order

After an initial phase of acclimatization in the convent of Oberschönenfeld, Sister Annunziata began to internalize the rhythm of monastic life and to accept it. Instead of feeling restricted and ordered about, she experienced relief. She recognized that rules could help:

- Because they relax you; what has been decided once and for all as a matter of principle does not need to be reconsidered every day. As a result you can concentrate on what is essential.
- Because they provide protection and support.
- Because time goes more slowly as it follows a particular order. Instead of being swept along by it, you follow its rhythm.

About moderation and the middle way

The rules governing monastic life aim to create equilibrium in the structure of the day, and also in every aspect of life, including clothes, work, eating, and sleeping. In the Bible, "earthly desires" that are excessive are associated with godlessness; in contrast, Christians must not only live a "righteous and pious" life but also one that is "prudent for this world." With moderation, people will not lose their way — in the same way a pendulum's oscillations to right and left become increasingly small until it finally comes to rest in the middle.

• Because they provide a feeling for what is important — which also means breaking these rules sometimes.

Sister Annunziata explained the last point further: "If I know someone is having problems and I might be able to help, then I must speak to her, because I am not allowed to hide behind the obligation of silence. I have a responsibility towards myself but also towards my fellow sisters."

Rest against unrest

The monks' Rule, said the Benedictine monk Ambrose Tinsley, is "geared to meet our existential needs." It seems to benefit people in spite of its strictness. The nuns of Oberschönenfeld have just one and a half hours of free time a day! And of this, a half hour must be spent in contemplation. That does not leave much time for anything else. Yet this is an important time of the day for the nuns. They know that they do not have to worry that the day has passed by and that they did not have a single minute to themselves. Another thing they do not need to worry about is overtime. Every activity has a beginning and a well-defined end. A task that is not completed must be completed at a later time. It is quite amazing, an old monk once told me, that "in spite of all our interruptions and prayers we always manage to complete our work."

As soon as these fundamental rules have been accepted, the hectic pace of life suddenly slows down. An appropriate tempo is also part of the correct rhythm. For instance, Sister Hildegard chose the right tempo when she read at the meal. She was perfectly confident about the pauses in the sentence.

Indeed, how much time could I save by rushing? (Saving time: an interesting concept...) I run to catch an earlier train — but end up all sweaty. While the computer is starting up I use the time to have a quick bite — but the pickle falls out of my sandwich. I resolved to compose my notes calmly and write them legibly so as not to lose any wonderful quotations. St. Francis de Sales used nature as an example: "Rivers that flow gently through the plain can carry large ships with heavy cargo; the rain that falls gently on the field makes it fertile. But roaring streams and raging torrents flood the land and are not suitable for ships, while heavy downpours and cloudbursts devastate the fields."

"He who rushes runs the danger of stumbling."
Solomon

The external order also has a deeper meaning. It leads to inner order. People who keep to a well-balanced tempo are in fact also practicing the basic elements of silence:

- LETTING GO. For example, those who have decided not to work in the evening will learn not to constantly think about work or the office, although it can take a while to internalize and apply this self-imposed rule. But in the end this results in having some "free" time and the necessary peace and quiet to enjoy these hours of leisure.
- PAUSING. When you make pausing for reflection a regular part of your everyday routine, it becomes twice as valuable. Life seems less superficial and more intense.
- INNER COMPOSURE. "Achieving silence" has an effect that is more like rest and relaxation. It seems to inherently lead to new ideas and discoveries, to a new experience and the intensification of the self. But this does not happen automatically; it requires daily practice.

About letting go and relaxing

Relaxing can be absolutely vital in many situations. People who stretch their

In the convent of Oberschönenfeld gardening is seen as a way of praying

bows too far will one day become overstretched themselves. The solution is letting go. For those who are prepared to do so, the phrase acquires a new meaning, because it marks the start of healing. To wait a moment. Letting go is associated with waiting, with care, including that of one's own person. The monks here quote a sentence from the gospel in order to help them let go more easily: "Let your will be done, not mine!" Though these words sound so familiar, they are difficult to say. Saying them implies giving up one's own will and freedom. Yet those who are prepared to say these words will paradoxically experience great freedom and relief: from restlessness, from problems, and from too many worries.

A Taoist proverb says: by doing nothing, everything gets done. Now, this does not mean just letting things take their own course or not becoming

At least at night

Denied the peace of night, no one can survive without ultimately becoming ill and going to pieces. "At least at night let your heart rest," Bishop Dom Helder Camara therefore admonished, "at least at night stop running; calm down those desires that drive you mad; try to let your dreams go to sleep. Surrender yourself finally and unreservedly into God's hands."

involved. Doing nothing should be understood as follows: looking for emptiness, the space in between, free time. This is found not only in monasteries and convents but also when we pray, meditate, or walk, when we attend a religious service or look at the sky. This "doing nothing," this emptiness, might seem at first glance to have no use at all. There is no movement, no productivity, and no net product. And yet: it is precisely in this in-between space, in this apparent vacuum, in the lines that have not yet been written, that things are rearranged and moments of strength, inspiration, and enlightenment appear. You are finally absolutely in the present, the only time (unlike the past and the future) that is real, that we can actually perceive and have at our disposal — and that we give too little heed to.

Quite suddenly, there is something before you that is intended just for you. An idea, or even an object. You suddenly have a good idea. Or you have a vision that looks like the solution to a problem and shows you how your life could proceed. When correctly used, this apparent standing still is in reality an unusually productive time: a hole in time through which the angels can slip through, or something like the buttonhole in your jacket that is needed to button it up.

But for this we also need silence, emptiness, and detachment from the normal world in which we have become all too enmeshed. In this silence we can hear ourselves, and we can hear God's word and inspiration. It is the famous rustling in the wind that can only be heard in total silence. We need not go to the desert for this—often such nothingness is simply the patient enduring of the little, ordinary, everyday difficulties that occur in life.

Exercise: The daily routine of the abbey of Oberschönenfeld

For the Cistercian nuns, everything has its place: silence, prayer, meditation, meal times, and work. You could take their day as example and try to bring more structure into your everyday life. Just try it out:

5:30 A.M.   Time set aside for personal meditation or prayer, then early coffee in the refectory.

6:30 A.M.   Lauds, the first of the canonical hours.

7:00 A.M.   Celebration of the Eucharist.

7:45 A.M.   Terce, second of the canonical hours; followed by breakfast in the refectory. End of the period of silence. The abbess hands out the tasks for the day.

8:30 A.M.   Work in the garden, bakery, bookshop, and bread shop.

12:00 MIDDAY Sext, third of the canonical hours

12:30 P.M.   Lunch in silence with reading, followed by a walk together to the cemetery.

1:15 P.M.   Free time, which must include a half hour of personal spiritual reading.

2:30 P.M.   Work time.

5:15 P.M.   Voluntary rosary praying in the chapel.

5:30 P.M.   Vespers, fourth of the canonical hours.

6:00 P.M.   Evening meal in silence with reading.

6:30 P.M.   Vigil, fifth of the canonical hours.

8:00 P.M.   Compline, sixth of the canonical hours.

8:30 P.M.   Start of the period of silence.

Silence

In another dimension: snowy peaks above the clouds near Oberstdorf, Allgäu

Taking the first step to inner peace

Step 1: Not speaking

Anselm Grün wrote: "Absolute tranquility is a step too far for us. It is only promised to us in death." Often even a small amount of silence is a great effort. A friend who spent a whole week in a Zen monastery, remaining silent throughout, said that in the only hour of the day that talking was allowed he burst out furiously: "I want to get out of here!" Nevertheless he stayed until the end.

Nuns spend a large part of their lives encloistered, in an area to which outsiders have no access. After the last prayer of the canonical hours each nun goes to her cell for the start of the "great silence," as Sister Annunziata described it. It lasts until the following morning. When the sisters see each other then, they do so without a word of greeting. It is only after breakfast that they are allowed to speak, and the next period of silence starts again at lunchtime. In fact, all mealtimes are silent. Usually the sisters also refrain from speaking when walking in the cloister.

The abbess of Oberschönenfeld, Ancilla Betting,

wrote that we try "today to be or to become a little like St. Benedict and St. Bernard and their companions were in the past: listening, loving, believing, persevering." She did not include "speaking."

Where they can, the sisters look for aids to help isolate themselves from the world. For instance, the habit represents seclusion both to themselves and to others. In the past, Trappists only communicated among themselves through sign language, and Carthusian monks, although living in a community, lived as if on their own in their tiny, Spartan cells. Their meals were handed to them through a flap next to the door. They ate, prayed, and contemplated God, in silence, voluntarily.

"If we want to live in peace, the peace must come from ourselves."

Jean-Jacques Rousseau

St. Benedict believed that silence was a prerequisite for the spiritual development of monks. He warned them against talking too much. Now and again we must even refrain from good conversation for the sake of silence. "Perfect followers will rarely be allowed to speak even in good, solemn, constructive conversations because of the importance of silence. It is indeed written: 'In many conversations you will be unable to escape sin.'" And elsewhere it is written: "Speaking and teaching are for the master, silence and listening are for the follower."

It is not the case that silence serves only a disciplinary function; it can also reveal other possibilities. St. Benedict equated it with listening, and explained it as follows: Silence gives you the opportunity to learn, to develop further, and to experience something new.

Step 2: Silence creates space

The sisters remain silent not because they do not like talking but because they like it too much, since they too like to have fun. Sister Annunziata told me about evenings in the convent when the nuns had a special celebration, on a saint's day or a sister's name day. On such occasions the nuns are allowed to speak and, contrary to the rule, they also spend the evening together. Sister Annunziata continued: "I often feel these evenings are like giggling parties." She also told me about mornings when the convent is full of guests. Then, in addition to all the organizational work of greeting the guests, making beds, and arranging meals, she also had to talk constantly, which she willingly did. But at midday she was horrified and thought to herself: *You haven't thought of God at all today!*

The first thing that a person keeping silence experiences is that it clears a space that had previously been occupied by talking. Silence frees this hitherto occupied space, and this space is vitally important in order to achieve peace and tranquility. Because:

- Those who speak are noisy. Those who are silent disturb neither themselves nor others.
- Those who speak are part of a dialogue. They are confronted with the lives of others, with what is important in these lives but also with what is unimportant. Those who speak direct their attention outward. Those who are silent direct their attention inwards.
- Those who speak are part of the world and the society in which they live. Those who are silent move away from it. They put some distance between themselves and the world. They leave their place for a while and admit a

Create silence

From *The Treasure of the Soul* by Søren Kierkegaard:

If I were a doctor and someone asked me: "What do you think should be done?" I would answer: "The first thing, the absolute condition that will enable something to be done, and thus the first thing that must be done: create silence, introduce silence. The word of God cannot be heard… create silence." Everything makes a noise; and in the same way that one says of a strong drink that it makes the blood boil, so in our time everything, even the most insignificant undertaking, the most unimportant communication, is only intended to excite the masses, the public, the din! And man, this clever creature, has become as it were sleepless in order to go on finding ever newer ways of increasing the din, in order to spread the roar and the meaningless as quickly and as much as possible … O create silence!

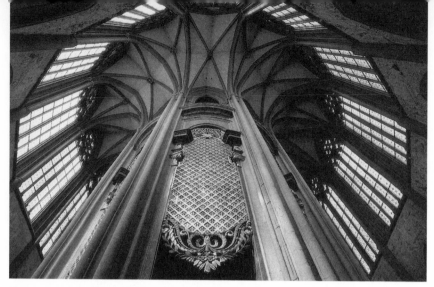

Eternity starts on Earth (Monastery of Zwettl)

sense of otherness into their lives.

This "otherness" can only be perceived in an atmosphere of peace. It is something full of mystery whose value is manifest in this very peace and that cannot be described in words but only experienced. The rules of the Carthusian order say: "The benefit and divine pleasure derived from the solitude and silence of isolation from friends can only be known by those who experience it." Silence is therefore not a torment for the Carthusian monks, but the beginning of blissful happiness.

It is the desert that we ourselves have created. In its vast space we rest and relax. It is not a luxury that you simply treat yourself to when you have time to spare. It is indispensable for a balanced life in accordance with the guidelines of moderation and the middle way.

Step 3: Awakening of ears and eyes

As soon as we stop speaking our other senses come into play, listening to the real self, the inner voice. In the same way that we cannot hear birds singing when we are at a busy road junction, so we have little chance of perceiving ourselves as we really are if we are always prattling with others and confronted with things that are not related to ourselves.

St. Francis of Assisi needed silence in order to hear the voice within himself and to better follow his path. For seven years he continually asked himself: "What do I want and what does God want of me?" Eventually, as he was sitting deep in prayer in a dilapidated church, he heard a decisive voice: "Francis, don't you see how broken down my house is? Go and rebuild it again!" Immediately it became clear to the saint what he had to do. As is written in the Old Testament: "When deep silence is enveloping the universe and it is midnight, this is when your almighty word descends from heaven" (The Book of Wisdom 19:14).

Step 4: Making contact with the mystery

Looking is associated with peacefulness, with silently noticing and perceiving things. I was looking at my surroundings like someone on vacation who finds everything about the new environment fascinating. I was now looking at my inner self with the same inquisitive gaze. Who was inside there? Then I was looking — at yet another level — at God. This is what St. Augustine meant when he said that through silence we get in touch with our longings again, instead of our cravings and addictions. The Benedictine monk Anselm Grün explained this as follows: "When I perceive my longing for God as the goad that keeps me alive, then everything falls into place. Whether I find success or not is no longer important."

"Give every day the chance to be the most beautiful in your life."
Mark Twain

This is the secret that the Carthusians experience as "divine pleasure," which they are unable to perceive in everyday life. We are bombarded daily

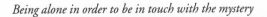

Being alone in order to be in touch with the mystery

289

The hour of silence
by Thomas Merton

"There must be an hour in the day when a man who must speak becomes silent. There must be an hour when a man of decisions puts aside his decisions, as if they had all vanished, and in which he learns a new wisdom: to distinguish the sun from the moon, the sea from the land, and the night sky from the curve of a hill."

with an endless stream of information, but this obscures what is really important — that mysterious "otherness," the source or the seed of life. The space created by silence opens up the possibility of making contact with this force again. This contact can give us great peace. The medieval Augustinian monk Thomas à Kempis found it more worthwhile to be "enclosed by four walls, taking care of one's salvation than to be performing miracles in the market and thereby lose sight of it." For "God and the holy angels will come to him" who follows this path.

I once got to know some autistic twins, Konstantin and Kornelius Keulen, who were both unable to speak but were able to communicate through a computer. The two boys always stressed how important silence was to them, and in this isolation they produced amazing ideas and writings. When Konstantin was eight, he wrote: "Living without speech gives me inner security… He who speaks destroys his world."

A tiresome intermediate stage: the arrival of the demons

Silence consciously undertaken is not simply an exercise. The resulting boredom is the least of the least of the problems, because there is no doubt that at the beginning — but also in the later stages — the long-ignored inner self will fly into a rage and go berserk. As happened to St. Anthony, we may be attacked by violent demons and fighting them will require a lot of energy. It will not be easy. "In your cell you will find what you all too often lose when you are outside," Thomas à Kempis said. "But when you are rarely in it, you will only remain in it very reluctantly." The only way of overcoming this reluctance is to try again and again. To practice being silent.

Sister Annunziata said that often when you are silent, a thousand things go through your head, and it is hopeless to try and push them out of it. But on other days, silence is simply the most beautiful thing that you could experience. "When I am successful, I do not rack my brains but just let things remain as they are."

"The world consists of numerous opportunities to love."
Søren Kierkegaard

Speaking

In order to be silent in the right manner, you must also use the right words when speaking. St. Francis of Assisi advised his brothers that "when they go into the world they must not scold… but they must be gentle, peaceable, and unassuming, obedient and humble, while they speak with propriety to all."

When necessary, monks have an obligation to use words. So, St. Benedict recommends that the abbot discuss problems. "Wavering brothers" should be comforted by the others through conversation so that they are not overcome by deep sorrow. And "he who has nothing to give another can at least give him a good word." St. Benedict also quoted the Bible: "A good word is better than the best gift."

Exercise: Now be silent!

This exercise is both easy and difficult.
Take time and be silent. Find a place where you cannot be reached, not even by a cell phone.
Now very consciously, try
- not to speak,
- to create space for yourself and for God,
- to rest in this space,
- to listen to and look at your inner self,
- to make contact with the mystery.

But remember that you may experience a lack of enthusiasm, anger, boredom, and frustration. These are the demons who want to prevent you from achieving inner peace.

Retreat

Architectural tranquility: Romanesque cloister in the former convent of St. John the Baptist of the Premonstratensian order, Steingaden, Upper Bavaria

Finding a quiet place

"I went to the woods because I wished to live deliberately, to front only the essential facts of life, and see if I could not learn what it had to teach."

Henry David Thoreau

St. Bernard, an early member of the Cistercian order and its most important as well as its most controversial personality, loudly denounced the images of saints in the Roman Church, the embellishment of cloisters and any kind of ornamentation or inlaid decoration, "whose floor that must be walked upon is a flurry of pattern." In ornament we would see "such a wonderful variety of different creatures" that we "would prefer to busy ourselves with them and marvel at such beauty all day long rather than think about God's law." According to St. Bernard's ideal, bare spaces and rooms would promote concentration. In the regulations about building and art issued by the General Chapter of 1134 it was said: "We do not allow any pictures or sculptures in our churches or anywhere in our monasteries, because these would attract our attention and therefore frequently detract from the good practice of meditation…"

The church in Oberschönenfeld is baroque. It is richly decorated with paintings, decorative elements, and a wealth of gold. There are statues of saints, angels, and representations of Jesus. The whole building is filled with works of art, and there are wonderful frescoes on the ceiling as well as an Infant Christ from Prague, dating from 1754. When I tactfully asked Sister Annunziata how this church fitted in with the order's philosophy, which was one based on simplicity, she replied frankly as usual: "The church was a blow to me when I arrived here. All this rococo can be quite oppressive, and there is not much to be seen of what St. Bernard advocated."

A house of emptiness and order

The baroque church at Oberschönenfeld was a reflection of the spirit of the time, newly built after a period of war and destruction. Sister Annunziata and the other nuns accepted it and even came to love it. On the other hand, its original architecture was exclusively geared to meeting the needs of conventual life, reflecting the position of the Cistercians as a strict contemplative order. The convent complex, a closed entity consisting of solid buildings with red pitched roofs, looks peaceful and light. The yellow-ochre and white façade gives it a reserved friendliness, open and closed at the same time. Then there is the little door through which the visitor enters the large convent — very symbolic for a community that wants as little contact as possible with the outside world but yet welcomes guests.

"I can discover a beautiful oasis anywhere in the large desert of life."
Heinrich Heine

Everything in its construction has been carefully thought out, down to the smallest detail. As a result, the architecture makes the order's strict daily routine as smooth as possible, thus contributing enormously to the silence and peace of the community.

The Rule leaves the nuns very little time to do what they like, and they tend to stay within their enclosed part of the convent. Thus, as a guest and a small human being, I have this large building with its long, bright corridors almost entirely to myself. Or rather: this large house has me. The house draws one into its emptiness, which must be endured. I soon felt a little abandoned, but this undisturbed emptiness also brought a great sense of relief. No one runs, no one is in a rush, there are no radios with cheap jingles or computers making noises, and everything is in its place. The books

Empty corridor in the convent of Oberschönenfeld

are in the bookcases and the flowers on the window sill. Indeed, there is not much more here. As Sister Annunziata said of her convent: "The place works, we do not need to do anything more." The atmosphere is clearly good for the soul. In the same way as the nuns' day is structured, so is the convent, a basic principle that was already present in the Creation. God gave order to the world, distinguishing between night and day, and separating land from water. This was not a neutral system but a meaningful one: "God saw that it was good." (Genesis 1:10)

How St. Benedict built his house

Throughout the centuries, the Christian West has been "greatly influenced by the spread and power of monasteries," as the author Wolfgang Urban observed. "Monasteries were the silent, powerful centers of society." This was why St.

Benedict also stipulated in his Rule what a monastery should look like. Again the aim was isolation from the outside world and its distractions. It "should, whenever possible, be built in such a way that all the necessary amenities, namely, water, mill, and garden, should be situated within the monastery complex; so that the various types of craft can be practiced there. So the monks will not need to leave the monastery, because that is usually not good."

The layout within the monastery was planned to provide particular places for each activity of the day: praying, reading, eating, and sleeping. It also included a place for the sick and a place for guests. In addition, it was very important that the monks should be able to go quickly from their work to the place where they pray, from the place where they pray to where they eat. There was no need to go long distances, which would have been inconsistent with their understanding of a concentrated life.

"A real yearning has been satisfied here, silence, solitude, but also a sense of community and daily encounters."

Le Corbusier, visiting the Carthusian monastery of Ema near Florence

Besides the practical aspects there were also spiritual requirements. The external appearance had to reflect the values of the community. This was mirrored in the hierarchy of the individual buildings. "The church, the house of God and the place where the gospel is read, had to be the largest, the most magnificent, and the most dominant building of the monastery complex," notes Wolfgang Braunfels in his book *Monasteries of Western Europe*. Most churches face east and this is the case at Oberschönenfeld, the nuns and sisters praying towards the rising sun, the light that is the symbol of Christ. Second in importance was the eleventh-century chapter house. Although not included in St. Benedict's Rule, in this building a chapter of the Rule was read every day. Here the monks were encouraged to read constantly and to internalize the monastery's regulations. Then came the refectory, a place that catered not only to physical but also spiritual needs. The other parts of the monastery were also intended to promote the faith of the community, whether in the cloisters, the dormitory or bedrooms, or through paintings on the walls, the stained glass windows, and the decoration of the floor.

In the Middle Ages a uniform monastic architecture developed, inspired by this pattern and culminating in the monastery of St. Gallen. Its plan, probably drawn up by Abbot Haito of Reichenau, stipulated precisely what activity should take place where. As the monks also performed social tasks — running schools, looking after guests, and brewing beer — the monastery had to provide special places for these activities. But all these public places were situated on the outer perimeter of the monastery complex. This was to preserve the

Cloister with column decorated with statues of the Evangelists in the cathedral of Ste. Marie in St-Bertrand-de-Cominges, Haute Garonne, France

atmosphere of peace in the community. In addition, special silent places were created in which one could not only restore and reenergize oneself, but where one could also become aware of the link between one's own existence and the cosmos: places such as a little chapel, recesses in the corridors, benches, and summerhouses in the garden. The element of water was present in the form of fountains, and nature was represented in carefully laid-out gardens.

The cloister, the heart of the monastery

The cloister is the heart of the monastery. Its architecture and design encourage silence. Today it stands as a fascinating architectural jewel where one can hear and almost touch silence. Here the perception of one's own self that is usually suppressed within us can develop.

The ideal cloister is a square arrangement of covered ambulatories, built in the form of arcades round the inner courtyard of the monastery. It usually consists of four sides that open up onto a carefully tended garden. The cloister may also be used for processions within the monastery as well as for meditation and relaxation. The little adjoining garden represents a piece of paradise on Earth, a symbol of eternal bliss.

Originally all the buildings of the monastery could be entered from the cloister (and usually only from there, and only through one door). There was no communication between the individual rooms. As a result, movement was guided along particular routes that influenced the layout of the building. In the words of the ancient monastic building regulations, the aim was "to avoid at all cost anything that could disturb the peace, tranquility, and contemplative atmosphere of the monastery, such as loud shouting, slamming doors, noisy footsteps, and so on. It is very important not to break the silence in such places, but particularly in the church, cloisters, and scriptorium."

Walking around the cloister and through its uniform arcades can be in itself a form of meditation. One can find here many topics for reflection:
- the endless road on which humanity finds itself;
- the incessant forward momentum;
- the endeavor to move forward without the compulsion to reach a goal;
- the light in the cloister and also the darkness caused by the columns and arches;

Martha and Mary

The seclusion behind monastery or convent walls, the peace and silence, are often mistakenly seen as an escape from the world. In the parable of Martha and Mary, Jesus shows us the importance of simply being. This does not mean indifferent passivity but rather alert attentiveness. And often those who remain silent in their apparently inactive life are much more energetic and intense than those who are active, always rushing to do things but never getting to the point.

Jesus arrived in a village and was warmly welcomed by Martha and Mary. While Martha was busy preparing to feed their guest, Mary sat down at his feet and just listened to him. When Martha asked him whether it did not worry him that she was having to do all the work on her own, Jesus replied: "Martha, Martha, you are worried and distracted by many things; there is need of only one thing. Mary has chosen the better part, which will not be taken away from her" (Luke 10:38).

- the internal and external, which belong together in the form of action and contemplation;
- the link between the building that protects and the openness of nature, between the solid house and the cascades of light.

The frugality of the Cistercians

The Cistercians were established as an order in 1098, separate from the other orders, pursuing greater isolation from the outside world, greater poverty, and stricter observance of the Rule, because they believed that monastic principles were no longer being properly followed elsewhere. When they did this they saw no reason to abandon the system of the cloister, although they modified other features of monastic architecture.

In Münsterschwarzach, breaks are as much part of the day as work and prayer

This was first of all reflected in the choice of site. Other monasteries were built on hilltops, visible from afar, close to heaven, and true to the word of Christ: "You are the light of the world. A city built on a hill cannot be hid." In contrast, the Cistercians preferred to be concealed. But this too is a path that reflects an aspect of Jesus, namely his "life in seclusion." This refers to the work of God that is not visible from the outside; the inner, humble path of faith. Accordingly, the Cistercians built all their monasteries in locations similar to that of the motherhouse of Cîteaux in France, on the edge of a river in a valley, away from human settlements. The same ground plan and lay-

Holy numbers

Cloisters reveal examples of the monastic interest in numbers and measurements, whose symbolism is extensive. One finds, for example, four arches with three supports. When multiplied this gives the number of apostles: twelve. That such correspondences were intentional has been pointed out by Rolf Legler, who refers to an inscription at the monastery of Vaison-la-Romaine dating from 1150 that reads, rather cryptically: "I beg of you, brothers, pass through the region of the North wind when you walk through the cloister; then you will come to the South. The triple fiery ones will set fire to the four-fold nest so that it will be added to the twelve stone vessels. Peace be on this house."

This means that the North should be overcome because it is in a sinful state, while the South, which is the site of the church and salvation, is the goal. The number three corresponds to the Holy Trinity, while the number four corresponds to the four cardinal points symbolizing the earth.

out was followed in all their monasteries. The churches were built without towers, and houses opposite the monastery gate were forbidden, as were stained glass windows. A document of 1134 stipulated that: "Stained glass windows must be removed within a time limit of two years, otherwise the abbot, prior, and cellar master must fast forthwith every sixth day on bread and water until the windows are changed." Crosses could only be made of wood, and walls could not be plastered. "We see Cistercians wearing gray-white wool and linen habits that are neither bleached nor colored walking among pale grey walls," wrote Wolfgang Braunfels. But paradoxically, it was the best qualities of the Cistercians that led to the decline of their high ideals. Braunfels explained this as follows: "The great effort and hard work expected from the monks brought about prosperity. With prosperity came worldly obligations." Meanwhile the rejection of decoration and pictures concentrated their ambition onto working in stone: "Where color and statues were forbidden, stonemasonry reached new perfection."

It was not only their appearance in habit or veil, but the buildings of the monks and nuns, every space and every detail, that contributed to the realization of the ideal. The monks were aware that true peace and silence could only be achieved in quiet places. Only when external tranquility is guaranteed can we collect ourselves, relax, concentrate on ourselves, and search for the divine. Ultimately these places of tranquility were meant to offer an

Exercise: A place of peace

Experience a day of peace. Take a break from work or leave the office earlier than usual. Go for a stroll on your way home.
You can find places of tranquility everywhere, not just behind the walls of a monastery or convent:

- *It may be a church, even if it is situated on a busy street. You have probably walked past one for years and at most checked the time on its clock. Inside it will be cool, with a dim light, and it will be quiet.*

- *Or an old churchyard. Every day at midday the nuns of Oberschönenfeld go and pay a visit to the cemetery. Here they not only benefit from the peace and quiet, but they also encounter death — and with it also life.*

- *Or you can sit on the bank of a river whose smooth, flowing water will draw your gaze, while the sound of it rushing by will drown the noise of voices and the barking of dogs — and you will find yourself meditating.*

Earthly foretaste of the eternal city that John predicted in the last book of the bible, Revelation: "And in the spirit he carried me away to a great, high mountain and showed me the holy city Jerusalem coming down out of heaven from God. It has the glory of God… And the city has no need of sun nor moon to shine on it, for the glory of God is its light" (Revelation 21:10–11, 23).

When looking for a place of peace in one's immediate surroundings, Sister Scholastica of the Oberschönenfeld monastery recommends choosing a particular place and a particular time. If you have to decide every day where and when you will pray, you will not be able to concentrate so well on the actual experience. This place could also be a little corner in your own dwelling that you have set aside for prayer with a cross, an icon, or a picture. It may also be an entire forest. Many people prefer to walk while they meditate. The old monks reflected on their faith, meditated, and repeated prayers while walking. Or they concentrated on a sentence or image, or just gazed at nature. But it is important that you should feel good in your "desert place," that it should suit you.

You can always find a special place; in fact, we carry it within ourselves to a certain extent, as the Carmelite nun Edith Stein wrote in 1938: "God is indeed within us, the entire most Holy Trinity. If only one could understand how to build a well-closed cell within one's inner self and withdraw to it as often as possible, then one would want for nothing anywhere in the world."

On listening

The cross is a symbol of the power of humility

The benefits of humility and obedience

False humility and its consequences

"Humility is man's own dignity before God."

Gertrud von le Fort

Sister Annunziata was twenty-eight years old when she completed her novitiate and solemnly promised to practice the three evangelical counsels or counsels of perfection.

At an age when other women were having their first children, she took a vow of chastity.

While her contemporaries in the outside world were doing all they could to emancipate themselves from their parents and other authorities, she took a vow of obedience.

And while young people in the outside world were saving to buy property, she gave away everything she owned and took a vow of poverty.

The fundamental attitude behind this radical departure from the world is humility, not a particularly popular virtue. Today, humility, along with obedience, is not highly regarded. We associate the concept with anxious, weak people, submissive and without a will of their own — puppets who can even become dangerous when the wrong people pull the strings. As is well known, this attitude can lead to the oppression of entire peoples. In this connection, André Louf, the abbot of a French Trappist monastery, speaks of neurotic humility. Louf gives the example of a fictitious monk who in his enthusiasm to follow the rules of the order projected the image of the perfect monk. But because he had to live up to his own expectations, he was under constant pressure. This was not conducive to inner peace.

It is therefore easy to understand that this monk would rebel at some point, particularly because this kind of humility involved the suppression of his true nature. He ended up angry and defiant, rejecting all guidance. His life had become a struggle to shake off authority, and his peace of mind had vanished.

"I will listen for the word of God."

Psalm 85:9

"We are subject to the same anxiety," André Louf observed, "fearful that we will become enslaved by authority. So we throw away all obligations: we want freedom at any price and sever all connections."

For Louf, this is the point that we have reached today. "No doubt we understand that our neurotic humility is very damaging, even crippling. But now we can no longer accept any form of humility." The large number of people leaving the Church is part of this phenomenon. People rebel against submission that they see as a meaningless pretense. They have lost a sense of its value, and representatives of the Church often make it difficult for them to recognize its importance.

Why true humility helps us achieve calmness and find ourselves

Sister Annunziata had absolute confidence in God, and her humility was entirely directed towards Him. What did this involve? "To see my own limitations and to accept my weaknesses. The point is that I accept myself," she explained. Those who accept the aspects of themselves that they do not like can improve without constant self-reproach. They can be compassionate towards themselves and as a result find inner peace.

Sister Annunziata smiled. In the past she had wanted to change the world and convert everyone. She gave up on this a long time ago, not out of frustration or failure, but because she found humility in reality. "I do not aim

Humility requires courage

for things," she quoted from the psalms, "that are too wonderful for me and too high."

Sister Annunziata learned, on the one hand, not to take herself too seriously in her role on Earth but, on the other hand, to take her own development extremely seriously, because that was the only key to peace, to life in general. "Where are you if you do not feel at ease with yourself? And if you run all round the world but miss out on your salvation, what is the use of all this haste and running?"

"For all who exalt themselves will be humbled, and those who humble themselves will be exalted."
Luke 14:11

Thomas à Kempis asked. And he continued: "When you have found peace and you really want to be in harmony with yourself and your God, then you must let go of everything else and only concentrate on yourself." This did not mean dwelling on oneself or leading a selfish way of life, but searching for one's own path.

The philosopher and mystic Simone Weil found her own humility while traveling: "In 1937 I spent two wonderful days in Assisi. When I was there alone in the little twelfth-century Romanesque chapel of Santa Maria degli Angeli, that unparalleled wonder of purity where St. Francis so often prayed, I felt compelled by something stronger than myself to throw myself to my knees for the first time in my life." To quote Thomas à Kempis again: "What is the use of being able to have erudite debates about the Holy Trinity if you do not have humility…?"

The telephone occupies a rather unimportant place in the convent of Loccum

Such humility need not be put on show. "True humility will not appear humble," wrote St. Frances de Sales. We keep coming back to this point: if one wants to find peace, one must concentrate on finding one's own path, not someone else's, no matter what other people think of it.

Humility leads to inner peace because it teaches one:

- *to accept one's own weaknesses:*
  Being aware that I have faults does not mean that I always have to be at odds with myself. I can try to work on my weaknesses, but in a gentle way.

- *to go through life realistically:*
  I know that my possibilities are limited and that I cannot save the whole world. If I try to do what is within my power, I shall feel in harmony with my goals. And as a result I shall find it easier to go forward.

- *to concentrate on oneself:*
  I can only achieve peace if I perceive myself as a whole person. If, on the other hand, I only look outwards and orient myself by other people, I shall not find the way that is suitable to me.

- *to experience truth:*
  If I manage to follow my own way, as the monks say, then I am in touch with the Divine. My actions are not for show but dictated by an inner logic and aesthetic.

It must hurt

St. Benedict was fully aware that humility and obedience could only be achieved at the cost of great pain. In his Rule he urged the monks to climb a twelve-runged ladder of humility. The ladder was, as it were, the link between heaven and Earth, with angels going up and down it, just as Jacob had seen in his dream in the Bible. Proceeding step by step, the important thing was not doing what you wanted to but showing obedience, "even when it is difficult and unpleasant." In addition, the monk should refrain from speaking and even "consider himself more humble and lowly than everyone."

Recommendations like these seem strange and outdated to us. Self-development is now a top priority. To make sacrifices, to submit sometimes, to accept frustration, or even to accept pain and suffering, is usually seen as

Obedience has to do with listening

The obedience that goes hand in hand with humility should not be seen as slavish submission. "It is a kind of dialogue," Sister Annunziata explained. "Obedience involves listening." In other words, it means being alert to the divine, the essence within us, as well as being alert to one's fellow human beings. St. Benedict wrote in the second chapter of his Rule: "In this way, through the effort of obedience, you will return to what you left behind through the sluggishness of disobedience."

Obedience means distinguishing the important from the unimportant

When some nuns declared a few years ago that they could no longer pray at twenty to five in the morning, Sister Annunziata was not very happy. She had always liked these early morning solemn prayers. But she fell into line with the decision of the majority. "We live together. If I am always in the opposition, it does not do me or the others any good."

Obedience means doing what is necessary

A few years ago I visited a hermit in his retreat. Heinrich Engelmann lived alone in a hut in the Ruhr. There he meditated in silence for several hours every day. When his mother became seriously ill, he did not hesitate and went back to the noisy city of Dortmund, where he looked after her for several years. When his mother died, he made her coffin himself and then returned to his retreat. While striving to achieve humility, it is often necessary to discard self-will.

This can easily be misunderstood. Heinrich Engelmann showed what this really meant: he had put aside his own decision to live in isolation and taken on the responsibility for his mother. This "peace within himself" went hand in hand with making the right decision. In due course he was able to return to his life of seclusion.

Obedience means not worrying

In the Sermon on the Mount, Jesus pointed out that humility and obedience can also mean liberation and inner peace: "Do not worry about your life, what you will eat or what you will drink, or about your body, what you will wear." These words are often criticized. They seem to say that we should not worry about the future but should instead spend our money as we like, and indulge in parties instead of working. But this is not what Jesus meant. It is more about making the right assessment about things. If our material well-being is the only thing that we think about, then we will become chronically anxious. "Is not the life more than meat, and the body more than raiment?" Jesus continued.

Worrying is not productive. We seize up. Then we can't perceive what others need. Jesus: "Which of you by worrying can prolong your life by even a little?"

In the training undergone by monks, it is said that they are allowed to look after their interests but only insofar as it is in their power, which is limited. In all humility and obedience, a monk should leave everything else to God, who also feeds the birds without them having to sow or harvest.

negative or embarrassing. But at the same time we fail to recognize the fundamental importance of suffering, and by suppressing it, we miss out on a necessary experience. Indeed, struggling and enduring is essential to achieve maturity and to become strong. It can truly be said that there is no progress or real achievement without pain and suffering.

A degree of pain is necessary in order to push back the outer walls. Pain is necessary to see what lies behind things, what is really happening, to acquire true knowledge, and to penetrate to the heart of the matter. No life is without pain. Buddha went as far as to say: "Life is suffering." In yoga, the pain starts mundanely with the stretching of stiff calves, shoulders, and thorax. On an intellectual level this can be interpreted as overcoming boundaries and pushing towards the essential — towards the goal. As Jesus said: "One who endures to the end will be saved."

I became aware of my own weakness during the birth of my son Paul. Beforehand I had imagined that I would be courageous and able to take the pain. Secretly I was proud of having rather a high pain threshold, and I

"Man is never greater than when he submits."
Pope John XXIII

Humility means going your own way
by Peter Bichsel

At court there were strong, clever people. The king was the king, the women were beautiful and the men brave, the priest was devout, and the kitchen maid was hardworking. Only Columbine was nothing. If somebody said: "Come on, Columbine, fight with me," Columbine would say: "I am weaker than you." If someone said:

"Do you trust yourself to jump over the stream?" Columbine would reply: "No, I do not trust myself to do that." Then when the king asked: "Columbine, what do you want to become?" Columbine replied: "I do not want to become anything, I am already something, I am Columbine."

wanted to demonstrate it at the birth. Then the contractions started and became increasingly worse. At first I resisted well, but there came a point when I could not go on any longer; I simply gave up. I was worn out, finished; I felt wretched. I'd fall asleep for a few minutes and then wake up again. It seemed as if the pain would go on forever. This continued for about an hour. I just lay there and tried to push everything away. But then I felt a surge of energy. Suddenly the contractions became stronger. The pain was still much too much for me but, cursing loudly, I held out somehow and the labor continued. An hour later my wonderful baby came into the world.

Exercise: meditate on humility

You can do this in various ways:

- *Choose a picture that expresses humility and allow it to work on you.*
- *Take on an attitude of humility by kneeling and lowering your head. Holding this posture for a while is in itself no easy task.*
- *Look for a quotation that appeals to you, perhaps something by St. Teresa of Ávila, who described humility as "change into truth." Repeat the phrase aloud or silently over and over again and listen to it within you.*
- *Write the word "humility" on a piece of paper and draw lines joining it to related concepts or words that come into your head.*

Finding peace in daily life

This too can be a desert: a track through the fields near the abbey of Oberschönenfeld

*The peace of the soul
and the noise of the world*

*T*here are always some days in the convent, said
Sister Annunziata, when things are completely chaotic
and you are far from enjoying peace of mind. If guests
happen to telephone then and explain longingly: "I
would like to spend a few quiet days in the convent,"
the nun answering would often say: "Yes, so would I,
really!"

So what would a perfect day be like for you, I
asked the sister, and suggested an answer: there
would be no telephone calls, hardly anything to do,
no one tugging at your habit, and you would have
all the time you wanted to be silent, to immerse yourself in prayer, and to enjoy the peace. But Sister
Annunziata shook her head vigorously: "No, no. A
perfect day can also be very hectic, the telephone may
ring umpteen times, and I may have to deal with people I would much prefer not to see. But if I succeed
in keeping a peaceful mind throughout the day and
direct my thoughts to God, not allowing Him to vanish from my heart — then the day is a unity, such as
I wish for."

When St. Benedict demanded that prayer should dominate the day, he did not mean that monks and nuns should drop everything and pray all day long with hands clasped. After all, according to St. Benedict's definition, every action can be performed as a prayer to God. Inspired by their faith, the sisters therefore try to approach life, in whatever form, with fearlessness. This implies treating life respectfully and attentively without becoming distracted. Again, there are rules that help them in this: stabilitas, simplicity, and change.

1. *Stabilitas*: Finding one's own place

Enjoying peace of mind in everyday life means remaining true to oneself. St. Benedict also required *stabilitas loci* from the monks. Basically, this refers to the promise to spend one's entire life in a particular monastery and to remain tied to one place. But *stabilitas loci* also means to remain true to oneself and one's chosen way of life. Like silence, this commitment to a place acts like a medicine that can lead to inner peace, because many factors causing restlessness are immediately ruled out by *stabilitas*:

"Let all things be done with moderation."
St. Benedict

- The constant moving from one place to the other, but also from one opinion to another, from today's fashion to tomorrow's.
- The daily questions: Perhaps I would prefer to move to the country? Or am I a city person? Am I in the right job or should I change?
- The numerous small decisions that we have to make every day because of excessive mobility; the constant weighing up of choices that is so exhausting, and the constant questioning of things that could simply be left as they are, because we cannot change them anyway.

"The word *stabilitas* is derived from the Latin *stare*, to stand," abbess Ancilla Betting explained. That means "that man has his position and his place, and that he knows what and who he is." Knowing oneself "at home" is essential if we are to find our true identity. The nun continued: "*Stabilitas* is a challenge because it inevitably confronts every man with himself, it asks about his location, his position, and whether he has a position." In addition: "Remaining true to yourself is not possible without 'becoming steadfast.' And by 'becoming steadfast' everyone is allowed to be how he is." The abbess

One needs to practice to find peace in meditation

continued: "The best and the innermost will only develop fully if one can grow and mature freely and without pressure."

Sister Annunziata stressed that *stabilitas* was a challenge, especially when nothing at all happens. No new discovery is made, and there are no spectacular experiences when praying or meditating. Then it is difficult to remain true to your path, not to doubt. When you learn a new sport, initially you make rapid progress. A soccer player learns to control the ball, how not to end up on his back when shooting, and to use his body to keep the ball from an opponent. But when he has a certain command of the game, his progress will seem much slower, and sometimes he will even feel he is going backwards. This is why the search for stability requires considerable patience and faith.

But if you have both patience and faith, *stabilitas* can create space, make you alert, and lead to inner strength. You have probably had days when you feel in complete harmony with yourself. You could even be sitting in a dark office from morning till night, yet feel great. On those days, you are sharing some of the monks' peace.

2. Simplicity — in the here and now

According to research, the majority of people spend more time thinking of the past or the future than the present. They dream of tomorrow and work out what might happen (and never does happen). Or they dwell on what happened yesterday, agonizing about decisions and developments that cannot be changed any more. Thus they end up as prisoners of history, which literally takes over their life. In the Bible, when God saved Lot and his family from Sodom's depravity he ordered them not to look back. Whoever looks back will become ossified, turned into a column of salt or an old grouch who takes no pleasure in the present, the only time that we really have.

To maintain one's peace of mind and stay in the present are among the most important tasks of daily life in the monastery. "I only have the present moment," Sister Annunziata explained, "and it is the art of spiritual life to shape it meaningfully." This includes not only the big things but equally the smallest ones. The image of an old woman came to my mind. I was watching as she was eating ice cream. She was sitting on a chair in the early spring sun, with her coat on and a handbag on her lap, her hair slightly tangled. In front of her was a small portion of ice cream with whipped cream, and it was the only thing on this crowded cafe terrace that occupied her. She slipped the spoon slowly into the ice cream, put it in her mouth, and with relish let the ice cream melt on her tongue. She took a long time over this, but she must have enjoyed it enormously. To give things time, treating them with respect and attention; this too is part of peace. St. Francis de Sales explained it as follows: "Conscientiousness and care do not disturb the peace and serenity of the soul, but anxiety, haste and agitated bustle do."

There is an interesting pattern in the history of the abbey of Oberschönenfeld: the fact that all the abbesses have died just before they could finish their life's work. None of them could ever complete it. Mother Willibürgis died in 1262, shortly before the completion of the first convent church built of stone that she had begun. Abbess Ursula died in 1522 just before

For monks, reading is also a form of meditation

Meeting oneself

by Anselm Grün

Jesus sent his disciples off to drive away impure spirits. Proudly they came back and told him what they had done and learned (Mark 6:30). Then he invited them to accompany him to an isolated spot where they could be on their own. They were to rest: "They had had no leisure even to eat."

Jesus invited his disciples to detach themselves from the world for a time. He wanted them to come with him to an isolated place where others did not have access. Jesus had evidently noticed that he and his disciples could not always just give. They also needed their own space where they could concentrate entirely on themselves. In Greek this is called *kat'idian*, meaning "They must exist for themselves." It can also be interpreted that they must feel at home with themselves, live with themselves, or meet themselves.

For any kind of work or any meeting with others, we need spaces in which we can also encounter ourselves. Otherwise we will lose ourselves. If we no longer have any contact with ourselves, our encounters with others will be empty. We will not really be able to help them.

Jesus invited the disciples to rest. The Greek word for this is *anapausasthe*. People can have rest during a break. Many people complain that they cannot find peace, but when they are on

new altars were erected in the church, and Mother Hildegardis, who had commissioned the baroque architect and master builder with the rebuilding of the convent church, died in 1722 without having seen the result.

This may tell us something: to do things as well as we can simply because they are waiting to be done or because they are necessary, not in order to be praised, to change the world, to go down in history, or to become famous. Even when we fail. "In our journey through life it does not matter whether holiday, they cannot bear the calm. They stop themselves from achieving inner peace. Evidently it is not just a matter of external peace and quiet. In order to find inner peace, one must confront one's own truth. Those who cannot bear their own company will not experience peace of mind. Constant activity is a way of avoiding inner stillness.

The early monks believed we should let our thoughts and feelings stream through us. We should give something to them and take something from them. If we try and drive them away they will pursue us. We must view them with affection. Only then will they give us peace and leave us in tranquility.

We are not as friendly and relaxed as we would like. We are far from having reached our middle way. We keep being thrown off the middle of the road. Humility is needed to recognize this. We need compassion and sympathy for that which is within us. So I wish that you all will enjoy living with yourself in solitude and find pleasure in reaching it, in order to become one with yourself and God, which is the reason for life.

Father Anselm Grün is the cellarer of the Benedictine abbey of Münsterschwarzach and a highly regarded Christian author.

> *"Come away to a deserted place all by yourselves and rest a while."*
>
> Jesus Christ

we achieve all the goals we have set ourselves," said the Benedictine monk Ambrose Tinsley, "but that we should show patience when we do not succeed in something and then make a new start."

3. Change — in order to begin anew

Much of what we hear about peace from the heads of convents and monasteries or from counselors sounds fascinating and convincing. Much of this

Inspiration in the cloister. A painting class in the convent of Geras

we ourselves have been aware of for a long time, and meanwhile some of the teachings and mnemonic phrases have become part of our general awareness of what we should really do. But we seldom succeed in achieving this peace. Sister Annunziata said she had 359 days in the year that were not perfect. Thomas à Kempis even said: "If only we could have lived just one day well and properly on Earth!" The Bible also warns us that we will fail again and again. Eve could not resist temptation and ate the forbidden fruit. On the other hand, the Bible also shows that it is possible to turn away from evil and follow another path, to turn back and find oneself, to find one's own peace. The town of Nineveh repented and was spared by God from terrible destruction. Perhaps this is the secret.

Turning back simply means mending our ways and returning to the straight path from which we keep straying — changing our behavior. But we can only increase our peace of mind if it is accompanied by greater understanding. This also seems to be the secret.

As a child I always found confession awful. You went to confession, said a few Our Fathers and Hail Marys, then off you went and sinned again. The process was very like going to the dentist: before going you were anxious and afterwards you were happy to have survived it. You quickly rattled off the prayers, helped mother do the dishes, and it was all over.

But doing penance is meaningless if it remains a purely formal act. "On the other hand, reformers rightly pointed to the fundamental concept of God's salvation in Christ and appealed to the determination of life through the mind," wrote the theologian Otto B. Knoch. "Turning one's life around is only possible through the mind and inner understanding." The people in the city of Nineveh not only fasted and wore their penitential robes, but the king also announced: "All of you must change and turn away from your evil doing and the injustice that clings to your hands."

Today, as in the past, it is not a question of fear and intimidation but of conscious change. Only the experience of an about-face, say the monks, is of value and can lead to peace. Then we will no longer be tossed here and there but will suddenly live our lives quite differently, with an inner certainty of what is important. Within this context the concept of sin seems quite different. Otto B. Knoch defines it as the "not-realization of one's own self."

A fresh start for everyone –
Why a bishop can never live like a Carthusian monk

In their vows, the Cistercian nuns promise that they will make a new start every day. Abbess Ancilla Betting explained: "This expresses the fact that monastic life is never finished, but that it is constantly in process and is subject to constant change. This daily fresh start gives each nun a way of life that helps her reach maturity as an integrated being, which is what she is aiming for....She can experience this renewal if she opens up to God every day."

Life is perpetual striving. Here Sister Hildegard was referring to the "letting go," the "abandoning of oneself to God" that must be practiced to one's last breath. To illustrate what she meant, Sister Hildegard told the story of an old monk who cried out on his deathbed: "I am now slowly beginning to become a monk!" He could also have said: "I am beginning to become a man," because conversion is possible for everyone anywhere. "I therefore address my words to you, whoever you are, if only you resist your self-will," St. Benedict wrote in his prologue. And St. Francis de Sales also pointed out that change only has value if it is compatible with daily life. "Real piety does not spoil anything; on the contrary, it makes everything perfect. If it cannot be combined with an honest profession or trade, then it is definitely not real." He stressed the importance of the individual way: "Would it be normal if a bishop wanted to live like a Carthusian monk? Or if a married couple cared as little about money as the Capuchin friars? Can a workman spend all day in church like the monks? On the other hand, can monks in the contemplative orders be available to everyone like the bishop?"

Monastic advice for peace and relaxation from morning till evening:

1. Start the day with meditation or prayer. This gives you a good rhythm for the rest of the day, prevents restlessness, creates order in the mind, and promotes concentration.

2. Then prepare yourself mentally for the day before you. St. Francis de Sales advised: "Reflect on the fact that the present day was given to you so that through it you can earn eternal life. Make up your mind to make good use of the day in achievement.... Consider in advance what jobs, transactions, and opportunities you will encounter today to serve God, what temptations might come your way..."

3. Short periods of meditation or prayer during the day will help you to deal with the effects of stress, to regain your strength, and to concentrate on the essential. This could be simply: "God, help me," which is what Sister Annunziata asked when she felt uncertain during her early days in the convent. Sister Scholastica suggested that quick prayers could be used in situations of everyday life, such as when the telephone rings. The New Testament includes quite a few of these short prayers: "God, be merciful to me, a sinner," prayed the tax collector, while the blind beggar who was cured by Jesus asked, "Jesus, son of David, have mercy on me." There are other ways. Make the sign of the cross, repeat a familiar word several times, or pause for a short time on the stroke of the hour. As abbot

Gregor Hanke said: "These little aids influence our work like a plus sign in a math assignment that makes something positive."

4. Try to look at unpleasant things, difficult tasks, and disagreeable people from another point of view. As Thomas à Kempis said: "There is no creature so small and insignificant that it does not reveal a trace of God's goodness."

5. See the symbolic value of ordinary daily events. Red traffic lights can be a welcome mini-pause during which you can relax a little and slow down the hectic pace. The bicycle ride home marks the break between work and leisure. This gives the mind the chance to rid itself of stress, freshen up, and prepare itself for the evening.

6. In the evening, reflect on the day. Concentrate especially on the good things. At least for today, make peace with yourself and the world.

Exercise: A 180-degree turn

Doing a mental about-face is hard work. It takes a lifetime. In order to understand the effort it takes, Father Johannes Pausch suggests standing up and making a 180-degree turn. We do that countless times throughout the day but this time we will concentrate on every movement.

First our head turns, followed by the shoulders and torso. "Then we lower the weight onto one foot (the left), lift the other foot (the right), face it in the same direction as the left foot, and transfer the weight onto the right foot. We have turned a little. The process is repeated until we have completed the turn, the complete about-face. Repeat this exercise several times and always try to be aware how many movements of the body are necessary to make an about-face."

Prayer

Monks in the choir stalls at the daily office in St. Ottilien monastery

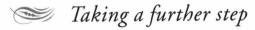

Taking a further step

*F*or monks and nuns, one of the most important steps towards achieving peace is prayer, whose close link with silence and composure is clearly visible in the external posture. The monk who is praying clasps his hands, lowers his head, does not look at anything, or even closes his eyes. He sits, kneels, or stands — he rests.

In the last few months, whenever I thought about this chapter, I became a little uncomfortable. For a long time I had thought of praying as something rather pompous and sanctimonious, and now I was about to recommend it. But then I suddenly realized that several times a week I was almost praying when I sat down and started my yoga exercises. My hands would be clasped and my eyes closed. In the convent I noticed how seriously the nuns took their prayers, in a way that was anything but sanctimonious. My only difficulty was in imagining the personified God of Christianity. Then Sister Annunziata told me about an experience that she had had. At the beginning of a week of meditation she had asked herself the questions: "Who do I really mean when I say God?" (This time she

"Do not pray hastily in order to say many prayers but make sure that the prayers that you do say come from the heart!"

St. Francis de Sales

added: "Strange that I should have asked that question. I had been here for quite a while…") She had found an answer: "He could still be God, beyond me, greater than me, but one who gives me the feeling of being loved, of being called." A pleasant solution that invites us to let go. We should not rack our brains trying to grasp the ineffable.

Praying therefore means getting in touch with this mystery, encountering it and perceiving oneself as a part of it, this force, this energy. For believers, this energy has a name and has become a person they can picture very clearly: Jesus Christ. Prayer is a spiritual experience, not an external event, and not sanctimonious at all.

Praying helps

People pray in all religions, and according to Christian Schütz, the abbot of the Benedictine abbey of Schweiklberg, prayer is an integral part of being human. According to Christian beliefs, it is also essential for experiencing human life in all its complexity. Schütz continued: "Prayer is implicit in the ability to speak. In prayer man uses language to go beyond himself, his universe, and the whole of reality, while at the same time confronting his finiteness and imperfect state."

Scientists have also investigated the concept of prayer in many studies. For example, Dale Matthews, professor at Georgetown University, analyzed and evaluated 325 studies on the subject of prayer from all over the world. His findings were that in over seventy-five percent of cases, praying was beneficial both for the body and the soul. In Maryland, 90,000 people were studied and it was found that churchgoers suffered less from heart problems, emphysema, and cirrhosis of the liver, and that suicide rates too were lower. After examining thousands of patients, Herbert Benson, cardiologist at Harvard University, established that praying and meditation were very good for the circulation of the blood and for the nerves. Then a study by Luciano Bernardi of the University of Padua revealed that saying rosaries and mantras improves patients' health, even that of nonbelievers. The breathing of the patients examined slowed down, which in turn had a positive effect on their general health.

Christian prayer: engaging one's whole being

Prayer is a mystery. We cannot quite unravel the forces that are activated by praying, but we can investigate them and experience them. Jesus himself put prayer at the center of his life. "We cannot understand the way of the Son of God and of man without acknowledging how important prayer was for him," Christian Schütz wrote. Jesus prayed constantly. He prayed before crises, important decisions, and his arrest. Over and over again he urged people to do the same. In the Sermon on the Mount, the Lord's Prayer occupies a central position. And the Lord also gave instructions on how to pray: "When you pray, do not do like the hypocrites," he said, "they go and pray in synagogues and on street corners so that people can see them.... But when you pray, close the door behind you; then pray to your Father who is hidden. Your father who can also see what is hidden will repay you."

Like Jesus, the early Christian communities said the Lord's Prayer and the 150 psalms of the Old Testament when they prayed. The same prayers are still said at the canonical hours in monasteries and convents today. Throughout their lives in the convent or monastery, nuns and monks continue singing. The words of the 150 psalms contain everything that concerns humanity, ranging from birth, love, and happiness to suffering, murder, and manslaughter; these psalms are so fundamental and wide-ranging that they are quoted over and over again in the Bible. Rainer Maria Rilke said that the Canonical Book of Hours was: "One of the few books in which you can completely immerse yourself, however distracted, disorganized, and troubled you are."

The people in the Old Testament psalter who pray do so in many ways: they call, cry, lament, thank, and praise. The question is, said Sister Annunziata, "to what extent shall I succeed in bringing what constitutes my rational self into dialogue with God." The believer must open up completely and be honest in prayer. For Sister Hildegard, this meant offering everything to God. This brings relief and liberation and is purifying at the same time.

A joyful noise

A prayer should reach deep down, be a real experience, and help us make progress on our chosen path. "Nothing should take priority over religious services," St. Benedict wrote, and *ora et labora* also means that prayer must extend to work and carry on throughout the day. Sister Annunziata says that when she is in the choir, she manages to forget about the soup that she has just served up to the guests and to concentrate entirely on her singing. She becomes someone else there, as she stands side by side with the other nuns, on festival days dressed in her habit, the *cuculla,* a flowing white mantle with wide sleeves that cover her folded arms. When she sings in her strikingly clear, pure voice, she is a different person from the person who just returned from a brisk walk in the woods, standing firmly and naturally in her place like a stylite on top of a tall pillar. Every movement is intentional and there is no hesitation or uncertainty. Melody and word, form and content, go together. Is this peace? "When I manage really to achieve this…" Then she finds peace for at least that moment, a peace that can also be creative. She might hear a psalm that she has been singing for years and suddenly understand and experience it in a completely new light.

An example she gave was a line in Psalm 137 that many people have had difficulty with: "Happy shall they be who take your little ones and dash them against the rock!" Sister Annunziata tried to reconcile this: "An explanation could be that the children referred to in the psalm were actually evil thoughts that are smashed against Christ."

The Benedictine monk Nikolaus Nonn, lecturer in Gregorian chant and liturgy says: "Silence and listening, responses and addresses…the elements that make up the offices said at the canonical hours resonate deeply within me and continue to provide new answers to old questions." But this is only one dimension. When the "togetherness" of the nuns works, the choirmaster and the choir interact perfectly, and when each singer keeps up and they all follow the rhythm, a second dimension opens up. A contemplation that goes beyond mere words.

"But know that the Lord has set apart the faithful for himself; the Lord hears when I call to him."

Psalm 4:3

"In the choir the monks have developed a sacramental dimension for prayer," Ambrose Tinsley wrote. Nikolaus Nunn sees the prayers of the offices as "the form of contemplation practiced by the West."

Staircase in the convent of Habsthal

He explains: "The air I breathe enters my body and I offer this air... back to God in the form of psalms. The remaining air that I have breathed in flows out, new air flows in.... The exchange between cantor and the praying community ensures that I do not get out of breath but... that I can reflect on the life-stream of breathing."

For me the most beautiful office is Vespers — in Latin. In that language the singing sounds so much stranger, more sublime, solemn, and mysterious. But on some days my thoughts would wander, and I would suddenly wonder why so many nuns wear glasses. Sister Annunziata was very familiar with this wandering of the mind. "As our day goes, so goes our singing in the choir. Some days we are all in harmonious voice, other days we are all going in different directions. Singing expresses my attitude and outlook." And on good days it seems that the choir is drinking in the air.

The holy reading

The liturgy of the canonical hours is one form of monastic meditation; the other is the holy reading. St. Benedict made it very clear that the source of this reading was to be the Holy Scriptures. Each monk and nun had to be completely familiar with them. The founder of the order required that the monks should read for two to three hours a day, and during Lent a particular book of the Bible was included in the program.

Faith had to permeate every aspect of the cloistered life, as shown, for example, in the readings at mealtimes. So when the nuns were eating and

Prayer of the week

Sister Annunziata could not say whether she had a favorite prayer. But she became so fascinated by a saying of Paul Claudel that she spent a whole week pondering it:

"God: the origin in which all things begin. The present, which carries everything. The end point, into which everything flows."

Extracts from the Rule of St. Benedict are read every day in the chapter house of Oberschönenfeld

sister Hildegard read to them from the Book of Kings, they were taking in spiritual as well as physical nourishment. In this connection Ambrose Tinsley pointed out that it is not necessary "that the mind should understand every single word." This could lead to exhaustion and frustration. Indeed, it is much more important to experience prayer as a whole. As St. Augustine said: "What is spoken with the mouth must become alive in the heart." Only repetition makes it possible to understand and perceive impressions that we had never imagined were there.

Naturally the kind of reading prescribed by St. Benedict had nothing to do with novels or the speed reading that is today taught in seminaries. The slow rhythm and repetition were fundamental. St. Benedict was speaking here of meditation: everything was aimed at making the words work deep down.

With body and soul

The aim of prayer in early Christianity was not only to pray with the mind but to achieve a union of body and soul through meditation. A widely read text dating from the thirteenth century entitled *The Nine Ways of Prayer of St. Dominic* showed the founder of the predicant order in various positions of the body. For the saint, prayer was the embodiment of faith. He sought contact with the Absolute through various positions of his body: the repeated bowing in front of the cross as a form of greeting resulted in the letting go of oneself and the acceptance of the love of God. He lay prostrate on the ground (*prostratio*) to make himself humble and docile towards the Holy Spirit. By standing, punctuated by genuflections, he expressed an attitude of respect towards listening and receiving new stimuli, comfort, and calmness. Often St. Dominic stretched his whole body towards heaven. Sometimes he prayed with open or clasped hands (as a mirror of his soul, as a mark of thanks). At other times he prayed with his arms spread out in front of the cross, which reflects the shape of the human body, as a sign of patient waiting for the power of redemption. Often he sat quietly in front of his crucifix. He smiled. He was silent. He listened. He was completely at peace.

In order to achieve this, the monks used a very special technique: they whispered to themselves when reading. The copying of whole books in the scriptorium also had two motives. The first aim was to disseminate books by making copies of them, especially the Bible, while the other objective, for the monk copying, was to absorb the words. A sentence has a different effect depending on whether one reads it or writes it, as the mystic William of St. Thierry explained: "Other people must believe in God, learn about him, and worship him. It is our business to love him, to be in harmony with him, to enjoy him."

The aim of prayer is to draw closer to God. In this context, one should consider the statement made by Karl Rahner, one of the most important Catholic theologians of the twentieth century, that the Christ of the future would be a mystic, one who has experienced something — or he would not exist at all.

Exercise: The prayer of light

Authors who write about prayer usually reach a point beyond which they can go no further. This is when they must deal with the experience of prayer rather than the theory. When the Irish Benedictine monk Ambrose Tinsley had the sense that words were no longer enough, he became aware of the light that shines on the path every day, "but particularly when the going gets difficult." The monk continued: "Often it seems to fall short, but then just at this moment we are reminded that this is the light of life, that the light of God is always there..."

When I look out my window at this moment I see a roof with a thin covering of snow, illuminated by a milky winter light, a dark, not unfriendly light. Look at the light at this very moment! It will never be the same as it is now. Try to discover the mystery of this light, or take it with you in a prayer.

Meditation

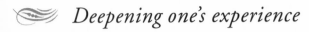

Deepening one's experience

"The most uncomfortable kind of motion is that of going into oneself."

Karl Rahner

*A*uthors who write about meditation stress repeatedly the impossibility of describing subjective experience in a way that is comprehensible to others. When we cannot even describe the taste of a strawberry or a slice of bread and butter, how could we express the taste of God? Personal experience is always at the heart of things. You may be prompted and guided by books and teachers, but in the end you have to rely on your own experience. The first effects that are perceived may still be familiar. Peter Raab, an expert on meditation, wrote: "Many people will find it easy to understand that at first they experience deep relaxation, and that attentiveness and concentration increase." But few people can really imagine that "discursive, restless thoughts will calm down, without the person who is meditating falling asleep or dozing…"

Christian meditation

When we speak of "meditation" we think mainly of silent, still contemplation, something like a picture. One may have certain stereotypes. In traditional

Christianity this kind of contemplation was practiced in spiritual exercises, especially in sixteenth-century Spain. While keeping silent, in contrast to the meditating techniques of the Far East, the person meditating would visualize a loving being before him, God or Jesus Christ himself. In the next higher level of meditation, contemplation and deep musing followed by inner vision replaces thought. This is the "prayer of silence" (Johannes von Gott). One stops thinking and is aware only of the presence of God. It is no accident that the term "temple," referring to that sacred precinct that in ancient tradition symbolized the presence of God, is part of the word "contemplation."

"The duty of other people is to believe in God... your duty is to taste God..."

William of St. Thierry

How do prayer and meditation differ from each other? In reality, it is hardly possible to distinguish between the two. After the Second Vatican Council, meditation was defined as a means of praying in order to reach the reality of God. When one remembers that the canonical hours are also a kind of meditation, then meditation can be seen as a deeper level of prayer.

Ultimately, one includes the other. Both prayer and meditation can be practiced by speaking aloud or purely interiorized when the words are just thought or, at the highest level, left out altogether. The overriding goal is to move from external silence towards inner peace, from inner peace towards the higher level, the so-called vision of God, and thence to the union with God, enlightenment itself. As the Spanish mystic St. Teresa of Ávila explained, enlightenment is a mystical experience that few are rewarded with. And yet it can occur just by reciting the Lord's Prayer.

When Athanasius wrote that the desert father St. Anthony "prayed almost constantly because he had learned that one must pray silently for oneself," he was indicating permanent concentration on God. Even then monks meditated, for instance by reciting verses of psalms or short prayers from the New Testament over and over again or silently repeating them in the mind. The practice of repetition became known as *ruminatio*, from the Latin *ruminare*, to chew over. It was the meditative repetition of the same thought that led to Gregorian chant. According to the abbot Emmanuel Jungclaussen, the repetitive nature of prayer was actually "the original form of Christian

Symbols can be of help on the way to inner peace

meditation" which arose as a response to the biblical injunction: "Pray at all times and do not let up."

The Jesus Prayer

As previously mentioned, the most important obligation of the early monks, the Hesychasts, was constant remembrance of God through unceasing prayer. The inner wakefulness needed for this was achieved using quick, fervent prayers such as verses of the psalms that were constantly repeated or short sentences from the New Testament such as "Jesus, son of David, have mercy on me" (Luke 18:35). They were also called "one-word" prayers. As meditation developed, the name of Jesus increasingly became the central point of the prayer. The sentence "Lord Jesus Christ, have mercy on me" appeared for the first time in the sixth century in the biography of St. Dositheus, and the monks on Mount

Sinai had already developed a special technique to give the Jesus Prayer a transformative effect through corresponding rhythmic breathing.

In the nineteenth century, "a monk of the Eastern Church" wrote a book entitled *The Way of the Pilgrim*, which disseminated the Jesus Prayer more widely throughout the Christian world. In it he described the practice of this meditation method (see Exercise), which is based on appealing to Jesus with uninterrupted concentration, using a formula such as "Lord Jesus Christ, have mercy on me," the words "Jesus Christ," or the continuous repetition of the single word "Jesus." In the eyes of the anonymous author this phrase said it all: Jesus was "present as Redeemer." In addition, "Where Jesus is, there is the Church; he who is always in Jesus, he is always in the church." And: "In the same way that the holy name grows in us, we grow in the knowledge of the divine mysteries."

To meditate it is important that you have no specific purpose, only that you turn your concentration inwards without any expectations. For a long time Sister Annunziata believed that she needed to have a deep mystical experience, such as an encounter with Jesus calling her to follow him. At some point she managed to free herself from this pressure: "Today I look back, and I see how far I have progressed on my own path, and I believe that God in this way showed me where I belonged." It was precisely this relaxed contact with her faith that helped her further her spirituality. It happened during a period of intensive meditation that she was "given two brief moments." The first time, she was meditating about a cross bearing a figure of Christ and the second time she was just sitting with a cup of coffee: "And suddenly it became clear to me. So completely clear."

The spiritual exercises of St. Ignatius

Every month, each nun in Oberschönenfeld has one "desert day." After terce, at about 7:45 A.M., she is released from all obligations and she can use that time until Vespers at 5:30 P.M. as she chooses, but with prayer as the absolute focal point. Sister Hildegard of the bread shop says she is often completely drained by loud talking, so she really soaks up the silence of the desert. Sister Annunziata told us that in the past she had used this time mainly to read the scriptures. "I used to believe that I had to produce something." Now that has changed completely; her prayers are influenced by the spiritual exercises of St. Ignatius and she tries to pray in a way that suits her best personally. This may entail meditation on a picture, sitting in silence before a crucifix, or contemplation of a word.

In the sixteenth century Ignatius of Loyola, a Spanish knight and founder of the Jesuit order, wrote about spiritual exercises based on his own experience. In recent years a modified version has circulated in many convents and monasteries and attracted a lot of interest. Many who are looking for a spiritual connection find in these exercises a kind of tool that they can use effectively on their own or, even better, under guidance. The best example of the success of this technique, which is also called the teaching of differentiation by the mind, was the foundation of the Society of Jesus. Ignatius and his comrades-in-arms were not sure whether their mission needed them to found an order, or whether it could be carried out in the form of a loose

"Never concentrate on your neighbor's faults. Instead always be prepared to excuse them. And conversely: always be deft at accusing only yourself."
Ignatius of Loyola

Buddhist monk meditating

connection. After fruitlessly weighing up all the arguments, on Ignatius's advice they sought for a solution in prayer and contemplation. We know the result.

The long exercises of St. Ignatius last for thirty days, and the shortened exercises for five days. Their objective is to help individuals in their personal decision-making processes. The aim is to discover through meditation what God has chosen for us.

"Many people live in continuous self-doubt," explained Sister Scholastica, who runs the classes at Oberschönenfeld. "It is a major step for you to make friends with God, to make yourself aware: I am loved. I am allowed to be here."

During the period of these spiritual exercises, participants must pray for half an hour a day. It starts with

- arrival, followed by letting go,
- noticing the chair on which you are sitting,
- being aware of your body,
- and finally, concentrating on your breathing.

Without such composure to get in the right mood there can be no meditation. St. Francis de Sales also recommended: "Start each prayer, whether silent or oral, by placing yourself in the presence of God." First you can say the sentence: "I am here." The participants in the exercises are then presented with several options: a quotation from the Bible, the life of a saint, or a picture. Sister Scholastica explained: "each person should choose what moves him most. If a participant is walking along a stream, he may include the stream in his prayer." Allowing it to work, absorbing it.

In the next conversation with the class teacher, the participant discusses the experience. Every evening, each participant ends the day in a fifteen-minute "prayer of loving attentiveness." Again, it is a matter of:

- accepting oneself,
- seeing goodness without the addition of a "but,"
- becoming aware of all the positive things of the past day.

In this way the participant will develop a new perception of everyday life. Asking what is irritating and why it is so. Recognizing one's own way. This fairly subjective approach will contribute to the development of a greater

Monk at prayer in the monastery of Melk

understanding of what is needed. One begins to make the right decisions. As a result, life is no longer seen as the basis for an indictment of the world but, according to Josef Sudbrack, Jesuit and author in the field of mysticism and meditation, it is inspired by the "optimism of Christian faith," as Ignatius understood it. The Orthodox monk speaks in this context of the "full presence" of humanity and adds with regard to the Jesus Prayer: "The all-enveloping presence is everything. Without it the name (Jesus) is nothing. He who can live permanently in the presence of our Lord does not need the name any more. It is only a stimulus and a temporary aid."

The rosary

It is vitally important for prayer and meditation that each person should use the tool that sits most comfortably in the hand. For many people this may

On meditation

What is meditation? Sister Scholastica, a nun at the convent of Oberschönenfeld, told the following story on this subject. A missionary in Africa noticed how a local man went to chapel every day, where he spent two or three hours in silence on a bench. The missionary had no idea what he was doing. Eventually he walked up to the man and asked him: "What are you doing there?" The African looked at him in surprise and replied: "Don't you understand? I am meeting God. He is looking at me and I am looking at him."

be the medieval rosary whose use later almost fell into oblivion until it suddenly experienced a revival.

A rosary has fifty-three small beads and seven large beads that are threaded on a closed chain or string. Counting on the beads, one says the Creed, the Lord's Prayer, the divine virtues, and finally "Glory be to the Father," and then ten Hail Marys are recited five times. In each Hail Mary a saying is added after the name "Jesus" that looks at a certain aspect of the life of Christ. Thus one looks at the Son of God with Mary's eyes and meditates on the whole gospel in an extremely concentrated form.

St. Francis de Sales qualified the practice further: "The rosary is a very useful form of prayer, on condition that it is used properly." It can be misunderstand as an exercise of diligence, in which case the Hail Marys are rattled off as quickly as possible while only thinking of one's shopping list or forthcoming appointments. "Without contemplation, a rosary is a body without soul," declares the papal document *Rosarium Virginis Mariae.* But if instead one perceives the rosary as a tool for meditation, the constant repetition and rhythmical saying of prayers associated with the regular sliding of the beads through the hand can produce a state of deep contemplation. Especially in stressful situations and in moments of need, it is the quickest way to achieve peace and relaxation and, when practiced as a daily exercise, it provides a dependable support in everyday life.

Exercise: the Jesus Prayer

In his book *The Way of the Pilgrim*, the anonymous author, "a monk of the Eastern Church," gave instructions for the Jesus Prayer. Here are a few extracts:

- The name Jesus can be used on its own or inserted in a short or longer sentence. ("Lord Jesus Christ, Son of God, have mercy on me.")

- You can say the name of Jesus in the street, your workplace, your room, in church, and so on.

- As well as using the name freely, it is also recommended that set times and places be established for regular invocation of the name.

- The body's posture does not play a decisive part in this. However, the best posture is that which leads to the greatest physical relaxation and inner peace.

- Before you start saying the name of Jesus, relax, collect yourself, and pray to the Holy Spirit for inspiration and guidance.

- Begin simply. To learn to walk, you must take a risk and make the first step; to learn to swim, you must dare to throw yourself into the water.

- Do not think that you are invoking the name; only think of Jesus. Say his name slowly, gently, and calmly.

- When invoking Jesus' name, you must not repeat the name constantly without a pause. After saying the name it should resound in the succeeding seconds and minutes of peace and collectedness.

- It is natural that when invoking the name we should hope for and try to obtain some kind of "positive" or tangible result. In other words, seeing a sign that we have made real contact with the person of our Lord. But we must avoid excessive craving for such experiences.

- Such sober "waiting" for the name of Jesus will provide blessing and strength for us.

READING 8

I and we

*Those who are at peace with themselves will also find peace with others.
(Abbey church of Neresheim)*

Living in peace

Love your neighbor and yourself as well

"Loving a person means seeing him as God intended him."

Fyodor Dostoyevsky

When I met the hermit Heinrich Engelmann for the first time a few years ago, I had no idea what kind of person I would find. I had never in my life encountered a hermit, and saints such as St. Anthony were unknown to me. I was surprised when the door of the hut opened and a little man embraced me warmly. He had two chairs, one of which he offered me, while he took the other. We sat there until evening, drinking tea, talking, and gazing out of the large window. I was not an intruder but a guest; my host was attentive, alert, and patient. His search to discover the essence of things had led him to live a life of solitude, but he came out of this solitude with a strong presence and welcomed me as a friend. His views and faith went far beyond an interest in his own person. Such an individual gives other people a good feeling. He accepts you, and he lets you be who you are. There is a word to describe this: love.

"Love your neighbor as yourself," Jesus urged. When these words are quoted today, the emphasis is usually on the words "your neighbor." But the sentence also includes the word "self" that, according Sister Annunziata, has not been interpreted correctly for a long time. Yet it is so important! First you must love yourself. If I do not love myself, how can I love others? Loving oneself does not mean going through life enamored of oneself but accepting oneself as a part of a whole, perceiving oneself with all one's strengths and weaknesses. In fact, you will get on with others in the same way that you get on with yourself. According to Sister Annunziata, the better you know yourself, the easier you will be able to cope on your weak days when you are feeling oversensitive. You will then be able to avoid certain things that might overwhelm you.

"A person who carries peace within himself spreads more blessings around him than one who is very learned."

Thomas à Kempis

St. Francis de Sales pointed out that we should be gentle with ourselves and never "rage at ourselves or our weaknesses." It is true that we must dislike and be sorry for our faults, but this dislike should not make us bitter or angry. Self-criticism should be combined with self-love, otherwise it will only be an unproductive, destructive waste of energy, which is taking the easy way out. When I rant and rave about my faults and shortcomings, I give the impression to myself and others that I am doing something: Look how upset I am about my imperfections! So I feel comforted instead of trying to change things. Changing things takes much more effort.

Monk in the beer garden at Andech

There can be no peace without love

"Love — and do what you like!"

Sister Annunziata had plenty of opportunity to examine where she stood with her "self" and her "neighbor" in this community, with its tensions and explosive forces. Abbess Ancilla Betting explained that communal living can "often be uncomfortable because the large number of young and old women living in close proximity leads to tension and conflict." Like any family, "monastic communities are constantly striving to practice neighborly love."

Sister Annunziata told us that on days when she has sorted things out in her mind, she is not bothered much by others and she accepts people as they are without question. St. Paul described love in his letter to the Corinthians; he said it must be above all one thing: kind. "If I have prophetic powers, and understand all mysteries and have all knowledge," the apostle added, "and if I have all faith, so as to move mountains, but do not have love, I am nothing" (1 Corinthians 13:2). And St. Augustine quite simply declared love to be life's motto: "Love — and do what you like!" he asserted, because a deed that is dictated by genuine love cannot possibly lead to false goals.

"Never allow someone you meet not to be happier after meeting you."

Mother Teresa

Trusting in the Creation tells us that the love of God is the most important duty for Christians. "You shall love the Lord your God with all your heart, and with all your soul." The result of this love that goes in both directions —

Being kind to yourself

Those who want live in harmony with their environment must also find peace with themselves. St. Bernard wrote a letter to Pope Eugene III telling him to observe the following:

"If the whole of your life and experience is concentrated on activity and you do not include time for reflection, shall I praise you? … You too are human. In order to ensure that your humanity is fully developed and complete, you must also have an attentive heart not only for others but also for yourself…. Although everyone has a right to a share of you, you too are a person, and you have a right to yourself. Why should it only be you who has no share of yourself? … Indeed, how can those who do not get on well with themselves get on with others? Remember: be lenient with yourself. I am not saying, do that always, I am not saying, do that often, but I am saying, do it now and again. Be to yourself as you are to others, or in any case be so after you have been so to others."

the faithful not only loves but also feels loved — is a feeling of inner strength and independence. Those who feel safe and secure do not have to worry about the world's love concerning their actions by constantly striving to satisfy the taste, desires, and opinions of others, as many do. Thomas à Kempis wrote: "We could all have peace and serenity if we did not torture our hearts and heads with what others are saying and doing, which in fact does not concern us."

Inner peace and the rules of love

The strict routine in monasteries and convents prevents many potential conflicts. Because decisions do not have to made, questioned, and debated over and over again, there is no reason to argue about them. But the monks are very inventive when it is a matter of stirring up trouble in the community. This is why St. Benedict gave very precise, detailed instructions for communal living:

- First of all, it is essential that no should be forced to live in the monastery, quite the contrary: "If someone wants to join the community… we don't make it easy for him… We talk to him about the toughness and difficulty of the road to God." But if he decides to join anyway, he cannot "shake off the yoke of the Rule any more."
- All brothers are consulted on important decisions. The abbot must listen to the opinion of the monks, and the monks for their part must not defend their views "arrogantly and stubbornly." In organizational matters, the abbot has the authority to ensure that the monks live together without too much friction, but at the same time he is on the same level as the rest of the brothers.
- Humility and obedience apply to everyone without exception. As an external expression of this equality, the abbess of Oberschönenfeld washes the feet of the novices at their investiture, just as Jesus did for the disciples shortly before his death.
- The monks must "recover peace before sunset after an argument," just as the Bible requires: "Do not let the sun go down on your anger" (Ephesians 4:25).
- No brother is allowed to defend another on his own authority "because this could lead to very serious irritation;" on the other hand, he may not "exclude or strike another unless the abbot has given him authority."

This may sound harsh, yet St. Benedict always placed the needs of people before anything else. The sick in particular should not lack for anything. They should have a bath as often as it makes them feel good. They are also allowed "to eat meat to restore their health." The brothers should care for the unpleasant, demanding sick with the same patience. In turn, the sick are urged not to make those who care for them "miserable by making excessive demands." All this corresponds to the words of Jesus: "What you have done to the lowest of my brothers you have done to me."

Inner peace and responsibility

Whether in a religious order or outside it, taking responsibility is particularly important for the smooth functioning of a group. In a monastery, the abbot is like a father to the whole community, based on the patriarchal

Statue of Christ with dove, convent of St. Marienthal

principle, but at the same time all the brothers are responsible for each other, that is to say in accordance with their functions. Responsible behavior also includes speaking their minds, but not about trivial matters such as the

Love the wrong people
by Thomas à Kempis

"There is no great merit in living with good, gentle people. It is easy because it is naturally pleasant for us. Everyone likes to live in peace and loves those people who are of the same mind more than others.

But living in peace with difficult, unpleasant, undisciplined people or with people who are contradictory, that shows compassion, that is praiseworthy..."

Exercise: spoil a friend

Jesus washed the feet of his disciples. You too should help a family member or friend by spoiling them on a normal day from morning till evening. Prepare and serve them their favorite breakfast. Do the tasks that they do not like doing at all. Do not interrupt them when they speak. Go to the cinema with them, go shopping or cycling together — whatever they choose to do. Do not make remarks that would upset them. And, on your part, ignore the things that would normally make you irritated. Do not do any of this expecting gratitude and praise or in the hope of them doing the same for you. Perhaps you should even arrange matters so that you keep your plan to yourself without the person being aware of it at all.

lumps in the vanilla pudding. Sister Annunziata decides intuitively when things are important enough to be said. This ability to separate the important from the banal requires a certain inner peace. As a young nun, for instance, she was rarely able to express her own point of view clearly to the others. She often remained silent because of her belief that she should leave others as they were and not play judge. "But what is the point if things keep seething within me, perhaps for years, and then still come out? Now I make the effort more often to say what I think and as a result to let people know who I am."

> *"Self-love makes us perceive the wrongs we suffer more harshly than they really are."*
> St. Francis de Sales

For St. Francis of Sales there was a limit to patient silence: when truth suffered as a result. Those unjustly accused must defend themselves quietly and reject the accusation, but at the same time be on their guard that their pleading does not become an end in itself. "If someone accuses you... do not get excited about it.... After you have done your duty towards truth, you must also do your duty towards humility. In this way you will not ignore your concern for your good reputation, nor your dutiful love of humility and a peaceful heart."

The rhythm of life

Time to rest

Living a full life

"Whether we live or
whether we die, we are
the Lord's."

Romans 14:8

*P*eople who want to achieve lasting peace must be in harmony with their lives. They must follow the rhythm that has been predetermined for them. It starts with birth and ends with death. In order to accept the rhythm of life, it helps:

- to look at ourselves; our own development, if we allow it, can help us understand what constitutes life;
- to avoid unnecessary struggles with ourselves and others, as we can do nothing against age or death;
- to feel complete and live without anxiety for the future.

In, out, pause

The smallest rhythmic cycle in our life is breathing. It took me a long time before I realized that one breath does not consist only of breathing in and out, but that the correct rhythm also includes a pause after breathing out. I did not find this out on my own. The breathing process is therefore made up of an active part and a passive part, the pause.

In yoga, it is said that we only have a certain number of breaths at our disposal, which is why we should be economical with our breaths. We can lower the frequency through special exercises, meditation, or sport. But there will be time when we have no breath left. The truth is that we too will die. This is a thought that terrifies most people, while for others it is such an impertinence that they want to forget about it completely. Franz Werfel compared this attitude to death with an "industrial accident on a busy skyscraper building site." "One of the toiling workmen falls from the top of some tall scaffolding and his colleagues just pause for a second, staring nervously downwards, in the knowledge that this could happen to them today or tomorrow."

About life and death

By contrast, Jesus saw death not as an evil but as a necessity that guides us through human life to eternal life. "When a grain of wheat does not fall to the earth and die, it remains alone; but when it dies, it produces further wheat." St. Benedict told the monks that "every day they must think of death, because it can come at any time." Although this may seem a very sobering thought, it is the only realistic approach. Things that we believe we need so badly and the apparently important tasks that dominate our day suddenly fall into perspective when we think of death. This leads to a serious attitude to life, but one that, for the very reason that it is realistic, can be extremely happy.

"If you carry your cross reluctantly you place on the cross a second cross."

Thomas à Kempis

Heinrich Spoerl wrote a fairy tale about a young peasant who was sitting under a tree as he waited impatiently for his beloved. A little man gave him a magic button. Every time the man turned it to the right, he could jump forward in time. He turned it, and his beloved arrived. He turned it again,

The nuns at Oberschönenfeld have placed death in their midst

and they celebrated their wedding. He turned it again, and they were lying in their bridal bed. He turned it again, and he had a house and children. He kept on turning and turning it, and then he was dying. Horrified, he realized that he had wasted his life and tried desperately to turn it the other way. And indeed, he was sitting once more under the apple tree, and he was extremely happy to wait.

If I am aware of the finiteness of time I can enjoy every day as something

Take the time

Take the time to work —
that is the price of success.
Take the time to think —
that is the source of power.
Take the time to play —
that is the secret of eternal youth.
Take the time to read —
that is the road to wisdom.
Take the time to be friendly —
that is the road to happiness.

Take the time to dream —
it moves your vessel towards a star.
Take the time to love and be loved —
that is the privilege of the gods.
Take the time to look back —
the day is too short to be selfish.
Take the time to laugh —
that is music for the soul.

Irish blessing

unique. "This means living in the present and not tomorrow or in the future," Sister Annunziata explained. Research carried out at Bar-Ilan University in Israel has shown that when people think of their own death, they also feel closer to their partners. It is partly the anxiety that draws them closer together but also the awareness that this valuable Earthly love will come to an end at some time in the future.

"If I accept death I shall also understand life better, which means dying a little every day," Sister Annunziata explained. "Every parting is like a little death, if I do not succeed in something, if I have to give up a plan, or if a human relationship breaks down. That too is part of being human."

The nuns of Oberschönenfeld have placed death right in their midst. During their daily walk to the cemetery following the midday office, they not only think of the dead nuns but also of their own deaths. Death is as present in their minds as life. It is therefore no coincidence that the chapter house in the convent was designed to remind the nuns of death. It is built completely of stone and in the middle is a large, dark wooden board. No one is allowed to walk on it because it is reserved for something very special: it is here that a nun is laid out when she dies. But it is also where the investiture of the novices takes place. They leave their old lives behind — that too is a kind of dying — and start new ones: in a new place, with new clothes and even a new name. Birth follows death.

The richness of the celebrations

In this way, the life of every nun is constantly reduced to its basic values. Each one wants to get closer to the essence of human life, to things that cannot be seen, such as "love" or feelings and personality, things that are much more important than the material aspects of our world. But nuns, too, have to work to achieve this. Symbols, rituals, and customs help the faithful on their path towards deeper dimensions. All these traditions give a clear structure to the life of the individual and the community. On the one hand, they connect life to Earth, and on the other, they raise life above it, because they give life a place in the universe and go back to its source. Like breathing, like each individual day, the year in convents and monasteries has its own precise rhythm, based on the life of Jesus, on the stages in His life: birth, the passion, death, and resurrection — reflecting the full experience of being human. However, the aim is not only to draw attention to the particular event but also to celebrate it, with great extravagance, processions, and vestments. Celebration plays an important part in the structure of the year. It breaks up the everyday routine, it is an opportunity to rest, and it is an outlet. As well as allowing the soul to "swing," it also elevates it.

Christmas—the celebration of life

The ecclesiastical year starts with Advent. Although in the past this period had overtones of repentance, nowadays it is a time of anticipation for the nuns. It is the start of something new in the midst of the bleak winter. The candles on the Advent garland announce it: Christ is born. When Christians celebrate His birth at Christmas, they also celebrate their own, and the uniqueness of each life. In the same way that we constantly lose the proper feeling for life, many of us misinterpret the spirit of Christmas, turning it into

The conch shell, symbol of the pilgrim

a festival of gifts, of family arguments, and even of feelings of hostility. When the nuns in Oberschönenfeld celebrate Midnight Mass and all the candles are burning, that is the highlight for them, said Sister Annunziata. Christmas involves us; it has to do with feelings, with happiness, and it is exhilarating.

The Passion — the time of suffering

The Passion before Easter is the time of suffering, of fasting, an ideal time to go into the desert and, as St. Francis de Sales suggested, to lay in "supplies of peace and humility."

With the tradition of praying the Stations of the Cross that occurs in the days before Easter, the agonizing Stations are reconstructed, from the Condemnation to the Crucifixion and the Entombment. Jesus set an example of how to endure suffering. He accepted His suffering and as result overcame it, thus giving the cross a new meaning as a symbol of liberation: "If any want to become my followers, let them deny themselves and take up their cross daily and follow me." As Anselm Grün put it, it is crucial to accept that "suffering is necessarily part of one's finite life, one's limitations and weaknesses, and one's mortality." Ultimately this also the easiest way. Thomas à Kempis wrote: "If you carry your cross reluctantly, it is like putting a second cross on top of it, you make the burden even heavier, and you still have to carry it." People who are constantly quarrelling, always angry, and feeling mistreated stand in their own way, and as a result they carry twice the weight. But on the other hand, taking up the cross means being concerned about what is essential.

Easter — the key to peace of mind

The cross becomes even more burdensome; on Holy Saturday we must carry it with the body of Jesus to the tomb. Then at last, on Easter Sunday, the angel proclaims the Resurrection, the victory of life over death. Easter is the key to Christianity, the key to Christian peace of mind. The event that transcended temporality is the foundation of all spirituality. The Resurrection had tangible consequences on Earth. The letter to the Romans says: "Just as Christ was raised from the dead by the glory of the Father, so we too might live in newness of life…" This event of the Resurrection is so crucial that it is commemorated in every Catholic service with the Eucharist.

The symbol of Easter is light. Parishioners gather round Easter bonfires, and in many places flaming Easter wheels are rolled down hills. The Emmaus Walk is still practiced, especially in Southern Germany. It is a walk during which the participants pray and sing. After Christ's Resurrection, the disciples went to Emmaus, sad and uncertain. They had heard about the Resurrection and found the tomb empty. They could not find Jesus. On the way to Emmaus, they were joined by a stranger to whom they told the whole story. It was only when they sat with him at the table, where he divided the bread and handed a piece to each one, that they recognized him as Jesus.

Christ's ascension and Pentecost — to heaven and back

Christ ascended to heaven forty days after Easter. Before the very eyes of the disciples, Jesus was finally "lifted up, and a cloud took him out of their sight." It was only in the fourth century that Christ's Ascension was declared a holy day in its own right. Before that it had been celebrated together with

There must be well-established customs
by Antoine de Saint-Exupéry

The little prince met a fox in the desert who explained to him the meaning of customs. "For instance, if you come at four o'clock I can begin being happy at three o'clock. And as time goes by, the happier I shall feel. At four o'clock I shall already be excited and worried: I shall experience how valuable happiness is. But if you come at any time I can never know when my heart is there… There must be well-established customs."

"What is a well-established custom?" the little prince asked. "It too is something that has fallen into oblivion," the fox replied. "It is what separates one day from another, one hour from the other hours…"

Pentecost, the day on which the Holy Spirit descended from heaven onto the disciples in the form of tongues of fire. It is true that there is a close link between these two events. Both events establish a connection between us and heaven, giving our life a new dimension. Anselm Grün explained: "Those who can see heaven as their home, for them many things of their lives are put into perspective, for them success and possession and health are no longer the most important things in life. They can face everything more calmly and without anxiety." Heaven is both the base camp from which the mountain climber starts his ascent and the summit that he must reach.

Lavender growing at the monastery of Senanque

Glossary of terms

abbey Independent convent for monks and nuns who live according to the Rule of St. Benedict

abbot/abbess Derived from Aramaic/Greek *abbas*, meaning father. The abbot (of a convent for men), or abbess (convent for women), is the head of an independent Benedictine convent (abbey) and is usually chosen for life

apostolate Missionary duty to pass on the faith by living according to the Christian faith and through pastoral care

asceticism Training in the spiritual life

breviary Texts of the prayers said at the canonical hours (Book of Hours), especially for private praying

catechism Instruction in the faith

cellarer The administrator or manager of the whole monastic economy

chapter 1. A part of the Rule; 2. Assembly of the community of monks in the chapter house

choir Part of the church (usually in the apse) in which the divine office is conducted

cloister From the Latin *claustrum*, derived from *claudere*, meaning to close or close off. 1. Open or closed, square-shaped passage round a garden inside a monastery, used for processions. 2. The name most frequently used for the place where monks and nuns live

contemplation Christian examination and reflection; concentration on life and the message of life. Contemplative orders are orders whose main occupation is meditation and silent reflection

enclosure Closed off part of a monastery or convent, not accessible to outsiders

Gregorian chant Music in a distinctive key sung as a single vocal line in religious services. It was introduced by Pope Gregory the Great in connection with his liturgical reforms

guardian The superior of a Franciscan community

habit The garment worn by monks or nuns

hermit Someone who lives in a hermitage or in solitude. In the early days of monasticism it was the epitome of monastic life

hermitage The place where hermits live

horary prayers From the Latin *hora*, hour. Prayers said at the canonical hours, that is, at particular times of the day: vigil (the previous evening), matins (in the morning), lauds (second morning prayer), terce, sext, and nones (at nine, twelve, and three o'clock; sext and nones are sometimes combined as the midday prayer), vespers (evening prayer), compline (prayer before the night rest)

lectio divina Spiritual reading

liturgy Celebration of the Eucharist and the divine office according to the ecclesiastical calendar

meditation Spiritual exercise that helps in finding the way of moderation, inspired by a word, text, or image

monastic Way of life and culture adopted by monks. The word monastery is derived from the late Greek *monazein*, to live alone

monk From the Greek *monachos*, hermit

novitiate Trial period for monks and nuns

nun From the Latin *nonna*. Female member of a monastic community

oblates Lay people who have a feeling of belonging to a certain monastic community and live their daily life according to the rules of that community

order Religious community of members bound by vows to devote themselves to religious aims

padre From the Latin *pater*, father. A professed monk or monk who has taken vows

postulate Period of application for membership of a religious order, lasting for up to six months.

poverty One of the three classic monastic vows ("evangelical counsels"), the others being chastity and obedience

prior/prioress Representative of the abbot or abbess

profess The taking of vows for a certain period or for life

provincial The head of a monastic province

refectory Dining room of a convent or monastery

Rule The rules of a community. Through the constitution of each order they are adapted to the circumstances of the times

spiritual exercises Spiritual program spread over several days under the direction of a leader. It leads to a new encounter with Christ and the finding of the way of moderation

vespers Evening service

vow A promise. The classic monastic vows are poverty, chastity, and obedience

Appendix

All retreat centers listed provide the option for public and private retreats for both genders. Additionally, the retreats have the option of being self-led (more relaxing) or guided (often more spiritually rigorous).

ALABAMA

Benedictine Sisters Retreat Center
Sacred Heart Monastery
   916 Convent Road
   Cullman, AL 35055
   (256) 734-8302
   Contact: Sr. Therese Haydel OSB, Dir.
   E-mail: retreats@shmon.org
   www.shmon.org
The church is run completely by women but the retreat is open to all genders. Yoga and massage therapy also available.

St. Bernard Abbey Retreat Center
   1600 St. Bernard Dr. SE
   Cullman, AL 35055
   (256) 734-8291
   Contact: Brother Andre OSB
   E-mail: BAndre@stbernardabbey.com
   www.stbernardabbey.com
Hosts several group retreats that are all male, but private retreats are available for all genders.

ARIZONA

Sisters of St. Benedict
Our Lady of Guadalupe Monastery
   8502 West Pinchot Ave.
   Phoenix, AZ 85037
   (623) 848-9608
   Contact: Sr. Lydia Armenta OSB
   E-mail: bensrs@aol.com
   www.benedictinesistersphoenix.org

Tolomei Retreat House
Holy Trinity Monastery
   P.O. Box 298
   St. David, AZ 85630-0298
   (520) 720-4016 or (520) 720-4642
   ext.17
   Fax: (520) 720-4202
   Contact: Br. Benedict Lemeki OSB, S.
   Corinne OSB
   E-mail: trinitylib@theriver.com
   www.holytrinitymonastery.org

ARKANSAS

Hesychia House of Prayer
  204 St. Scholastica Road
  New Blaine, AR 72851
  (479) 938-7375
  Contact: Sr. Louise Sharum OSB
  www.stscho.org/hesychia.html

Coury House
Subiaco Abbey
  340 N. Subiaco Avenue
  Subiaco, AR 72865
  Contact: Br. Mel Stinson OSB
  E-mail: couryhouse@subi.org
  www.subi.org/couryhouse.htm

Benedictine Spirituality
and Conference Center
  P.O. Box 3489
  Fort Smith, AR 72913-3489
  (479) 783-1135
  Contact: Sr. Hilary Decker OSB
  E-mail: retreats@stscho.org
  www.stscho.org

CALIFORNIA

Prince of Peace Abbey
  650 Benet Hill Road
  Oceanside, CA 92054
  (760) 430-1305
  Contact: Br. Benedict OSB
  E-mail: abbeyretreat@aol.com

St. Andrew's Abbey Retreat Center
  P.O. Box 40
  Valyermo, CA 93563
  (661) 944-2178
  Contact: Guest Office/Secretary
  E-mail: retreats@valyermo.com
  www.saintandrewsabbey.com

COLORADO

Benet Hill Monastery
  3190 Benet Lane
  Colorado Springs, CO 80921-1509
  (719) 495-2574
  Contact: Sr. Josie Sanchez OSB
  E-mail: bpinescs@hotmail.com
  www.benethillmonastery.org

Benet Pines Retreat Center
  15880 Highway 83
  Colorado Springs, CO 80921
  (719) 495-2574
  Contact: Sr. Josie Sandhez OSB
  E-mail: bpinescs@hotmail.com
  www.benethillmonastery.org

Abbey of St. Walburga
  1029 Benedictine Way
  Virginia Dale, CO 80536-7633

Phone & fax: (970) 472-0612
Contact: Sister Scholastica OSB
E-mail: abbey@walburga.org
www.walburga.org

CONNECTICUT

My Father's House Spiritual Retreat Center
39 North Moodus Road
Moodus, CT 06469
(860) 873-1581
www.myfathershouse.com

DISTRICT OF COLUMBIA

Loyola Retreat House, Washington
9270 Loyola Retreat Rd
Newburg, MD 20664
macdonaldray.com/loyolaretreat.org

FLORIDA

Holy Name Monastery
P.O. Box 2450
St. Leo, FL 33574-2450
(352) 588-8320
Fax: (352) 588-8319
Contact: Sr. Mary Clare Neuhofer OSB
E-mail: retreats.holyname@saintleo.edu
www.floridabenedictines.org

St. Leo Abbey Retreat Center
P.O. Box 2350
Saint Leo, FL 33574-2350
(352) 588-8184
Contact: Mrs. Donna Cooper, Director
E-mail: abbey@saintleo.edu
www.saintleoabbey.org

IDAHO

St. Gertrude's Retreat Center
Monastery of St. Gertrude
HC 3 Box 121
Cottonwood, ID 83522-9408
(208) 962-3224
Fax: (208) 962-7212
Contact: Sr. Lillian Englert OSB
E-mail: Retreat@StGertrudes.org
www.StGertrudes.org

ILLINOIS

Saint Benedict's Abbey
[Ecumenical; assoc. OSB Confederation]
7561 West Lancaster Road
Bartonville, IL 61607
(309) 633-0057
Fax: (309) 633-0058
Contact: Fr. James Marshall OblSB at
(309) 633-0474
E-mail: sba@sbabbey.com
www.sbabbey.com

St. Joseph's Loft
Monastery of the Holy Cross
   3111 S. Aberdeen Street
   Chicago, IL 60608-6503
   (773) 927-7424
   Fax (773) 927-5734
   Contact: Br. Edward Glanzmann OSB
   E-mail: porter@chicagomonk.org
   www.chicagomonk.org

Benet House Retreat Center
St. Mary Monastery
   2200 88th Ave. West
   Rock Island, IL 61201
   (309) 283-2108
   Contact: Sr. Charlotte Sonneville OSB
   E-mail: retreats@smmsisters.org
   www.smmsisters.org

INDIANA

Kordes Center
   814 E. Tenth Street
   Ferdinand, IN 47532
   (812) 367-2777, (800) 880-2777
   Fax: (812) 367-2313
   Contact: Vanessa F. Hurst
   E-mail: kordes@thedome.org
   www.thedome.org/kordes

The Guest House
St. Meinrad Archabbey
   St. Meinrad, IN 47577
   (800) 581-6905
   Contact: Br. Maurus Zoeller OSB
   www.saintmeinrad.edu

Benedict Inn Retreat and Conference Center
   1402 Southern Avenue
   Beech Grove, IN 46107
   (317) 788-7581
   Fax: (317) 782-3142
   Contact: Sr. Mary Luke Jones OSB
   E-mail: Benedict@indy.net
   www.benedictinn.org

IOWA

Covenant Monastery
   1128 - 1100th St.
   Harlan, IA 51537-4900
   (712) 755-2004
   Contact: Sr. Linda Zahner OSB
   E-mail: lzahner@fmctc.com
   Rural setting for retreats & spiritual
   direction.

KANSAS

Sophia Center
Benedictine Sisters of Mount St. Scholastica
   751 South Eighth Street
   Atchison, KS 66002
   (913) 360-6173
   Contact: S. Rosemary Bertels OSB
   E-mail: sophia@mountosb.org
   www.mountosb.org/sophia.html

Benedictine Retreat Ministry
St. Benedict's Abbey
   1020 North Second Street
   Atchison, KS
   (913) 367-5340 ext. 2842
   Contact: Fr. Matthew Habiger OSB
   E-mail: matth@benedictine.edu
   www.kansasmonks.org

KENTUCKY

Mt. Tabor Retreat Center
   150 Mt. Tabor Road
   Martin, KY 41649
   Contact: Sr. Jan Barthel OSB
   E-mail: mtbenedictine@pcc-uky.cam-
   puscwix.net
   www.mounttabor.net

The Guesthouse Retreat House
Abbey of Gethsemani
   Trappist, KY 40051
   (502) 549-4129
   Contact: Rev. Alan Gilmore, OCSO
   www.monks.org

LOUISIANA

Abbey Christian Life Center
St. Joseph Abbey
   St. Benedict, LA 70457
   (504) 892-3473
   Contact: Rev. Thomas Perrier OSB
   www.stjosephabbey.org

Our Lady Queen Monastery
   50252 Antioch Road
   Tickfaw, LA 70466-9747
   (985) 345-1202
   Fax: (985) 345-2630
   E-mail: OLQMTLA70@aol.com
   www.ourladyqueenmonastery.org

MAINE

Living Water Spiritual Center, Winslow
  93 Halifax Street
  Winslow, Maine 04901
  Phone: (207) 872-2370
  www.e-livingwater.org
Also offers Buddhist meditation, nature
programs, interfaith dialogue, ecumenical
worship, and spiritual practices from many
different disciplines.

MASSACHUSETTS

Retreat and Spirituality Center
Glastonbury Abbey
  16 Hull Street
  Hingham, MA 02043
  Contact: Thomas O'Connor OSB
  E-mail: office@glastonburyabbey.org
  www.glastonburyabbey.org

St. Scholastica Priory
  271 North Main Street
  P.O. Box 606 - Route 32
  Petersham, MA 01366-0606
  (978) 724 3213
  Fax: (978) 724-0033
  E-mail: sspriory@aol.com
  www.petershampriory.org

MINNESOTA

Benedictine Center of St. Paul's Monastery
  2675 Benet Road
  St. Paul, MN 55109
  Contact: Sam Rahberg
  E-mail: benedictinecenter@
    stpaulsmonastery.org
  www.stpaulsmonastery.org

House of Prayer (Episcopal Diocese)
  P.O. Box 5888
  Collegeville, MN 56321
  (320) 363-3293
  Fax: (320) 363-2074
  E-mail: houseprayer@csbsju.edu
  www.ehouseofprayer.org

MINNESOTA

McCabe Renewal Center
  2125 Abbotsford Avenue
  Duluth, MN 55803-2219
  (218) 724-5266
  Fax: (218) 724-7138
  Contact: Sr. Lois Eckes OSB
  E-mail: McCabeRenCtr@aol.com
  www.duluthbenedictines.org

Mount St. Benedict Center
620 Summit Avenue
Crookston, MN 56716
Contact: Director
E-mail: lkraft@msb.net
www.msb.net

Spiritual Life Program
Saint John's Abbey
Collegeville, MN 56321-2015
(320) 363-3929
Fax: (320) 363-2504
Contact: Fr. Robert Pierson OSB
E-mail: SpirLife@csbsju.edu
www.saintjohnsabbey.org/retreats

Spirituality Center
Saint Benedict's Monastery
104 Chapel Lane
St. Joseph, MN 56374-0220
Contact: S. Dorothy Manuel OSB
E-mail: DManuel@csbsju.edu
sbm.osb.org/spiritualitycenter

MISSOURI

Abbey Center for Prayer & Ministry
Conception Abbey
37174 State Highway V V
Conception, MO 64433
(660) 944-2809
Contact: Trish Wiederholt or Karen

Ceckowski
E-mail: abbeycenter@conception.edu
www.conceptionabbey.org

NEBRASKA

Immaculata Monastery & Spirituality
Center, Missionary Benedictine Sisters
300 North 18th St.
Norfolk, NE 68701
(402) 371-3438
E-mail: center@norfolk-osb.org
www.norfolk-osb.org

St. Benedict Center
1126 Road I
Schuyler, NE 68661-0528
E-mail: retreats@stbenedictcenter.com
www.stbenedictcenter.com

NEW JERSEY

Benedictine Center for Spirituality
St. Walburga Monastery
851 North Broad Street
Elizabeth, NJ 07208
(908) 353-3028
Contact: S. Marita Funke OSB
E-mail: MaritaOSB@aol.com
www.catholic-forum.com/bensisnj/
bencenter.html

St. Mary's Abbey Retreat Center
230 Mendham Rd.
Morristown, NJ 07960
(973) 538-3231, ext. 2100
Contact: Fr. Beatus Lucey OSB
www.osbmonks.org

NEW MEXICO

Monastery of Christ in the Desert
P.O. Box 270
Abiquiu, NM 87510
(801) 545-8567
Contact: Guestmaster
E-mail:
CIDguestmaster@christdesert.org
www.christdesert.org

Pecos Benedictine Monastery
Retreat Reservations Office
P.O. Box 1080
Pecos, NM 87552-1080
(505) 757-6415, ext. 254
Fax: (505) 757-2285
Contact: Guestmaster
E-mail:
guestmaster@pecosmonastery.org
www.pecosmonastery.org

NEW YORK

Mount Saviour Monastery
231 Monastery Rd.
Pine City NY 14871-9787
(607) 734-1688
Fax: (607) 734-1689
Contact: Br. James Cronen OSB
E-mail: Guest@msaviour.org
www.msaviour.org

NORTH CAROLINA

Living Waters Catholic Reflection Center
103 Living Waters Lane
Maggie Valley, NC 28751
www.catholicretreat.org

NORTH DAKOTA

Hospitality Center, Annunciation
Monastery
7520 University Drive
Bismarck, ND 58504
(701) 255-1520
Contact: Sr. Gemma Peters OSB
E-mail: weaverosb@hotmail.com
www.annunciationmonastery.org

Benedictine Spirituality Center
Sacred Heart Monastery
8969 Highway 10
Box 364
Richardton, ND 58652
(701) 974-2121
Fax: (701) 974-2124
Contacts: Prioress Ruth Fox or Sister
Rita OSB
E-mail: home@
sacredheartmonastery.com
www.sacredheartmonastery.com

OHIO

Our Lady of the Holy Spirit Center
5440 Moeller Avenue
Norwood, Ohio 45212
Phone: (513) 351-9800
Fax: (513) 351-988
www.olhsc.org

OKLAHOMA

Benedictine Spirituality Center
Red Plains Monastery
728 Richland Road, SW
Piedmont, OK 73078-9324
(405) 373-4565
E-mail:
redplainsmonastery@wavelinx.net
www.redplainsmonastery.org

St. Gregory's Abbey
1900 West MacArthur
Shawnee, OK 74804
(405) 878-5491
Contact: Br. Benet Exton OSB
E-mail: bsexton@stgregorys.edu
www.monksok.org

OREGON

Mt. Angel Abbey Retreat
St. Benedict, OR 97373
Contact: Alexander Plasker OSB
www.mountangelabbey.org

Shalom Prayer Center
Queen of Angels Monastery
840 S. Main Street
Mt. Angel, OR 97362
(503) 845-6773
Contact: Sr. Joan Pokorny OSB
E-mail: shalom@open.org
www.open.org/~shalom

PENNSYLVANIA

Mount St. Benedict Monastery
6101 East Lake Rd
Erie, PA 16511
(814) 899-0614 ext. 402
Fax: (814) 898-4004
Contact: Sr. Carolyn Gorny-
Kopkowski OSB
E-mail: Spirituality@mtstbenedict.org
www.eriebenedictines.org

Monastic Guest House
St. Emma Monastery
1001 Harvey Avenue
Greensburg, PA 15601-1494
(724) 834-3060
www.stemma.org/retreat.htm

SOUTH DAKOTA

Blue Cloud Abbey Retreat Center
P.O. Box 98
Marvin, SD 57251
Contact: Fr. Thomas Roznowski OSB
E-mail: Abbey@bluecloud.org
www.bluecloud.org

Benedictine Ministry Outreach
Saint Benedict's
415 South Crow Street
Pierre, SD 57501
(605) 244-0969
Contact: Sister Adel Sautner OSB
E-mail: bennii@dakota2k.net

Mother of God Monastery
110 28th Avenue SE
Watertown, SD 57201
(605) 882-6631
Fax: (605) 882-6658
Contact: Sister Emily Meisel OSB
E-mail: monastery@dailypost.com
www.watertownbenedictines.org

Benedictine Peace Center
1005 West 8th Street
Yankton, SD 57078
(605) 668-6024; 661-3829 (mobile)
Contact: Jeanne Ranek OSB
E-mail: jeanne.ranek@mtmc.edu
www.yanktonbenedictines.org

TEXAS

Omega Retreat and Spirituality Center
216 W. Highland
Boerne, TX 78006
(830) 816-8470
Fax: (830) 249-3327
Contact: Mr. Andrew Anderson
E-mail: omegactr@gvtc.com
www.boernebenedictines.com

St. Benedict Monastery Retreat and
Spirituality Center
17825 S. Western
Canyon, TX 79015
(806) 655-9317
Fax: (806) 655-09736
E-mail: nuns@osbcanyontx.org
www.osbcanyontx.org
Contact: Sister Hildegard Varga, OSB

UTAH

Our Lady of the Mountain Retreat House
1794 Lake Street
Ogden, UT 84401-3016
Contact: Sr. Danile Knight OSB
E-mail: Olmrh@juno.com

VERMONT

The Benedictine Monks of Weston Priory
58 Priory Hill Road
Weston, VT 05161-6400
(802) 824-5409
Fax: (802) 824-3573
E-mail: guestbrother@westonpriory.org
www.westonpriory.org

VIRGINIA

Mary Mother of the Church Abbey
12829 River Road
Richmond, VA 23233-7206
(804) 784-3508
Fax: (804) 784-2214
Contact: Retreat Center
  Administrator, Bro. Jeffery Williams
  OSB, ext. 125
www.richmondmonks.org

WASHINGTON

The Priory Spirituality Center
500 College Street NE
Lacey, WA 98516-5339
(360) 438-2595
Contact: Sister Dorothy Robinson OSB
E-mail: spiritualityctr@stplacid.org
www.stplacid.org/spirit.html

WISCONSIN

Saint Bede Retreat and Conference
Center
  P.O. Box 66
  1190 Priory Road
  Eau Claire, WI 54702-0066
  (715) 834-8642
  Contact: Sr. Hildegarde Geraets OSB
  E-mail: sisters@saintbede.org
  www.saintbede.org

Holy Wisdom Monastery
  Postal Address:
  Benedictine Women of Madison
  P.O. Box 5070
  Madison, WI 53705-0070
  Street Address:
  4200 County Highway M
  Middleton, WI 53562-2317
  (608) 836-1631
  Fax: (608) 831-9312 (retreat center)
  Fax: (608) 836-5586 (monastery)
  E-mail: info@benedictinewomen.org
  www.benedictinewomen.org

St. Benedict's Abbey and Retreat Center
  12605 244 Avenue
  Benet Lake, WI 53102-0333
  Contact: Mr. George P. Freeman
  E-mail: BenetLake1@aol.com
  www.benetlake.org

Picture credits

AKG, Berlin: 56, 163, 223

Dr. Wilfried Bahnmüller: 176, 262, 272, 284, 292, 294, 297, 354

Staadiche Bibliothek Bamberg: 146

Bibliothèque Royale de Belgique: 64

Robert Boecker: 149

Hieronymus Bock, *Kreuterbuch* (Herbal) 1572, Monastery of Plankstetten: 181, 182, 185, 186, 189

Fischer, Louis, *Gandhi, Prophet der Gewaltlosigkeit*, Munich 1983: 15

Lucia Glahn: 130, 133, 136

Andrea Göppel: 4, 28, 45, 79, 115, 118, 214, 250, 269, 295, 314, 363

Robert Harding Associates: 13

Hans-Günther Kaufmann: 16, 21, 24, 34, 37, 94, 98, 106, 111, 113, 122, 154, 155, 158, 168, 173, 198, 204, 207, 213, 226, 230, 234, 238, 243, 304, 307, 348, 349, 364

Lois Lammerhuber: 22, 40, 47, 72, 76, 90, 108, 128, 139, 144, 171, 194, 196, 210, 216, 275, 277, 281, 300, 322, 326, 333, 343, 357

Rupert Leser: 60, 66, 69, 84, 102

Middle East Archive: 17

Mirko Milovanovic: 254, 258, 266, 288, 308, 319, 331, 336, 339, 352

Bernhard Müller: 7, 142

Private collection: 252

Provatakis, Theocharis, *Meteora*, Athens 1983: 10

Hans Siwik: 2, 27, 48, 52, 82, 87, 100, 150, 165, 220, 221, 248, 270, 289, 317, 341, 346, 360